From Needles to Hook

Complete Guide to Converting Knit Patterns to Crochet

Letter of Introduction

*W*hat a beautiful sweater pattern! That would be simply perfect to wear to next year's family reunion. My cousins would have a fit! What do I need to make this? Wait a minute. What's this? Oh no, it's knit! I wish this was done in crochet. I haven't a clue as to how to change this over into what I like to do best, and that's crochet. Toss that idea out, along with the afghan I liked last month, and the pillow I liked the month before that. Why isn't there a book on how to change these instructions?

Does this scenario sound familiar? Well, don't toss aside knit patterns any longer. The beautiful stitch patterns found in knitting can easily be translated into the language of crochet. The crochet genie has heard the many wishes asking for a tutorial on the subject of knit to crochet conversion and has provided the very publication to grant those wishes in the form of From Needles to Hook.

Starting with the basics, From Needles to Hook *provides the clues to solving the mystery of changing knit pattern stitches to crochet. Each chapter is designed to guide you from one step of the process to the other. The key is to discover which crochet stitches are the best substitutes for the knit stitches. Using simple addition, subtraction, multiplication and division, there won't be any knit pattern that cannot be converted to a similar crochet technique. Patterns for a sampler afghan, clothing and household items are scattered throughout to not only provide examples, but to also provide finished wearable and home décor accents. Upon completion, you will literally hold the proof of the technique in your hands.*

So, drag those knit patterns back out into the daylight and let the stitches flow from the needles to your crochet hook. Look that knit pattern right in the eyelet and don't let it give you any cable. You have seen the future and it is crochet.

KNIT
Crossed Stripes

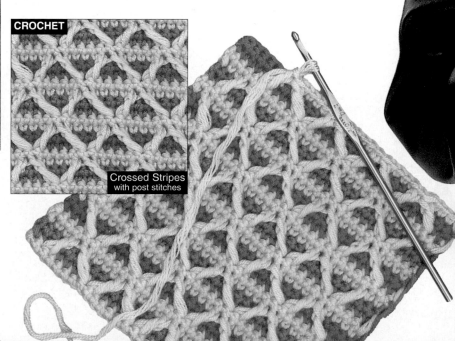

CROCHET
Crossed Stripes
with post stitches

*W*e have created a complete guide that will allow anyone to take just about any knitted pattern and make it in crochet.

Table of Contents

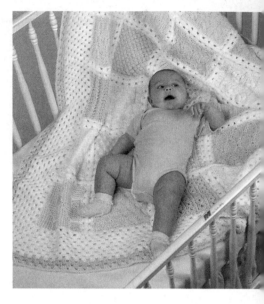

Editor	DONNA SCOTT
Acquisitions Editor	DEBORAH LEVY-HAMBURG
Associate Editor	DONNA JONES
Assistant Editor	SHIRLEY BROWN
Copy Editor	SHIRLEY PATRICK
Book Design	GREG SMITH
Production Artist	JOANNE GONZALEZ
Production Supervisor	MINETTE SMITH
Photography Supervisor	SCOTT CAMPBELL
Photographer	ANDY J. BURNFIELD
Photo Stylist	MARTHA COQUAT
Photo Assistant	CRYSTAL KEY

Chief Executive Officer	JOHN ROBINSON
Publishing Marketing Director	DAVID J. McKEE
Book Marketing Manager	CRAIG SCOTT
Product Development Director	VIVIAN ROTHE
Product Development Manager	CONNIE ELLISON
Publishing Services Manager	ANGE VAN ARMAN

Customer Service	1-800-449-0440
Pattern Services	(903) 636-5140

ISBN: 1-57367-124-X
First Printing: 2002
Library of Congress Catalog Card Number:
2002104514

Printed in the United States of America.

Visit us at
NeedlecraftShop.com

Every effort has been made to ensure the accuracy
and completeness of the instructions in this book.
However, we cannot be responsible for human error or for
the results when using materials other than those specified
in the instructions, or for variations in individual work.

Chapter One

Converting Knit to Crochet

*T*o get started, there's what you need to know about the basic principles of converting knit to crochet. You'll learn about the most important factor in your success— gauge—and how it relates to yarns, hook sizes and more.

Yarns and Gauges

How many times have you seen a knitted design or stitch pattern you'd really love to make, but you only crochet, or you don't have the time to spend on a knitted item?

It's fairly easy to convert simple knit patterns to crochet by following a few basic principles. The first time you convert a pattern, it's best to choose a simple design with a basic stitch pattern and save the intricate stitch patterns for later, after you have practiced the technique.

There are several things to consider when converting knit stitch patterns to crochet. Let's carefully examine some of them.

SUBSTITUTING YARNS

Using the same type yarn and the same stitch gauge, knitted stitches will be softer and less bulky than crocheted stitches, so it is best to use a size or two smaller yarn for the crocheted piece. For example, if you are converting a pattern knitted in worsted yarn to crochet, try working to the same stitch gauge using sport or baby yarn for a softer texture.

*Chunky yarn:
8 sts = 2"*

Here is a list of suitable yarn substitutes:

Knit with:	Crochet with:
Chunky	Worsted
Worsted	Sport
Sport	Baby or fingering
Baby	Two strands of size 10 thread

If working with novelty or variegated yarn, it's best to choose a plain stitch design and reserve the intricate stitch patterns for plain yarns. It's very disappointing to put all that effort into a beautiful stitch pattern, then not be able to see the pattern because the novelty yarn obscures the stitches.

MATCHING GAUGES

The single most important factor in determining the finished size of a knit or crochet item is **gauge.**

When converting from knit to crochet, the main thing to remember is that regardless of the stitches used for the item, the **crochet stitch count and the stitch gauge should remain the same** as the original knitted pattern, otherwise, the finished item may turn out to be an undesirable size.

Knit and crochet rows are not the same height in proportion to the stitches, so you will need to **adjust the number of rows** in each section to achieve the proper size. It is best to add or subtract rows in multiples of two, so that you are at the proper end of the row to ensure correct shaping and stitch patterns in following rows.

When working a knitted stitch pattern over several rows **to establish a design** such as cables, basketweave, eyelet or yarn-over designs, etc., you must allow for these design repeats when deciding how many rows to add or subtract for your crocheted item. You will need to end on the same side of the work (right or wrong side) at the end of the design repeat as the original pattern is written.

Since each of us crochets or knits differently, there is no standard for knowing exactly how much a hook or needle size will change the gauge or finished size. The yarn you choose and the tension you hold on the yarn will create looser or tighter stitches; for smooth, even stitches, it is important to keep this tension the same throughout the item.

This means that gauge is the responsibility of the crocheter or knitter and must be consistent throughout the entire item to assure an accurate finished size.

Considering the basics and importance of gauge, making a few gauge swatches using various stitches will enable you to determine which hook and yarn to use for the proper finished size. These swatches will also help you determine which stitches to use to achieve the desired effect for each section in the item, such as ribbing and body section stitches of a sweater. Experiment with various stitches to achieve the desired effect (this will be covered in more detail in "Stitches for a Similar Look").

What to do with these swatches? If you still feel gauge swatches are a waste of time, here are a couple of suggestions for putting them to good use.

If you are making a jacket or sweater, make each swatch about 4" square. Choose the best two swatches to make **shoulder pads** for the garment. Fold each swatch in half diagonally to form a triangle, insert a layer of quilt batting if desired, and sew the edges together. Attach the shoulder pads to the inside along the shoulder seams.

Another good use is to always make your swatches the same size—about 3" square or 4" square. Save all your swatches, sorting them according to yarn types. When you have enough of one yarn type to make a nice **afghan** or **pillow** or **place mat** or such, sew or crochet them all together and work a nice crocheted border around the edge.

As you work it is important to **check your gauge often**. Sometimes when we measure over two or three inches, we seem to get an accurate gauge count, but the best way is to measure the entire piece from time to time as you are working on it. Measure from side to side across an entire row (do not stretch or scrunch the piece) and divide by the number of stitches in that row; this gives you an accurate overall stitch gauge. For an accurate overall row gauge, measure from the beginning row to the last row and divide by the number of rows worked.

If the necessary crochet gauge is too heavy or stiff, you can change to a smaller yarn or a larger hook to achieve a more appealing texture. Using the same hook, a larger yarn produces a larger gauge; a smaller yarn a smaller gauge, thus a larger or smaller finished item. ●

Worsted yarn:
8 sts = 2"

Sport yarn:
9 sts = 2"

Stitches for a Similar Look

In this section we will address several crochet stitches used to mimic specific knit stitches. A few basic knit stitches and their crochet counterparts are:

1 K st or 1 P st	= 1 sc st
K or P 2 sts tog	= sc 2 sts tog
K in front lp then in back lp of same st	= 2 sc in same st
6 st st rows	= 4 sc rows

STOCKINETTE STITCH

For knitted **stockinette stitch,** work one row of knit stitches and one row of purl stitches alternately for the needed number of rows, with the **knit** side of the stitches showing. This forms a good smooth background fabric.

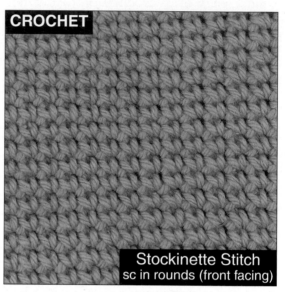

CROCHET

Stockinette Stitch
sc in rounds (front facing)

KNIT

Stockinette Stitch

Stockinette stitch can be duplicated in crochet by working rows of smooth flat crochet stitches. Single crochet stitches and half-double crochet stitches work best, especially if worked in unturned rows or rounds with the **front side** of the stitches showing. If the rows are turned, small ridges are formed. While this creates a good effect, it is not as similar a look as the same stitches worked in rows or rounds without turning.

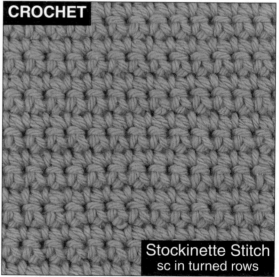

CROCHET

Stockinette Stitch
sc in turned rows

For knitted **reverse stockinette stitch,** work one row of knit stitches and one row of purl stitches alternately for the needed number of rows, with the **purl** side of the stitches showing.

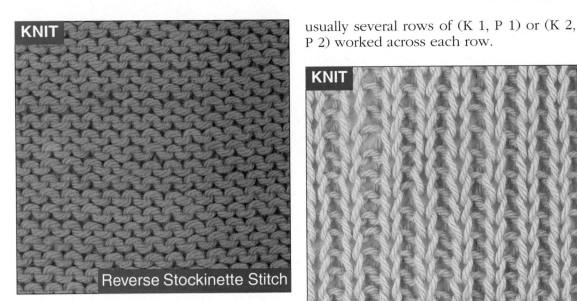

Reverse Stockinette Stitch

usually several rows of (K 1, P 1) or (K 2, P 2) worked across each row.

KNIT

Ribbing

For a similar look in crochet, work un-turned rows or rounds of single crochet stitches with the **back side** of the stitches showing. Turned rows of single crochet stitches can also be used for reverse stockinette stitch if it is not also used for stockinette stitch in the same piece.

Crocheted **back loop ribbing** and **post stitch ribbing,** two often-used versions, are worked in very different manners, but each has a finished look similar to knitted ribbing.

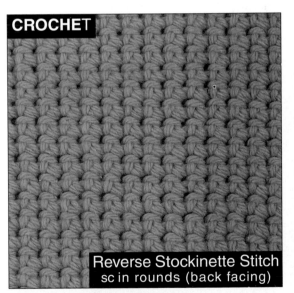

Reverse Stockinette Stitch
sc in rounds (back facing)

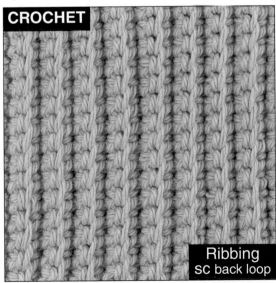

Ribbing
sc back loop

RIBBINGS

Ribbings are usually included in socks, sweaters, hats, gloves and many other items. The way that ribbing stitches are crocheted can be one of the major differences between the knitted pattern and the crocheted piece.

For **knitted ribbing,** the stitch pattern is

In knitting, when a knit stitch is turned over it becomes a purl stitch, and a purl stitch becomes a knit stitch. So it is in crochet with post stitches and back/front loops. A front post stitch becomes a back post; a back post stitch becomes a front post. A front loop becomes a back loop; a back loop becomes a front loop. When you turn and work back across a row, whether knitting or crocheting, the pattern **refers to each stitch as it appears when you are ready to work it.**

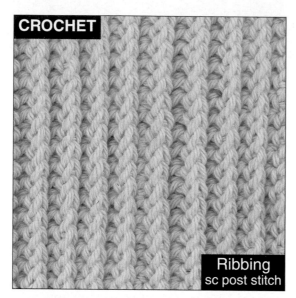

**Ribbing
sc post stitch**

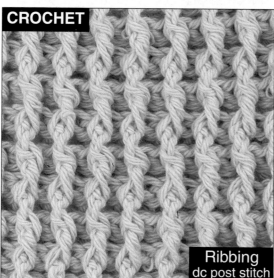

**Ribbing
dc post stitch**

Back loop ribbing is formed by **vertical** rows of stitches as follows:

Row 1: Ch to measure height of ribbing plus one ch extra, sc in second ch from hook, sc in each ch across, turn.

Row 2: Ch 1, sc in **back loop** of each st across, turn.

Repeat row 2 until the ribbing is the desired length, or if another section of

stitches is worked onto the ribbing, until the ribbing has the same number of rows as the next section has stitches, then turn the piece to the side and work one stitch into the end of each of the ribbing rows.

A variation of this method is to work around the back post of the stitches rather than in the back loops *(not shown).*

Post stitch ribbing is formed by **horizontal** rows of stitches as follows:

Row 1: Ch the same number of stitches as the knitted cast-on plus 2 extra chs, dc in the fourth ch from hook and in each ch across, turn.

Row 2: Ch 2, (dc **front post** around next st, dc **back post** around next st) across with hdc in top of ch-2, turn.— *Notice that when you turn the piece over, the stitches worked as **front posts now appear as back posts,** and the stitches worked as **back posts now appear as front posts.***

Row 3: Ch 2, dc front post around each front post and dc back post around each back post with hdc in top of ch-2, turn.

Repeat row 3 until the ribbing is the desired height. If another section of stitches is worked onto the ribbing, work one stitch into each of the ribbing stitches.

Vertical ridges and creases can be formed in much the same manner as post stitch ribbing. This effect is best achieved using half-double, double or treble crochet

KNIT

Vertical Ridges and Creases

GARTER STITCH

Knitted **garter stitch** is simply multiple rows of knit stitches.

KNIT

Garter Stitch

stitches. Work several front post stitches to form a front-facing vertical rib or ridge, then alternate with one or two back post stitches to form a vertical crease or valley; this stitch combination will produce a reversible fabric. For a non-reversible fabric, in the creases or valleys, use sc or hdc stitches worked into the tops of the stitches rather than post stitches.

For crochet garter stitch, use multiple horizontal rows of single crochet stitches or half-double crochet stitches worked into the **back loops** of the previous row.

CROCHET

Vertical Ridges and Creases
sc sts and dc post stitches

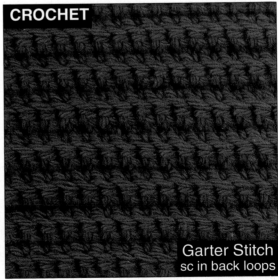

CROCHET

Garter Stitch
sc in back loops

BASKETWEAVE PATTERN

Knitted **basketweave** designs are made by working a few stockinette stitches, then the same number of reverse stockinette stitches alternately across the row for several rows to form small square or rectangular blocks of stitches, then switching the positions of the stockinette and the reverse stockinette blocks for the same number of rows to alternate the sections. Repeat this sequence to create the illusion of a woven fabric.

then work the same number of **back post** stitches; repeat this sequence across the row. Work two or three rows placing front post stitches in front post stitches and back post stitches in back post stitches to produce blocks of stitches similar to the knitted fabric, then reverse the positions of the front post and back post sections for the same number of rows to alternate the sections. Repeat this sequence to create the illusion of a woven fabric.

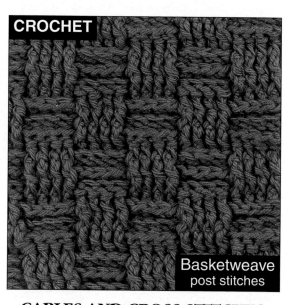

KNIT

Basketweave

CROCHET

Basketweave
post stitches

Crocheted **basketweave** designs can be formed in several ways. Here are two easy methods.

Work a few double or half-double crochet **front post** stitches,

CABLES AND CROSS STITCHES

Knitted **cables** are formed by slipping two or three stitches *(first half),* onto a cable

KNIT

Cables

needle or separate double-pointed needle and holding those stitches out of the way at back or front of the work while the next two or three stitches are knitted *(second half)*, then knit the stitches from the cable needle, causing the stitches to be crossed.

For a knitted **cross stitch,** skip one stitch *(first half)*, knit the next stitch *(second half)* and leave on the needle, then knit the skipped stitch and drop both stitches from left needle at the same time.

Crocheted **cables and/or cross stitches** can be formed by working over the same number of stitches used for the knitted cable or cross stitch as follows: skip the designated number of stitches *(first half)* and work a front post stitch around each of the next designated stitches *(second half)*, then work a front post stitch around each skipped stitch.

CROCHET

Cables
dc cross stitches

If the second half stitches are worked in **front** of the first half, the cable or cross stitch will cross left over right *(left cross)*; if they are worked in **back** of the first half, it will cross right over left *(right cross)*.

EYELETS

Simply stated, **eyelets** are holes worked into the fabric in a specific pattern.

Knitted eyelets are formed by working a yarn-over and a companion decrease, usually right beside the yarn-over, but it can be placed a few stitches away. A yarn-over without the decrease becomes an extra stitch or an increase. When knitting the yarn-over on the following row, take care not to twist the yarn-over strands—this will close the opening and the eyelet will be lost.

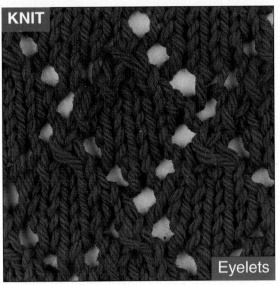

KNIT

Eyelets

Crocheted eyelets can be worked by simply making a chain-1 or chain-2 space and skipping a companion stitch on the previous row directly below the chain—no decrease is needed since skipping stitches maintains the same stitch count. If an increase is desired, then make a chain space as above but do not skip a companion stitch. ●

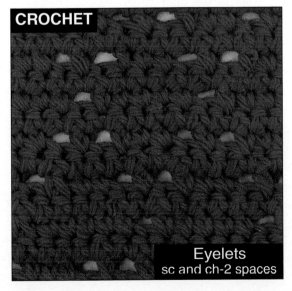

CROCHET

Eyelets
sc and ch-2 spaces

How to "Work In Pattern"

Knit patterns are usually written as a series of combined stitch patterns or design repeats with instructions for shaping where needed. Once the stitch combination and/or design repeat has been established, the remaining instructions may only say "work in pattern." This simply means to work the stitch pattern instructions exactly as previously stated, carefully keeping track of your stitches and rows.

To demonstrate how to work in pattern, we'll use a simple rib pattern with an 8-stitch repeat plus six extra stitches at the end of the row (*see Sample Knit and Crochet Patterns on next page*). For quick and easy comparison, we have placed the knit version in the left column with the crochet version beside it in the right column.

When instructions for shaping are incorporated into the established pattern, there are some helpful tips for keeping your place in the stitch pattern. These principles work the same whether for knit or crochet; even complicated stitch and design repeats can be mastered.

It's very helpful to keep a **notepad** handy to mark down the repeats and rows as they are completed.

Another tip for working in pattern is to **place a marker between each design repeat.**

When using markers in this manner, after stitches have been bound off or decreased, even after several decreases, you can see at a glance how many stitches you have left of an incomplete repeat. Then count from the marker to the decrease to determine what the next stitch should be.

For a decrease at the **end of a row,** whether you end with a complete or a partial repeat, simply work in pattern across to the last 2 stitches and work the decrease.

To find which stitch of the repeat is next after binding off across the **center of a row,** such as a neck opening, count the stitch pattern repeatedly across the bound-off stitches, then resume the pattern in the next st.

When **beginning a row** with a decrease or with bound-off stitches, resume working in pattern using the same procedure as for the second side of the neck shaping as demonstrated in the Sample Patterns.

At the beginning or end of the rows, when **adding stitches** using increases or cast-on stitches or chains, incorporate each new stitch into the pattern to become partial or full repeats (depending on the number of additional stitches), thus extending the stitch pattern across the rows.

Although knit and crochet patterns are written quite differently, with a little planning and forethought, a knit pattern can be nicely adapted for use in a crochet project as demonstrated in the following sample pattern. ●

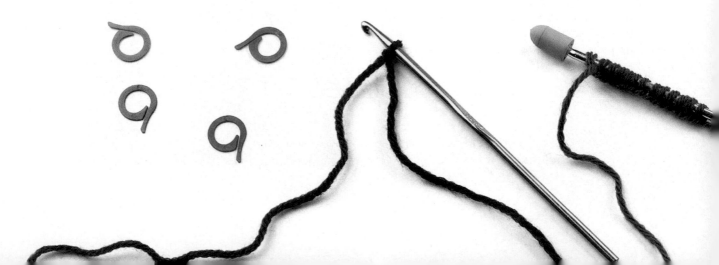

SAMPLE KNIT PATTERN

Cast on 62.
Row 1: K 6, (P 2, K 6) across.
Row 2: P 6, (K 2, P 6) across.
Pattern is established in rows 1 and 2.
Rows 3–80: Work in pattern.
Row 81: For **first side,** work in pattern across first 24 sts; for **neck,** with separate skein of yarn, bind off 14; for **second side,** work in pattern across.
Rows 82–84: Working both sides at same time with separate skeins of yarn, work in pattern with decrease at neck edge on each side in each row.
Bind off each side.

To Work in Pattern For Neck Shaping:

On row 81, the 14 bound-off stitches use one full repeat plus six stitches of the next repeat. Therefore, resume working in pattern by working the seventh and eighth stitches of the incomplete repeat, then continue in pattern across the remainder of the row.

On row 82, work across the first side to the last 2 sts and work the decrease; on the second side, work the decrease (this will use the first 2 stitches of the next repeat); work the next 6 stitches in pattern to complete the repeat, then resume pattern across the row.

On row 83, work across the first side to the last two sts and work the decrease; on the second side, the decrease will use the first two stitches, so begin with the third stitch to complete the partial repeat, then continue in pattern across the row.

On row 84, work across the first side to the last 2 sts and work the decrease; on the second side, work the decrease (this will use the third and fourth stitches of the partial repeat); work the last 4 stitches of the partial repeat, then begin a new repeat and continue in pattern across the row.

SAMPLE CROCHET PATTERN

Row 1: Ch 64, dc in fourth ch from hook, dc in each ch across, turn. *(62 dc made)*
Row 2: Ch 2 *(counts as first hdc),* hdcfp around each of next 5 sts, hdcbp around next 2 sts, (hdcfp around each of next 6 sts, hdcbp around next 2 sts) across to last 6 sts, hdcfp around each of next 5 sts, hdc in last st, turn.
Row 3: Ch 2, hdcbp around each of next 5 sts, hdcfp around each of next 2 sts, (hdcbp around each of next 6 sts, hdcfp around each of next 2 sts) across to last 6 sts, hdcbp around each of next 5 sts, hdc in last st, turn.
To **work in pattern,** repeat rows 2 and 3 alternately.
Rows 4–80: Work in pattern.
Row 81: For **first side,** work in pattern across first 23 sts, hdc in next st leaving remaining sts unworked, turn.
NOTES: For **beginning decrease (beg dec),** ch 1, hdc first 2 sts tog.
For **end decrease (dec),** hdc last 2 sts tog.
Rows 82–84: Work in pattern with **beg dec** or **end dec** *(see Notes)* at neck edge on each row. At end of last row, fasten off.
Row 81: For **neck edge,** skip next 14 sts on row 80; for **second side,** join with sl st in next st, ch 2, resume in pattern across last 23 sts, turn.
Rows 82–84: Work in pattern with beg dec or end dec at neck edge on each row. At end of last row, fasten off.

To Work in Pattern For Neck Shaping:

Row 82 On first side: Work beg dec and next 6 post sts of the partial repeat, then resume in pattern for remainder of row.
Row 83: Work in pattern across to the last 2 sts and work end dec.
Row 84: Work beg dec and the next 4 post sts of the partial repeat, then resume in pattern for remainder of row.
Row 82 On second side: Work in pattern across to the last 2 sts and work end dec.
On row 83, Work beg dec and the next 5 post sts of the partial repeat, then resume in pattern for remainder of row.
Row 84: Work in pattern across to the last 2 sts and work end dec.

Drawing and Working From Schematics

A schematic is a small-scale diagram of finished knit or crochet pieces before assembly. They are normally used for clothing patterns, but can also be used for quilts or afghans, toys, and other items that must be properly sized to fit together for assembly.

Schematics can offer valuable information at a glance about measurements of completed pieces, as well as shape and correct positioning of pieces for blocking and assembly.

When converting a knitted pattern that has complicated areas of shaping, if the pattern does not include a schematic, it is sometimes helpful to draw one for yourself. Draw a rough outline of the shape of each piece of the finished item—graph paper is often helpful. Calculate the number of stitches or rows needed in the various sections by multiplying the stitch or row gauge by the measurements of the section and mark each on the drawing. Then as you crochet the piece, compare the schematic to your work to be sure your piece is developing the proper shaping.

Use clothing schematics to your advantage by comparing body measurements of the person who will wear the garment to the dia-

gram. This will provide the information for a beautifully fitted garment before you ever pick up a hook or needles to begin.

These garment measurements are important to finished style and fit:

1. **Chest/bust:** Width across front or back at chest or bust (add front and back together for total).
2. **Bottom ribbing:** Width of ribbing.
3. **Shoulder:** Width of shoulder from neck edge to armhole edge.
4. **Armhole:** Depth from shoulder straight down to bottom of the armhole.
5. **Across back:** Width across the upper back at shoulders.
6. **Side body:** Length from bottom edge to underarm.
7. **Back length:** Length from bottom edge to base of neck at center back.
8. **Underarm sleeve:** Length of sleeve from underarm to bottom edge.
9. **Upper arm:** Circumference around sleeve at upper arm.
10. **Sleeve ribbing:** Width of sleeve ribbing.

Use schematics along with pattern instructions for added help in blocking, assembling and finishing your crocheted items. ●

Schematic

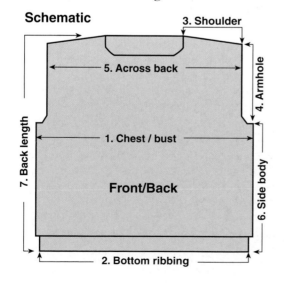

3. Shoulder
5. Across back
4. Armhole
1. Chest / bust
7. Back length
6. Side body
Front/Back
2. Bottom ribbing

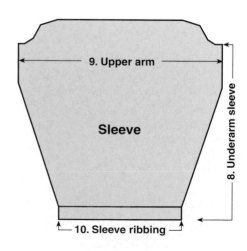

9. Upper arm
Sleeve
8. Underarm sleeve
10. Sleeve ribbing

Blocking, Seams and Joinings

BLOCKING

When each piece is completed, it should be blocked before assembly. Using the measurements listed on the pattern, or the schematic measurements if you are using one, shape the piece on a padded surface such as a blocking board or ironing board and pin in place with rust-proof pins. If you have kept an accurate gauge, the pieces will be the desired size and will easily match the measurements or schematic.

Block each piece by allowing steam from your steam iron or steamer to penetrate the fibers, but **do not touch it with the iron,** as this will flatten and distort the stitches. Pat the stitches into shape and allow the pieces to dry thoroughly before moving.

SEAMS AND JOININGS

Quality finishing is an important step in producing beautiful hand-crafted items. Even a well-stitched item will be less attractive if the seams are bulky or uneven.

Different seams should be used depending

on the type of yarn and stitches used. Also consider the location of the seam if making a garment or a shaped item such as a toy animal.

Experiment with several methods for each seam. After becoming familiar with the various seams, you'll be able to choose seams that make your crocheted items stand out among the very best.

When making a seam, match the stitches and rows unless the instructions state to ease or gather fullness; use yarn the same color as the pieces being sewn and if possible, change yarn colors when the stitch colors change.

A good seam to use to join pieces edge-to-edge is the **whipstitch.**

Whipstitch Seam

Thread a large tapestry needle with matching yarn and attach the yarn to both pieces at the beginning of the seam. To sew ends of rows together, (insert the needle from the **top** at end of the row on the first piece, then from the **bottom** at end of the row on the other piece and pull snug); move up to the next row and repeat between ( ). Continue in this manner across to the end of the seam. Secure and hide the yarn end.

Whipstitch can also be used to sew tops of stitches and/or starting chains together. Just insert the needle through the tops of the stitches or through the chain rather than through the ends of the rows.

Backstitches are commonly used for joining pieces where there is a seam allowance. This is helpful when a slightly larger piece is to be eased to fit a smaller piece, but it also adds more bulk to the seam.

Hold the pieces with right sides together and attach the yarn to both pieces at the beginning of the seam. Skip the next stitch

Backstitch Seam

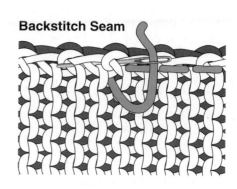

(or row), run the needle from the **bottom** through the next st and out at the top; go back and insert the needle from the **top** through the skipped stitch to the bottom in a looping manner and pull snug. (Skip one stitch past the last backstitch and run the needle through to the top, drop back and run the needle to the bottom next to the last backstitch to form another loop and pull snug); repeat between ( ) to the end of the seam. Secure and hide the yarn end.

Crochet **slip stitch** is another way of joining pieces with seam allowances.

Slip Stitch Seam

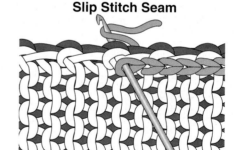

Hold the pieces with right sides together and attach the yarn to both pieces at the beginning of the seam. With the yarn held behind the work, insert the hook through the first stitch (or row) of both pieces and pull a loop of yarn through to the front; (insert the hook through the next stitch of both pieces and pull a loop through to the front and through the loop on the hook); repeat between ( ) to the end of the seam. Cut the yarn leaving an end to hide; pull the cut end through the loop on the hook and pull snug. Secure and hide the yarn end. ●

Chapter Two

A Sampler Afghan

*T*his sampler afghan consists of squares used as lessons throughout the chapters of the book. You'll find complete instructions for both knitted and crocheted versions. As you make your way through the chapters, you'll find square-by-square instructions for converting the knitted version to crochet and learn the logic behind each step. This way, when you finish your afghan, you'll be able to apply the same principles to other projects on your own.

Large Afghan

KNIT

Sampler Afghan
Designed by Darla Sims

GENERAL INFORMATION

*1: For comparison, instructions for **Knit Version** are in blue type; instructions for **Crochet Version** are in black type.*

2: Afghan can be made using only one color; simply disregard the color changes and work each Square using all same color yarn.

*3: If needed, **change to another needle or hook size** to obtain the proper gauge; before Edging, each Large Afghan Square should be 7" x 7"; each Baby Afghan Square should be 6" x 6".*

FINISHED SIZES

Baby knit or crochet Afghans are about 39" x 54"; each Square with Edging is 7½" x 7½".

Large knit or crochet Afghans are about 43" x 60"; each Square with Edging is 8½" x 8½".

CROCHET SPECIAL STITCH

Work each **front post (fp)** or **back post (bp,** *see Crochet Stitch Guide on page 191)* around designated st on **row before last,** pull up to height of row being worked. **Always skip one** st on last row for **each fp** or **bp.**

LARGE—KNIT VERSION

MATERIALS: Wool-Ease® yarns by Lion Brand® Yarn Company: **Chunky** Art. 630 for **Squares:** 42 oz. in desired colors—item shown uses about 14 oz. each Fisherman #099 (white), Foliage #187 (color A) and Willow #173 (color B). **Worsted** Art. 620 for **Edgings** and **Borders:** 25 oz. Fisherman #099 (white); tapestry needle; needles and crochet hooks: for **Squares,** cable needle and Nos. 10 *(small),* 10½ *(medium)* and 11 *(large)* knitting needles; for **Borders,** size H crochet hook *(or needles and hook needed to obtain gauges).*

GAUGES (see General Information No. 3): With **chunky yarn** and **needles** needed to obtain gauge for individual **Square,** each row of sts on Square = 7" across; finished square is 7" x 7". For **Edgings and Border,** with **H hook** and **worsted yarn,** 4 sc = 1", 3 dc and one ch in shell pattern = 1".

LARGE—CROCHET VERSION

MATERIALS: 50 oz. in desired colors of Wool-Ease® Art. 620 by Lion Brand® Yarn Company or **worsted yarn**—item shown uses Fisherman #099 (white), for multi-color version, 12 oz. color A, 12 oz. color B and 26 oz. white; tapestry needle; size G *(small),* H *(medium)* and I *(large)* crochet hooks *(or hooks needed to obtain gauges).*

GAUGES (see General Information No. 3): With **worsted yarn** and hook needed to obtain gauge for individual **Square,** each row of sts on Square = 7" across; finished Square is 7" x 7"; For **Edgings and Border,** with **H hook** and worsted yarn, 4 sc = 1", 3 dc and one ch in shell pattern = 1".

BABY—KNIT VERSION

MATERIALS: Yarns by Lion Brand® Yarn Company: 32 oz. in desired colors of Pound of Love Art. 550 or worsted yarn for Squares—item shown uses 14 oz. White #100, 9 oz. each Pastel Pink #101 (color A) and Pastel Green #156 (color B); 12 oz. White #100 Baby Soft Art. 920 or sport yarn for Edgings and Border; tapestry needle; needles and crochet hooks: for Squares, cable needle and Nos. 8 *(small)*, 9 *(medium)* and 10 *(large)* knitting needles; for Borders, size F crochet hook *(or needles and hook needed to obtain gauges)*.

GAUGES (see General Information No. 3): With **worsted yarn** and needles needed to obtain gauge for individual **Square,** each row of sts on Square = 6" across; finished Square is 6" x 6". For **Edgings and Border,** with **F hook** and sport yarn, 9 sc = 2", 9 sts and chs in shell pattern = 2".

BABY—CROCHET VERSION

MATERIALS: 35 oz. in desired colors of Baby Soft Art. 920 by Lion Brand® Yarn Company or **sport yarn:** item shown uses 15 oz. White #100, 10 oz. each Pastel Pink #101 (color A) and Pastel Green #156 (color B); tapestry needle; size F *(small),* G *(medium)* and H *(large)* crochet hooks *(or hooks needed to obtain gauges)*.

GAUGES (see General Information No. 3): With **sport yarn** and hook needed to obtain gauge for individual **Square,** each row of sts on Square = 6" across; finished Square is 6" x 6"; For **Edgings and Border,** with **F hook** and sport yarn, 9 sc = 2", 9 sts and chs in shell pattern = 2".

Knit or Crochet Afghan

1: To make **either size** Afghan in either **Knit** or **Crochet,** using yarns and gauges listed for individual item, make one Afghan Square of each Stitch Pattern as instructed in Chapters 3–6. The instructions for each Square begin on the pages listed below:

2: When all Squares with Edgings are completed, work **Assembly** and **Border** according to Basic Finishing beginning on page 28.

Baby Afghan

KNIT

CROCHET

Basic Finishing

Use as instructed for Knit or Crochet Version of Sampler Afghan

EDGING (work around each Square)
HELPFUL HINT FOR KNIT VERSION:

To stabilize ends of rows on each side of Square as you work rnd 1, work over a strand of matching-color yarn—use tail from cast-on or bind-off or a separate strand. After completing rnd 2, pull loose ends of separate strands to proper measurement and secure.

Rnd 1: Using crochet hook and white yarn for **Edgings and Border** *(see Materials for individual item)*, with right side of Square facing, join with sc in any corner st; working in ends of rows and in sts, evenly space 27 sc across to next corner st, (2 sc in corner st, evenly space 27 sc across to next corner st) 3 times, sc in same st as first sc, join with sl st in first sc. *(29 sc on each side)*

Rnd 2: (Ch 3, 2 dc) in first st, (ch 1, skip next 3 sts, 3 dc in next st) 7 times, ch 2 at corner; *3 dc in next st, (ch 1, skip next 3 sts; 3 dc in next st) 7 times, ch 2 at corner; repeat from * 2 more times, join with sl st in top of ch-3. Fasten off. *(24 dc and 7 chs on each side, 2 chs at each corner)*

ASSEMBLY

After all Squares are completed, assemble Afghan as follows: With wrong sides together, matching sts and working through both top loops of each dc and each ch, sew or slip stitch pieces together according to Afghan Assembly Diagram.

Continued on page 30

Afghan Assembly Diagram

Alternating Cables	Eyelet Cables	Diamonds	Mitered Corners
Hourglass	Beaded Rib	Tri-Color Checks	Bare Branches
Parallel Lines	Crossed Stripes	Basketweave	Baby Cables
Plaid Stitch	Diagonal Rib	Berry Stitch	Alternating Links
Bobble Tree	Flying Geese	Dash Stitch	Gum Balls
Entwined Cables	Boxed Cables	Zigzags	Diamond Columns

BORDER (work around entire Afghan)

Rnd 1: Using crochet hook and white yarn for **Edgings and Border** *(see Materials for individual item)*, join with sl st in second ch of any corner ch-2 sp, (ch 3, 2 dc) in same ch as sl st, *ch 1, (3 dc in next ch-1 sp, ch 1) across side to ch-2 sp at next corner, 3 dc in first ch of corner, ch 2, 3 dc in second ch; repeat from * 2 more times, ch 1, (3 dc in next ch-1 sp, ch 1) across to next corner, 3 dc in first ch at corner, ch 1, join with sc in top of ch-3.

Rnds 2–6: (Ch 3, 2 dc) in center of joining sc, *ch 1, (3 dc in next ch-1 sp, ch 1) across to ch-2 sp at next corner, 3 dc in first ch of corner, ch 2, 3 dc in second ch; repeat from * 2 more times, ch 1, (3 dc in next ch-1 sp, ch 1) across to corner, 3 dc in ch-1 at corner, ch 1, join with sc in top of ch-3 *(counts as ch)*.

For one-color Border:

Rnds 7–9: Repeat rnd 2.

Rnd 10: (Ch 3, 2 dc) in center of joining sc, *ch 1, (3 dc in next ch-1 sp, ch 1) across to ch-2 sp at next corner, 3 dc in first ch of corner, ch 2, 3 dc in second ch; repeat from * 2 more times, ch 1, (3 dc in next ch-1 sp, ch 1) across to corner, 3 dc in ch-1 at corner, ch 2, join with sl st in ch-3. Fasten off.

For Multi-color Border:

Rnd 7: (Ch 3, 2 dc) in center of joining sc, *ch 1, (3 dc in next ch-1 sp, ch 1) across to ch-2 sp at next corner, 3 dc in first ch of corner, ch 2, 3 dc in second ch; repeat from * 2 more times, ch 1, (3 dc in next ch-1 sp, ch 1) across to corner, 3 dc in ch-1 at corner, ch 2, join with sl st in ch-3. Fasten off.

Rnd 8: With color A yarn, repeat rnd 1.

Rnd 9: Repeat rnd 7.

Rnd 10: With color B yarn, join with sl st in second ch of any corner ch-2 sp, (ch 3, 2 dc) in same ch as sl st, *ch 1, (3 dc in next ch-1 sp, ch 1) across side to ch-2 sp at next corner, 3 dc in first ch of corner, ch 2, 3 dc in second ch; repeat from * 2 more times, ch 1, (3 dc in next ch-1 sp, ch 1) across to next corner, 3 dc in first ch at corner, ch 2, join with sl st in ch-3. Fasten off. ●

Chapter Three

Basic Knit and Purl Combinations

*B*asic knit and purl combinations are the building blocks for knitting. As you make the squares, you will learn how to interpret these in crochet. Then you can advance to the enticing lineup of projects.

Basic Knit and Purl Combinations

In knitting, alternating rows of basic knit and purl stitches form a flat, smooth fabric; the knit side of the fabric is stockinette stitch; the purl side of the same stitches is reverse stockinette stitch.

Other combinations of basic knit and purl stitches also form some high-low stitch patterns, such as garter stitch, basketweave, ribbing and geometric shapes.

In this chapter, we address some of the crochet stitches which can produce the look of these basic knit and purl combinations.

Tri-Color Checks

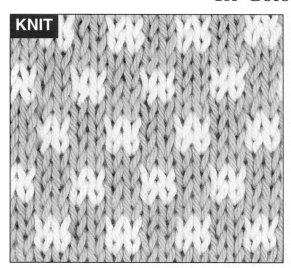
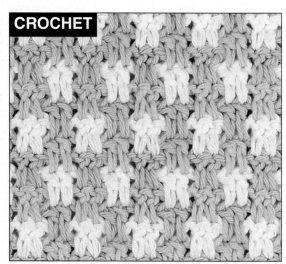

Plaid

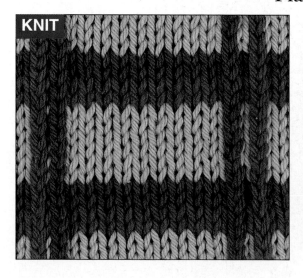

Basketweave

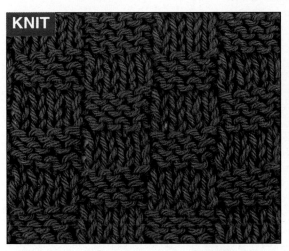

Alternating Links

Mitered Corners

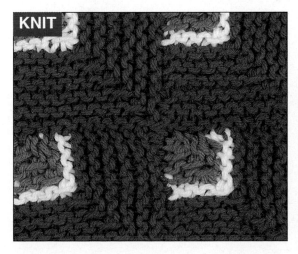

Tri-Color Stitch Pattern

Knitted stockinette stitches and slipped stitches worked in multiples of two rows each of three colors are used to create this check stitch design.

To duplicate the look in crochet, work one row of each color using half-double crochet stitches to resemble stockinette stitches. The slipped stitches are formed by working chain-2 spaces to hold their place; then on the next row and using the next color, double crochet stitches are worked over the chain-2 spaces into stitches of the row before last to create the look of the slipped stitches.

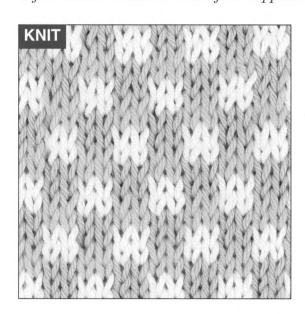
KNIT

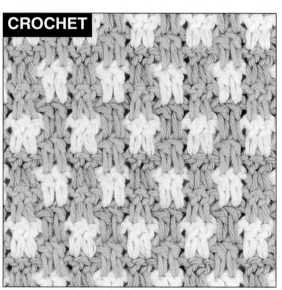
CROCHET

Afghan Square: Tri-Color Checks

READ BEFORE STARTING

*Refer to **Chapter 2** for instructions for using Squares to make either Knit or Crochet Version of Large Afghan or Baby Afghan.*

*For comparison, each Square has instructions for **Knit Version** in blue type, and instructions for **Crochet Version** in black type.*

KNIT VERSION

With medium needles and color B, cast on 26.

NOTES: *When slipping sts, carry yarn loosely along purl side of work; always slip sts as if to purl.*

CROCHET VERSION

Row 1: With medium hook and color B, ch 28, dc in fourth ch from hook, dc in next ch, (ch 2, skip next 2 chs, dc in next 2 chs) 5 times, ch 2, skip next 2 chs, dc in last ch, turn. *(First 3 chs count as first st—*

When changing colors, drop yarn; pick up again when needed.

Row 1: With color B, K 3, slip 2 *(see Notes)*, (K 2, slip 2) across to last st, K 1.

Row 2: P 1, (slip 2, P 2) across to last st, P 1.

Row 3: With color A *(see Notes)*, K 1, (slip 2, K 2) across to last st, K 1.

Row 4: P 3, slip 2, (P 2, slip 2) across to last st, P 1.

Row 5: With white, K 3, slip 2, (K 2, slip 2) across to last st, K 1.

Row 6: P 1, (slip 2, P 2) across to last st, P 1.

Row 7: With color B, K 1, (slip 2, K 2) across to last st, K 1.

Row 8: P 3, slip 2, (P 2, slip 2) across to last st, P 1.

Row 9: With color A, K 3, slip 2, (K 2, slip 2) across to last st, K 1.

Row 10: P 1, (slip 2, P 2) across to last st, P 1.

Row 11: With white, K 1, (slip 2, K 2) across to last st, K 1.

Row 12: P 3, slip 2, (P 2, slip 2) across to last st, P 1.

Rows 13–48: Repeat rows 1–12 consecutively.

Last row: With color B, K across.
Bind off.

Piece should measure same as gauge.

Work Edging in Basic Finishing on page 28.

26 sts and chs made)

NOTES: Fasten off at end of each row; join next color with sl st in first st.

Work in color sequence of: One row color A; one row color B; one row white.

Row 2: With next color *(see Notes)*, ch 2 *(counts as first hdc)*; working over ch-2 throughout, (dc in 2 skipped chs of starting ch, ch 2, skip next 2 sts on last row) 6 times, hdc in last st on last row, turn.

Row 3: With next color, ch 2, (dc in 2 skipped sts in row before last, ch 2, skip next 2 sts on last row) 6 times, hdc in last st, turn.

Next rows: Repeat row 3 until piece measures same size in length and width.

Last row: Ch 1, sc in first st, (dc in 2 skipped sts in row before last, sc in next 2 sts on last row) 6 times, sc in last st. Fasten off.

Piece should measure same as gauge.

Work Edging in Basic Finishing on page 28.

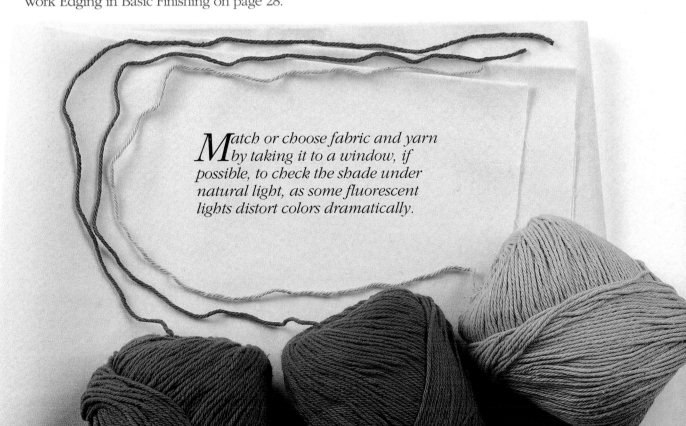

*M*atch or choose fabric and yarn by taking it to a window, if possible, to check the shade under natural light, as some fluorescent lights distort colors dramatically.

Tri-Color Beach Bag

Designed by Donna Jones

Heading to the beach in style is no problem at all with this whimsical tote made using the Tri-Color stitch pattern. This crochet stitch achieves the look of basic stockinette stitch with knitted-in color patterns.

FINISHED SIZE: About 2½" thick x 16½" wide x 17½" high, plus Strap.

MATERIALS: Yarns by Lion Brand® Yarn Company—Kitchen Cotton Art. 760 or cotton worsted yarn: 10 oz. Lime #174; 8 oz. each Sunflower #157 and White #100, small amount each Navy #110, Sage #181, Maize #186 and Cinnamon #135; MicroSpun Art. 910 or shiny sport yarn: 2 oz. Buttercup #158, small amount Mango #186; 1 yd. heavy white fabric; straight pins; iron and ironing board; sewing needle and thread; crochet stitch markers; tapestry needle; E and G crochet hooks *(or hooks needed to obtain gauges)*.

GAUGES: G hook, 16 sts in pattern = 4"; 4 rows in pattern = 1".
E hook, rnds 1–5 of Sun = 2" across; 5 sc = 1".

SIDE *(make 2)*

Row 1: Using cotton yarn, with G hook and lime, ch 70, dc in fourth ch from hook, dc in next ch, (ch 2, skip next 2 chs, dc in next 2 chs) across with dc in last ch, turn. Fasten off. *(First 3 chs count as first dc—68 sts and chs made)*

Row 2: Join sunflower with sl st in first st, ch 4 *(counts as first hdc and ch-2),* skip next 2 sts on last row; working over ch-2 throughout, (dc in 2 skipped chs of starting ch, ch 2, skip next 2 sts on last row) across with hdc in last st on last row, turn. Fasten off.

Row 3: Join white with sl st in first st, ch 2 *(counts as first hdc),* dc in 2 skipped sts on row before last, (ch 2, skip next 2 sts on last row, dc in 2 skipped sts in row before last) across with hdc in second ch of ch 4 on last row, turn. Fasten off.

Row 4: Join lime with sl st in first st, ch 4, skip next 2 sts, (dc in 2 skipped sts in row before last, ch 2, skip next 2 sts on last row) across with hdc in top of ch-2, turn. Fasten off.

Row 5: With sunflower, repeat row 3.
Row 6: With white, repeat row 4.
Row 7: With lime, repeat row 3.
Row 8: With sunflower, repeat row 4.

Rows 9–57: Repeat rows 3–8 consecutively, ending with row 3.

Row 58: Join lime with sc in first st, sc in next 2 sts, (dc in 2 skipped sts in row before last, sc in next 2 sts on last row) across with sc in top of ch-2. Fasten off.

GUSSET AND STRAP

Row 1: Using cotton yarn, with G hook and lime, ch 14, dc in fourth ch from hook, dc in next ch, (ch 2, skip next 2 chs, dc in next 2 chs) across with dc in last ch, turn. Fasten off. *(12 sts and chs made)*

Row 2: Repeat row 2 of Side.

Next rows: Repeat rows 3–8 of Side consecutively until piece measures about 75" long, ending with row 5.

Last row: Join white with sc in first st, sc in next 2 sts, (dc in 2 skipped sts in row before last, sc in next 2 sts on last row) across with sc in last st. Fasten off.

LINING

1: Using crocheted pieces as patterns, cut one piece of fabric to match each crocheted piece plus ¼" extra all around; if necessary for Gusset and Strap Lining, cut 4"-wide strips and sew end to end for length needed, separate seams and press flat, then cut out Lining from this piece.

2: With each Lining piece, press all outer edges ¼" to wrong side.

3: With wrong sides together, center each Lining piece over matching crocheted

piece and pin in place—**be sure to leave tops of sts or narrow edge of crocheted pieces exposed** for Assembly and to work border sts around Strap and tops of Sides after Assembly.

4: On each piece, using sewing needle and thread and taking care that stitches do not show on outside, sew each folded Lining edge in place leaving tops of sts and narrow edges exposed. On each Side piece, tack Lining and Side together here and there across piece to stabilize.

SUN

Rnd 1: With E hook and buttercup sport yarn, ch 2, 8 sc in second ch from hook. *(8 sc made)* Work in continuous rnds, do not turn; **mark first st** of each rnd.

Rnd 2: 2 sc in each st around. *(16)*

Rnd 3: (2 sc next st, sc in next st) around. *(24)*

Rnd 4: (Sc in next st, 2 sc next st, sc in next st) around. *(32)*

Rnd 5: Sc in each st around.

Rnd 6: (Sc in next 3 sts, 2 sc next st) around. *(40)*

Rnd 7: (Sc in next 2 sts, 2 sc next st, sc in next 2 sts) around. *(48)*

Rnd 8: (Sc in next 5 sts, 2 sc next st) around. *(56)*

Rnd 9: (Sc in next 3 sts, 2 sc next st, sc in next 3 sts) around. *(64)*

Rnd 10: Sc in each st around.

Rnd 11: (2 sc next st, sc in next 7 sts) around. *(72)*

Rnd 12: (Sc in next 4 sts, 2 sc next st, sc in next 4 sts) around. *(80)*

Rnd 13: (Sc in next 9 sts, 2 sc next st) around. *(88)*

Rnd 14: (Sc in next 5 sts, 2 sc next st, sc in next 5 sts) around. *(96)*

Rnd 15: (Sc in next 23 sts, 2 sc next st) around. *(100)*

Rnd 16: *Skip next st, (hdc, 2 dc, ch 1, tr, ch 2, sl st in tr, ch 1, 2 dc, hdc) in next st, skip next st, sc in next st; repeat from * around, join with sl st in first hdc. Fasten off.

Sunglasses

Rnds 1–3: Using cotton yarn, with E hook and navy, work rnds 1–3 of Sun.

Rnd 4: Work rnd 4 of Sun, sl st in next st. Fasten off.

Rnds 5–7: Using cotton yarn, with E hook and navy, work rnds 1–3 of Sun.

Rnd 8: Work rnd 4 of Sun, sl st in next st; **to join** sides, sl st in last sc on rnd 4. Fasten off.

Rnd 9: With E hook and mango sport yarn, join with sc in first sc past joining of rnds 4 and 8, (2 sc in next st, sc in next 2 sts) 10 times, skip sl st, sc in next st, (2 sc in next st, sc in next 2 sts) 10 times, skip sl st, join with sl st in first sc. Fasten off. *(82)*

Rnd 10: Working this rnd in **back lps** *(see Crochet Stitch Guide on page 191)*, skip first 20 sts on rnd 9, join mango with sl st in next st, sl st in next 41 sts leaving last 20 sts unworked. Fasten off.

Mouth

Using cotton yarn, with E hook and cinnamon, ch 24, sl st in second ch from hook, sc in next ch, sc next 2 chs tog, hdc in next ch, dc next 2 chs tog, dc in next 4 chs, sc in next ch, dc in next 4 chs, dc next 2 chs tog, hdc in next ch, sc next 2 chs tog, sc in next ch, sl st in last ch; working on opposite side of ch, sl st in first ch, sc in next 3 chs, 2 sc in next ch, sc in next ch, 2 hdc in next ch, hdc in next 9 chs, 2 hdc in next ch, sc in next ch, 2 sc in next ch, sc in next 3 chs, sl st in last ch. Fasten off.

Sun Assembly

Match bottom of joining sl st on rnd 8 of Sunglasses to center of rnd 1 on Sun; sew Sunglasses in place *(see photo).*

Sew Mouth to Sun centered about ¾" below Sunglasses.

SANDAL (make 2)

Rnd 1: Using cotton yarn, with E hook and sage, ch 15, 3 sc in second ch from hook, sc in next 5 chs, hdc in next 7 chs, 5 hdc in end ch; working on opposite side of ch, hdc in next 7 chs, sc in next 5 chs. *(32 sts made)* Work in continuous rnds, do not turn; **mark first st** of each rnd.

Rnd 2: 2 sc in each of first 3 sts, sc in next 7 sts, hdc in next 5 sts, 2 hdc in each of next 5 sts, hdc in next 5 sts, sc in next 7 sts. *(40)*

Rnd 3: (2 sc in next st, sc in next st) 3 times, sc in next 5 sts, hdc in next 10 sts, 2 hdc in each of next 6 sts, **mark sixth and seventh sts** of last 12 sts made, hdc in next 10 sts, sc in next 3 sts, sl st in first st. Fasten off.

Row 4: For **straps,** with E hook and maize, leaving 5" end, ch 9, hdc in rnd 2 between two marked sts, ch 9. Leaving 5" end, fasten off.

Lay straps flat with right side up; use 5" ends to sew to posts of sts at sides of rnd 3 *(see photo).*

STARFISH

Rnd 1: With E hook and maize, ch 2, 5 sc in second ch from hook, join with sl st in first st.

Rnd 2: (Ch 9; working in **back bar** of chs—*see illustration,* sl st in second ch from hook, sl st in next ch, sc in next 6 chs, sl st in next st on rnd 1) 5 times ending

Back Bar of Ch

with last sl st in joining sl st of rnd 1. Fasten off. *(5 arms)*

Rnd 3: Place cinnamon loop on hook; joining first st in any arm, (sc in ch-1 sp at end of arm, ch 1; working in **back lps** of sts and chs, sl st in next 7 sts, sc last sc and center of rnd 1 and first ch on next arm tog, sl st in next 7 chs, ch 1) 5 times, join with sl st in first sc. Fasten off.

ASSEMBLY AND FINISHING

1: On crocheted Side to be front of Bag, sew Sun to upper right about 2" in from top and side edges *(see photo).*

2: Arrange and sew Sandals and Starfish to front Side at lower left.

3: To assemble Bag, sew first and last rows of Gusset and Strap together to form ring.

4: For **Gusset,** with seam at center of row 1 on one Side, taking care not to stretch or gather either piece, pin ends of rows on Gusset and Strap to starting chain of one Side; pin ends of rows on Side to Gusset, leaving remaining rows free for Strap; sew together using tapestry needle and yarn.

5: Repeat step 4 with other Side on opposite ends of same rows on Gusset.

6: Join lime with sc in second st on top row of either Side, sc in each st across to last st, sc last st and first unworked row on Strap together; spacing sts so edge lays flat, sc in ends of rows across Strap to last row before Side, sc last row of Strap and first st on Side together, join with sl st in first sc. Fasten off.

7: Repeat step 6 on other Side and opposite ends of rows on Strap. ●

Plaid Stitch Pattern

*T*o duplicate this knitted Plaid stitch design, we use rows of single crochet stitches to resemble stockinette stitches and changing row colors as indicated for the knit pattern. The vertical stripes are worked the same for knit or for crochet.

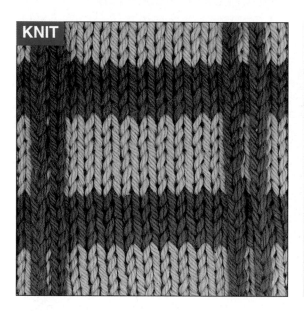

KNIT

CROCHET

Afghan Square: Plaid

READ BEFORE STARTING

Refer to **Chapter 2** for instructions for using Squares to make either Knit or Crochet Version of Large Afghan or Baby Afghan.

For comparison, each Square has instructions for **Knit Version** in blue type, and instructions for **Crochet Version** in black type.

KNIT VERSION

With medium needles and color B, cast on 24.

Rows 1–6: For **stockinette st (st st)**, work K rows and P rows alternately. At end of last row, drop color B; do not cut.

Rows 7–8: With color A, work in st st. At end of last row, drop color A; do not cut.

Rows 9–10: With white, work in st st. At end of last row, drop white; do not cut.

CROCHET VERSION

Row 1: With medium hook and color B, ch 25, sc in second ch from hook, sc in each ch across, turn. *(24 sts made)*

Rows 2–6: Ch 1, sc in each st across, turn.

Row 7: Ch 1, sc in each st across changing to color A in last st *(see Crochet Stitch Guide on page 191),* turn. Drop color B; pick up when needed.

Row 8: Ch 1, sc in each st across, turn.

Rows 11–30: Picking up dropped colors as needed, repeat rows 1–10 consecutively. Piece should measure same as gauge. Bind off with white. Cut all yarns.

*NOTE: For each **vertical stripe,** place loop of designated yarn on larger crochet hook; insert hook from front through center of designated cast-on st; holding yarn behind work and taking care that sts are worked loosely so piece is not distorted, yo with yarn and pull loop through to front of piece; working vertically across Square, (insert hook into center of st on next row, yo, pull through row and loop on hook) across to bind-off edge. Cut yarn leaving end to hide. Pull cut end through loop on hook; pull snug. Hide ends.*

First stripe: With color A, make a vertical stripe *(see Note)* in seventh sts from **right** edge.

Second stripe: With white, make a vertical stripe in eighth sts from **right** edge.

Third stripe: Repeat first stripe on **left** edge.

Fourth stripe: Repeat second stripe on **left** edge.

Work Edging in Basic Finishing on page 28.

Row 9: Ch 1, sc in each st across changing to white in last st, turn. Cut off color A.

Row 10: Ch 1, sc in each st across, turn.

Row 11: Ch 1, sc in each st across changing to color B in last st, turn. Cut off white.

Rows 12–29: Repeat rows 2–11 consecutively, ending with row 10.

Row 30: Ch 1, sc in each st across. Fasten off. Piece should measure same as gauge.

*NOTE: For each **vertical stripe,** place loop of yarn on larger crochet hook; insert hook from front through designated st on row 1; holding yarn behind work and taking care that sts are worked loosely so piece is not distorted, yo, pull loop through to front of piece; working vertically across Square, sl st in each row across. Fasten off.*

First stripe: With color A, work vertical stripe in seventh sts from **right** edge.

Second stripe: With white, work vertical stripe in eighth sts from **right** edge.

Third stripe: Repeat first stripe on **left** edge.

Fourth stripe: Repeat second stripe on **left** edge.

Piece should measure same as gauge.

Work Edging in Basic Finishing on page 28.

History of Plaid

*P*laid, or tartan style of cloth, is used to identify individual Clans. Originally the Scots were Irish invaders of the land from Irish Dairiada. The Norse invasions around 800 AD separated these Scots from the Irish and created a new country, Scottish Dairiada. It became what we now call Scotland. However, the style of dress remained the same in both countries until the middle of this millennium.

The clothing consisted of a shirt of linen, frequently embroidered and cut to the knees. The women wore them in a longer length that fell to the ankle. Over this, both wore a Brat, or cloak, of varying lengths pinned at the shoulder with a brooch. The higher a person's rank in society, the longer the brat. It was distinguished by its pattern of weave and colors. Today this pattern is called plaid.

In Gaelic, plaide means blanket. The word tartan, 'tiretaine' in French, means a type of cloth. The color system of rank was put in place by either the Tighernmas or Eochaid, the seventh and eighth of the Milesian line of Kings in Ireland. They lived about 800 BC and incorporated a system of distinguishing classes and professions by the colors of their clothing. A King or Queen would wear seven colors, a poet six, a cheiftain five, an army leader four, a landowner three, a rent payer two and a serf one color only.

While the original color system is no longer in use, the plaid has evolved from an individual identifier to one of an entire Clan. The Tartan and its pattern of weaves and color now identify the family. By passing the right to wear five-color plaid from the cheiftan to all family members, we now have the modern tartan.

Plaid Pillow

Designed by Donna Jones

A pillow is always a relaxing addition for some quality reading or quiet time.

FINISHED SIZE: About 12" square.

MATERIALS: Wool-Ease® Art. 620 by Lion Brand® Yarn Company or worsted yarn: 6 oz. Cranberry #138, 3 oz. each Fisherman #099 and Navy #111; 12" square pillow form; F crochet hook *(or hook needed to obtain gauge)*.

GAUGE: 9 sc = 2"; 9 sc rows = 2".

SIDE *(make 2)*

Row 1: With cranberry, ch 55, sc in second ch from hook, sc in each ch across, turn. *(54 sts made)*

Rows 2–5: Ch 1, sc in each st across, turn.

Row 6: Ch 1, sc in each st across changing to navy in last st *(see Crochet Stitch Guide on page 191)*, turn. Drop cranberry.

NOTE: *Do not cut dropped colors; pick up again when needed.*

Row 7: Ch 1, sc in each st across, turn.

Row 8: Ch 1, sc in each st across changing to fisherman in last st, turn. Drop navy.

Row 9: Ch 1, sc in each st across, turn.

Row 10: Ch 1, sc in each st across changing to cranberry in last st, turn. Drop fisherman.

Row 11: Ch 1, sc in each st across, turn.

Rows 12–51: Repeat rows 2–11 consecutively.

Rows 52–56: Ch 1, sc in each st across. At end of last row, fasten off all yarns.

VERTICAL STRIPES *(make on each Side)*

NOTE: *For each **vertical stripe,** place loop of designated yarn on hook; insert hook from front through designated st on row 1; holding yarn behind work and taking care that sts are worked loosely so piece is not distorted, yo and pull loop through to front of piece; working vertically across Square, sl st in each row across. Fasten off.*

First stripe: With navy, skip first eight sts from **right** edge, work vertical stripe along **ninth** sts from edge *(see photo)*.

Second stripe: With fisherman, work vertical stripe in **next** sts beside **previous** stripe.

Third stripe: With fisherman, skip next seven sts from **previous** stripe, work vertical stripe in **eighth** sts from stripe.

Fourth stripe: With navy, work vertical stripe in **next** sts beside **previous** stripe.

Next stripes: Repeat third and fourth stripes three more times for a total of ten stripes, leaving eight sts remaining along left edge.

BORDER *(make on each Side)*

Working around outer edge, with right side of piece facing, join cranberry with sc in any corner st, sc in same st, (sc in each st or in each row across to next corner, 3 sc in corner st) 3 times, sc in each st or in each row across to first corner, sc in same st as joining sc, join with sl st in joining sc. Fasten off.

ASSEMBLY

Hold Sides wrong sides together, matching stitches; working through both layers as one, join navy with sl st in first st; working from left to right, **reverse sc** *(see Crochet Stitch Guide)* in each st around, inserting pillow form before closing last side, join with sl st in first reverse sc. Fasten off. ●

Plaid Table Setting

Designed by Darla Sims

Brighten your breakfast table with this cheerful setting made with Plaid stitch.

FINISHED SIZES: Place Mat is 12" x 17"; Coaster is 6" square; Napkin Ring is 3¼" wide.

MATERIALS: MicroSpun Art. 910 by Lion Brand® Yarn Company or sport yarn: 5 oz. Lime #194, 2½ oz. each Purple #147 and Coral #103; tapestry needle; F and G crochet hooks *(or hook needed to obtain G hook gauge)*.

GAUGE: G hook; 9 sc = 2"; 9 sc rows = 2".

PLACE MAT

Row 1: With G hook and lime, ch 64, sc in second ch from hook, sc in each ch across, turn. *(63 sc made)*

Rows 2–5: Ch 1, sc in each st across, turn.

Row 6: Ch 1, sc in each st across changing to purple in last st *(see Crochet Stitch Guide on page 191),* turn. Drop lime.

Row 7: Ch 1, sc in each st across, turn.

Row 8: Ch 1, sc in each st across changing to coral in last st, turn. Fasten off purple.

Row 9: Ch 1, sc in each st across, turn.

Row 10: Ch 1, sc in each st across changing to lime in last st, turn. Fasten off coral.

Row 11: Ch 1, sc in each st across, turn.

Rows 12–51: Repeat rows 2–11 consecutively.

Rows 52–56: Ch 1, sc in each st across, turn.

Rnd 57: Working around outer edge, ch 1, sc in each st and in end of each row around with 3 sc in each corner, join with sl st in first sc. Fasten off.

Vertical Stripes

NOTE: *For each* **vertical stripe,** *place loop of designated yarn on hook; insert hook from front through designated st on row 1; holding yarn behind work and taking care that sts are worked loosely so piece is not distorted, yo and pull loop through to* front *of piece; working straight vertical lines across Square, (skip next row and sl st in next row) across. Fasten off.*

First stripe: With purple, skip first six sts from **right** edge, work vertical stripe in **seventh** sts from edge *(see photo).*

Second stripe: With coral, work vertical stripe in **next** sts beside previous stripe.

Third stripe: With purple, skip next five sts from **previous** stripe, work vertical stripe in **sixth** sts from previous stripe.

Fourth stripe: With coral, work vertical stripe in **next** sts beside previous stripe.

Next stripes: Repeat third and fourth stripes six more times for a total of ten stripes, leaving six sts remaining along left edge.

Border

Rnd 1: With F hook, join purple with sc in center st at any corner, ch 5, skip next st, (sc in next st, ch 5, skip next st) around, join with sl st in first sc. Fasten off.

Rnd 2: With F hook, working in **front** of rnd 1, join coral with sc in first skipped st, ch 5; working in **back** of rnd 1, sc in next skipped st, ch 5; (working in **front** of rnd 1, sc in next skipped st, ch 5; working in **back** of rnd 1, sc in next skipped st, ch 5) around, join with sl st in first sc. Fasten off.

COASTER

Row 1: With G hook and lime, ch 18, sc in second ch from hook, sc in each ch across, turn. *(17 sc made)*

Rows 2–3: Ch 1, sc in each st across, turn.

Row 4: Ch 1, sc in each st across changing to purple in last st *(see Crochet Stitch Guide on page 191),* turn. Drop lime.

Row 5: Ch 1, sc in each st across, turn.

Row 6: Ch 1, sc in each st across changing to coral in last st, turn. Fasten off purple.

Row 7: Ch 1, sc in each st across, turn.

Row 8: Ch 1, sc in each st across changing to lime in last st, turn. Fasten off coral.

Rows 9–13: Ch 1, sc in each st across, turn.

Rows 14–22: Repeat rows 4–12.

Rnd 23: Working around outer edge, ch 1, sc in each st and in end of each row around with 3 sc in each corner, join with sl st in first sc. Fasten off.

Vertical Stripes (see Note in Place Mat Vertical Stripes)

First stripe: With purple, skip first four sts from **right** edge, work vertical stripe in **fifth** sts from edge *(see photo)*.

Second stripe: With coral, work vertical stripe in **next** sts beside previous stripe.

Third stripe: With purple, skip next five sts from **previous** stripe, work vertical stripe in **sixth** sts from previous stripe.

Fourth stripe: With coral, work vertical stripe in **next** sts beside previous stripe, leaving four sts remaining along left edge.

Border

Joining in center st at any corner of Coaster, work same as Place Mat Border.

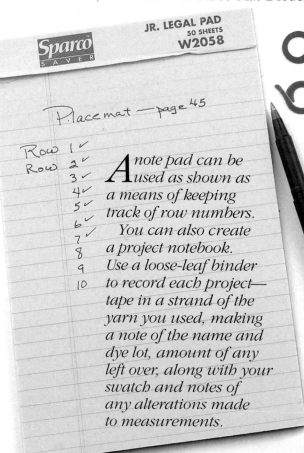

Placemat — page 45

Row 1 ✓
Row 2 ✓
3 ✓
4 ✓
5 ✓
6 ✓
7
8
9
10

A note pad can be used as shown as a means of keeping track of row numbers. You can also create a project notebook. Use a loose-leaf binder to record each project— tape in a strand of the yarn you used, making a note of the name and dye lot, amount of any left over, along with your swatch and notes of any alterations made to measurements.

NAPKIN RING

Row 1: With G hook and lime, ch 20, sc in second ch from hook, sc in each ch across, turn. *(19 sc made)*

Row 2: Ch 1, sc in each st across, turn.

Row 3: Ch 1, sc in each st across changing to purple in last st, turn. Drop lime.

Row 4: Ch 1, sc in each st across, turn.

Row 5: Ch 1, sc in each st across changing to coral in last st, turn. Fasten off purple.

Row 6: Ch 1, sc in each st across, turn.

Row 7: Ch 1, sc in each st across changing to lime in last st, turn. Fasten off coral.

Rows 8–10: Ch 1, sc in each st across, turn. At end of last row, fasten off.

Vertical Stripes (see Note in Place Mat Vertical Stripes)

First stripe: With purple, skip first five sts from **right** edge, work vertical stripe in **sixth** sts from edge *(see photo)*.

Second stripe: With coral, work vertical stripe in **next** sts beside previous stripe.

Third stripe: With purple, skip next five sts from **previous** stripe, work vertical stripe in **sixth** sts from previous stripe.

Fourth stripe: With coral, work vertical stripe in **next** sts beside previous stripe, leaving five sts remaining along left edge.

Sew ends of rows together to form tube.

Border

Rnd 1: With right side of tube facing, with F hook, join purple with sc in end of seam on last row, ch 5, skip next st, (sc in next st, ch 5, skip next st) around, join with sl st in first sc. Fasten off.

Rnd 2: With F hook, working in **front** of rnd 1, join coral with sc in first skipped st, ch 5; working in **back** of rnd 1, sc in next skipped st, ch 5; (working in **front** of rnd 1, sc in next skipped st, ch 5; working in **back** of rnd 1, sc in next skipped st, ch 5) around, join with sl st in first sc. Fasten off.

Rnds 3–4: Working in starting ch on opposite side of row 1, repeat rnds 1 and 2. ●

Basketweave Stitch Pattern

*K*nitted basketweave design is created by working four to six knit stitches then the same number of purl stitches alternately across the row for several rows to form a square of each stitch section, then the knit and purl stitch sections are reversed for the same number of rows; repeat this row sequence to give the piece a woven appearance.

To duplicate the look in crochet, work double or half-double crochet stitches in the front posts to represent the knit stitches and in the back posts to represent the purl stitches.

KNIT

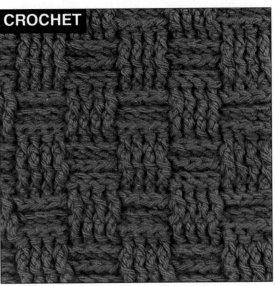

CROCHET

Afghan Square: Basketweave

READ BEFORE STARTING

Refer to **Chapter 2** for instructions for using Squares to make either Knit or Crochet Version of Large Afghan or Baby Afghan.

For comparison, each Square has instructions for **Knit Version** in blue type, and instructions for **Crochet Version** in black type.

KNIT VERSION

With medium needles and white, cast on 26.

Rows 1–4: K 1, (P 4, K 4) across to last st, K 1.

Rows 5–8: P 1, (K 4, P 4) across to last

CROCHET VERSION

Row 1: With small hook and white, ch 28, dc in fourth ch from hook, dc in each ch across, turn. *(26 sts made)*

Rows 2–3: Ch 2 *(counts as first hdc),* ***dc front post (dcfp,** *see Crochet Stitch*

st, P 1.

Next rows: Repeat rows 1–8 until piece measures same as gauge.

Bind off.

Work Edging in Basic Finishing on page 28.

Guide on page 191) around each of next 4 sts, dc back post (**dcbp,** *see Stitch Guide*) around each of next 4 sts; repeat from * across with hdc in last st, turn.

Rows 4–5: Ch 2, (dcbp around each of next 4 sts, dcfp around each of next 4 sts) across with hdc in last st, turn.

Next rows: Repeat rows 2–5 consecutively until piece measures same as gauge. Fasten off.

Work Edging in Basic Finishing on page 28.

Baby Bunting

Designed by Donna Jones

Wrap the new arrival in love with this soft bunting made with Basketweave stitch pattern.

MATERIALS: Babysoft® Art. 920 by Lion Brand® Yarn Company or sport yarn: amount desired color needed for size—*shown is Lilac #144;* 12" piece of ½"-wide satin ribbon; 14" of ⅝"-wide satin ribbon for **girl** only **or** 12" piece of 1"-wide satin ribbon for **boy** only; dress zipper in length needed for size; straight pins; sewing needle and thread; tapestry needle; crochet hook needed to obtain gauge for size.

GAUGES

Infant's 0–3 months: E hook, 11 dc post sts = 2"; 11 dc post st rows = 4".

Infant's 3–6 months: G hook, 9 dc post sts = 2"; 9 dc post st rows = 4".

SIZES

Infant's 0–3 months. Finished measurement: 12" across x 20" long, plus Hood.

Yarn: 14 oz.

Zipper: 18" long.

Infant's 3–6 months. Finished measurement: 14" across x 25" long, plus Hood.

Yarn: 18 oz.

Zipper: 22" long.

BODY

Row 1: With hook for size, ch 110, dc in fourth ch from hook, dc in next 25 chs, 4 dc in next ch, dc in next 52 chs, 4 dc in next ch, dc in last 27 chs, turn. *(First 3 chs count as first dc–114 dc made)*

Row 2: Ch 2, **dcfp** *(see Crochet Stitch Guide on page 191)* around each of next 2 sts, (**dcbp**—*see Stitch Guide*—around each of next 4 sts, dcfp around each of next 4 sts) 3 times, dcbp around next st, 2 hdc in each of next 2 sts, dcbp around next st, (dcfp around each of next 4 sts, dcbp around each of next 4 sts) 6 times, dcfp around each of next 4 sts, dcbp around next st, 2 hdc in each of next 2 sts, dcbp around next st, (dcfp around each of next 4 sts, dcbp around each of next 4 sts) 3 times, dcfp around each of next 2 sts, hdc in top of ch-2, turn. *(118 sts)*

Row 3: Ch 2, dcbp around each of next 2 sts, (dcfp around each of next 4 sts, dcbp around each of next 4 sts) 3 times, dcfp around each of next 2 sts, 2 hdc in each of next 2 sts, dcfp around each of next 2 sts, (dcbp around each of next 4 sts, dcfp around each of next 4 sts) 6 times, dcbp around each of next 4 sts, dcfp around each of next 2 sts, 2 hdc in each of next 2 sts, dcfp around each of next 2 sts, (dcbp around each of next 4 sts, dcfp around each of next 4 sts) 3 times, dcbp around each of next 2 sts, hdc in top of ch-2, turn. *(122 sts)*

Row 4: Ch 2, dcbp around each of next 2 fp, (dcfp around each of next 4 bp, dcbp around each of next 4 fp) 3 times, dcfp around each of next 3 sts, 2 hdc in each of next 2 sts, dcfp around each of next 3 sts, (dcbp around each of next 4 sts, dcfp around each of next 4 sts) 6 times, dcbp

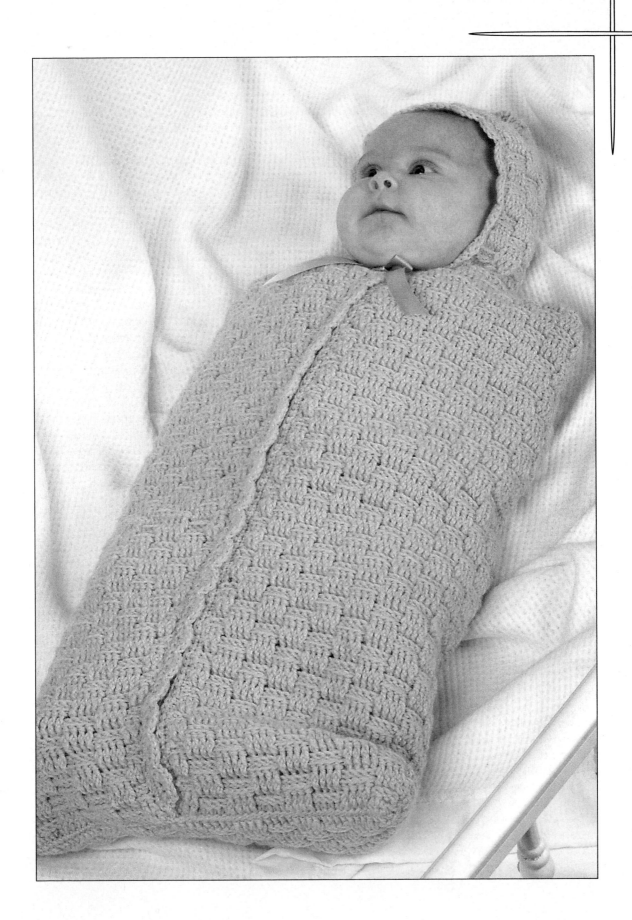

around each of next 4 sts, dcfp around each of next 3 sts, 2 hdc in each of next 2 sts, dcfp around each of next 3 sts, (dcbp around each of next 4 sts, dcfp around each of next 4 sts) 3 times, dcbp around each of next 2 sts, hdc in top of ch-2, turn. *(126 sts)*

Row 5: Ch 2, dcfp around each of next 2 sts, (dcbp around each of next 4 sts, dcfp around each of next 4 sts) 3 times, dcbp around each of next 4 sts, 2 hdc in each of next 2 sts, dcbp around each of next 4 sts, (dcfp around each of next 4 sts, dcbp around each of next 4 sts) 7 times, 2 hdc in each of next 2 sts, dcbp around each of next 4 sts, (dcfp around each of next 4 sts, dcbp around each of next 4 sts) 3 times, dcfp around each of next 2 sts, hdc in top of ch-2, turn. *(130 sts)*

Row 6: Ch 2, dcfp around each of next 2 sts, dcbp around each of next 4 sts, (dcfp around each of next 4 sts, dcbp around each of next 4 sts) 15 times, dcfp around each of next 2 sts, hdc in top of ch-2, turn.

Rows 7–8: Ch 2, dcbp around each of next 2 sts, dcfp around each of next 4 sts, (dcbp around each of next 4 sts, dcfp around each of next 4 sts) across to last 3 sts, dcbp around each of next 2 sts, hdc in top of ch-2, turn.

Rows 9–10: Ch 2, dcfp around each of next 2 sts, dcbp around each of next 4 sts, (dcfp around each of next 4 sts, dcbp around each of next 4 sts) across to last 3 sts, dcfp around each of next 2 sts, hdc in top of ch-2, turn.

Rows 11–54: Repeat rows 7–10 consecutively.

*NOTE: For **decrease (dec)**, dc next 2 sts tog.*

Row 55: Ch 2, dcbp around each of next 2 sts, (dcfp around each of next 4 sts, dcbp around each of next 4 sts) 3 times, dcfp around each of next 4 sts, **dec** 2 times *(see Note)*, dcfp around each of next 4 sts, (dcbp around each of next 4 sts, dcfp around each of next 4 sts) 7 times, dec 2 times, dcfp around each of next 4 sts, (dcbp around each of next 4 sts, dcfp around each of next 4 sts) 3 times, dcbp around each of next 2 sts, hdc in top of ch-2, turn. *(126 sts)*

Row 56: Ch 2, dcbp around each of next 2 sts, (dcfp around each of next 4 sts, dcbp around each of next 4 sts) 3 times, dcfp around each of next 3 sts, dec 2 times, dcfp around each of next 3 sts, (dcbp around

each of next 4 sts, dcfp around each of next 4 sts) 6 times, dcbp around each of next 4 sts, dcfp around each of next 3 sts, dec 2 times, dcfp around each of next 3 sts, (dcbp around each of next 4 sts, dcfp around each of next 4 sts) 3 times, dcbp around each of next 2 sts, hdc in top of ch-2, turn. *(122 sts)*

Row 57: Ch 2, dcfp around each of next 2 sts, (dcbp around each of next 4 sts, dcfp around each of next 4 sts) 3 times, dcbp around each of next 2 sts, dec 2 times, dcbp around each of next 2 sts, (dcfp around each of next 4 sts, dcbp around each of next 4 sts) 6 times, dcfp around each of next 4 sts, dcbp around each of next 2 sts, dec 2 times, dcbp around each of next 2 sts, (dcfp around each of next 4 sts, dcbp around each of next 4 sts) 3 times, dcfp around each of next 2 sts, hdc in top of ch-2, turn. *(118 sts)*

Row 58: Ch 2, dcfp around each of next 2 sts, (dcbp around each of next 4 sts, dcfp around each of next 4 sts) 3 times; for **shoulder decrease,** dc next 6 sts tog; (dcfp around each of next 4 sts, dcbp around each of next 4 sts) 6 times, dcfp around each of next 4 sts; for **shoulder decrease,** dc next 6 sts tog; (dcfp around each of next 4 sts, dcbp around each of next 4 sts) 3 times, dcfp around each of next 2 sts, hdc in top of ch-2, turn. Fasten off. *(108 sts)*

Fold last row at shoulder decreases with ends of rows together at center front.

For shoulder seam on each side, begin at shoulder decrease and sew 12 sts on each side of decrease together, leaving 30 sts at center back and 15 sts on each side of front unsewn for neck edge.

HOOD

Row 1: Skip first 3 sts on neck edge, join with sc in next st, sc in each st across front and back neck edge leaving last 3 sts unworked, turn. *(54 sc made)*

Row 2: For **beading row,** ch 4, dc in next st, (ch 1, skip next st, dc in next st) across, turn. *(Ch-4 counts as dc and ch-1; 28 dc, 27 ch sps)*

Row 3: Ch 3, dc in next 26 sts and ch sps, skip next ch sp, dc in last 27 sts and ch sps, turn. *(54 dc)*

Row 4: Ch 2, dcfp around each of next

4 sts, (dcbp around each of next 4 sts, dcfp around each of next 4 sts) 6 times, hdc in top of ch-2, turn.

Rows 5–6: Ch 2, dcbp around each of next 4 sts, (dcfp around each of next 4 sts, dcbp around each of next 4 sts) across with hdc in top of ch-2, turn.

Rows 7–8: Ch 2, dcfp around each of next 4 sts, (dcbp around each of next 4 sts, dcfp around each of next 4 sts) across with hdc in top of ch-2, turn.

Rows 9–27: Repeat rows 5–8 consecutively, ending with row 7. At end of last row, leaving end for sewing, fasten off.

Fold row 27 of Hood in half. Beginning at outer corners, sew tops of sts on row 27 together.

TRIM

Row 1: With right side of work facing, join yarn with sl st in end of row 1 on Body, ch 1, evenly space 3 sc across ends of every 2 rows across to corner *(87 sts in ends of rows)*, 2 sc in same st as last sc, sc in next 2 sts, skip row 1 on Hood *(inside corner)*, 2 sc in end of row 2, sc in end of each row across both sides of Hood to row 2 on other side, 2 sc in end of row 2 *(54 sts on Hood)*, skip row 1 *(inside corner)*, sc in next 2 sts on Body, 3 sc in next st at corner, evenly space 3 sc across ends of every 2 rows across to bottom *(87 sts in ends of rows)*, turn.

Row 2: Ch 1, sc in each st across to center st at next corner, leaving remaining sts unworked. Fasten off. *(88 sts)*

Row 3 for boy *(not shown)*: With front side of row 2 facing, join with sl st in first st on row 2, working from left to right, **reverse sc** *(see Crochet Stitch Guide on page 191)* in each st across; fasten off. Skip across and join with sl st in first st on row 1 of Hood, reverse sc in each st across ending in st at other end of row 1. Fasten off.

Row 4 for boy: With wrong side of row 1 facing, join with sc in remaining unworked center st next to Hood, sc in each st across to bottom edge. Fasten off. *(88 sts)*

Lap rows 2–3 on left side over rows 1–2 on right side; pin ends of rows together.

Row 3 for girl: Working down center front, skip Hood and join with sl st in next center corner st, sc in each st across front

edge to bottom, turn. *(88 sts)*

Row 4 for girl: Sl st in first st, (skip next st, 5 dc in next st, skip next st, sl st in next st) across to last 3 sts, skip next st, 5 dc in next st, skip last st, sl st in end of row 3. Fasten off. Skip across and join with sl st in first st worked into row 1 of Hood, (skip next st, 5 dc in next st, skip next st, sl st in next st) 13 times with last sl st in st worked in other end of row 1. Fasten off.

Lap rows 2–3 on right side over rows 1–2 on left side; pin ends of rows together.

ASSEMBLY AND FINISHING

1: Leaving row 4 loose, pin one side of zipper to back of row 2 and other side of zipper to back of row 3 with tops of stitches about 1/8" away from zipper teeth; using sewing needle and thread, sew in place at least 1/4" from zipper teeth.

2: With tapestry needle and yarn, sew remainder of rows 2 and 3 together below zipper.

3: With zipper at center, flatten row 1 on Body; sew starting chain together using yarn and tapestry needle.

4: Using 1/2" ribbon, fold one end under 1/4", fold under again 1/4", sew all layers of fold to back of Trim even with row 2 on Hood. Loosely weave other end of ribbon in and out through row 2 of Hood, leave 1/2" end and cut off remainder. Fold end under 1/4", fold under again 1/4", sew all layers of fold to back of Trim even with row 2 on Hood.

5: For **girl's bow** *(see photo)*, from 5/8" ribbon, cut a 1 1/2" piece for knot, fold each end under 1/4" and pin in place. Fold remaining ribbon into a 2 1/2"-wide bow leaving ends for streamers; tack all layers together at center. Trim streamer ends. Gathering center of bow slightly, wrap 1 1/2" knot piece around bow overlapping ends at back; sew in place. Sew bow to top of row 4 on Trim.

6: For **boy's bow tie** *(not shown)*, from 1" ribbon, cut a 1 1/2" piece for knot, fold each end under 1/4" and pin in place. Fold remaining ribbon into a 2 1/2"-wide bow leaving ends at back; tack all layers together at center. Trim ends into a V even with loops. Gathering center of bow as needed, wrap 1 1/2" knot piece around bow overlapping ends at back; sew in place. Sew bow tie to top of row 4 on Trim. ●

Winter Scarf

Designed by Darla Sims

Sometimes including a small accent can add just enough warmth.

FINISHED SIZE: 5½" wide x 50" long, plus Fringe.

MATERIALS: 9 oz. Plum #145 Wool-Ease® Art. 620 by Lion Brand® Yarn Company or worsted yarn; G crochet hook *(or hook needed to obtain gauge)*.

GAUGE: 16 dc = 4"; 8 dc rows = 4".

SCARF

Row 1: Loosely ch 24, dc in fourth ch from hook, dc in each ch across, turn. *(Ch-3 counts as dc–22 dc made)*

Rows 2–3: Ch 2 *(counts as first hdc)*, **dcfp** *(see Crochet Stitch Guide on page 191)* around each of next 4 sts, **(dcbp** around each of next 4 sts, dcfp around each of next 4 sts) across to last st, hdc in last st, turn. *(22 sts)*

Rows 4–5: Ch 2, dcbp around each of next 4 sts, (dcfp around each of next 4 sts, dcbp around each of next 4 sts) across to last st, hdc in last st, turn.

Next rows: Repeat rows 2–5 until piece measures 50" long or desired length, ending with odd-numbered row. At end of last row, fasten off.

FRINGE

For each **Fringe,** cut 8" strand of yarn, fold in half; insert hook from front through stitch, pull fold through stitch, pull ends through fold, pull snug.

Fringe in each st across first row and last row. Trim ends even. ●

*T*o hide yarn ends when adding a new ball of the same color yarn, work to about 10" or 12" from the end of the old yarn, lay the new yarn along top of the previous row and work a few stitches over this yarn; then as you work the next st, insert the hook into the stitch as usual, pull through with the new yarn and complete the stitch; continue to work over the old yarn for a few stitches, then cut off both exposed yarn ends and continue working with the new yarn.

To hide yarn ends when adding a different color yarn, work the first stitch of the new color as instructed, then lay both yarn ends along top of the previous row and work a few stitches to enclose the ends, then cut off both exposed yarn ends and continue working with the new yarn.

Alternating Links Stitch Pattern

*K*nit and purl stitches combine to form the illusion of chain links in this stitch pattern. To achieve the same effect in crochet, use single crochet stitches for the reverse stockinette stitch background and front post single crochet stitches worked into the row before last for the raised chain effect.

KNIT

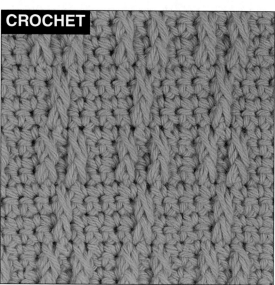

CROCHET

Afghan Square: Alternating Links

READ BEFORE STARTING

Refer to **Chapter 2** for instructions for using Squares to make either Knit or Crochet Version of Large Afghan or Baby Afghan.

For comparison, each Square has instructions for **Knit Version** in blue type, and instructions for **Crochet Version** in black type.

KNIT VERSION

With large needles and color B, cast on 26.

Row 1: *(Right side)* P 5, *K 1-**through the back lps (-tbl),** P 4; repeat from * across to last st, P 1.

Row 2: K 5, (P 1-tbl, K 4) across to last st, K 1.

Rows 3–4: Repeat rows 1 and 2.

CROCHET VERSION

Row 1: With small hook and color B, ch 27, sc in second ch from hook, sc in each ch across, turn. *(26 sc made)*

Row 2: Ch 1, sc in each st across, turn. ***NOTE:*** Work **all sc sts** into sts of **last row.**

Row 3: Ch 1, sc in first 5 sc *(see Note)*, **scfp** *(see Special Stitch on page 24)* around next st on row before last directly below

Row 5: P 4, (K 1-tbl, P 1, K 1-tbl, P 2) across to last 2 sts, P 2.

Row 6: K 4, (P 1-tbl, K 1, P 1-tbl, K 2) across to last 2 sts, K 2.

Rows 7–8: Repeat rows 5 and 6.

Rows 9–28: Repeat rows 1–8 consecutively, ending with row 4.

Piece should measure same as gauge.

Bind off purlwise.

Work Edging in Basic Finishing on page 28.

next st, (sc in next 4 sc; counting from last fp, skip next 4 sts on row before last, scfp around next st) 3 times, sc in last 5 sc, turn.

Row 4: Ch 1, sc in each st across, turn.

Row 5: Ch 1, sc in first 5 sc; scfp around first fp, (sc in next 4 sc, scfp around next fp) 3 times, sc in last 5 sc, turn.

Row 6: Ch 1, sc in each st across, turn.

Row 7: Ch 1, sc in first 4 sc, (scfp around st on row before last directly below next st, sc in next sc, skip next fp on row before last, scfp around next st, sc in next 2 sc) 4 times, sc in last 2 sc, turn.

Row 8: Ch 1, sc in each st across, turn.

Row 9: Ch 1, sc in first 4 sc, (scfp around next fp, sc in next sc, scfp around next fp, sc in next 2 sc) 4 times, sc in last 2 sc, turn.

Rows 10–29: Repeat rows 2–9 consecutively, ending with row 5. At end of last row, fasten off.

Piece should measure same as gauge.

Work Edging in Basic Finishing on page 28.

Button-Trimmed Slippers

Designed by Darla Sims

Using the Alternating Links stitch pattern you can crochet slippers to enhance those rare moments of leisure.

MATERIALS: Wool-Ease® Art. 620 by Lion Brand® Yarn Company or worsted yarn: 6 oz. White #100; 75–80 assorted white buttons; sewing needle and thread; tapestry needle; G crochet hook *(or hook needed to obtain gauge).*

GAUGE: 16 sts in pattern = 4"; 16 rows in pattern = 4".

SIZES

Small fits lady's shoe size 5–6.
Medium fits lady's shoe size 7–8.
Large fits lady's shoe size 9–10.

NOTE

Instructions are for size **Small;** changes for **Medium,** and **Large** are in [ ].

SLIPPER (make 2)

Row 1: *(Right side)* With G hook, ch 42 [48, 54], sc in second ch from hook, sc in each ch across, turn. *(41 [47, 53] sc made)*

Row 2: Ch 1, sc in each st across, turn.

*NOTE: Work each **long sc front post (lscfp,** see Crochet Stitch Guide on page 191) around designated st on row before last, pull up to height of row being worked. Always **skip one st** on last row behind each lscfp.*

Row 3: Ch 1, sc in first 5 sts, *lscfp *(see Note)* around st on row before last directly below next st, sc in next 5 sts on last row; repeat from * across, turn.

Row 4: Ch 1, sc in each st across, turn.

Row 5: Ch 1, sc in first 5 sts, (lscfp around next fp on row before last, sc in next 5 sts on last row) across, turn.

Row 6: Ch 1, sc in each st across, turn.

Row 7: Ch 1, sc in first 4 sts, (lscfp around st on row before last directly below next st, sc in next st on last row, lscfp around st on row before last directly below next st, sc in next 3 sts on last row) across with sc in last st, turn.

Row 8: Ch 1, sc in each st across, turn.

Row 9: Ch 1, sc in first 4 sts, (lscfp around next fp on row before last, sc in next st on last row, lscfp around next fp on row before last, sc in next 3 sts on last row) across with sc in last st, turn.

Next rows: Repeat rows 2–9 consecutively until piece measures same size in length and width. At end of last row, fasten off.

ASSEMBLY AND FINISHING

1: For each Slipper, with wrong side out, fold in half diagonally to form a triangle *(see illustration).* Using tapestry needle, sew together across one long edge from point *(at toe)* to corner *(at heel);* then sew up 3" from corner for back of heel.

2: Turn right side out.

3: For **flap** at top of foot, fold unsewn point back over center fold.

4: With sewing needle and thread, sew buttons randomly on flap. ●

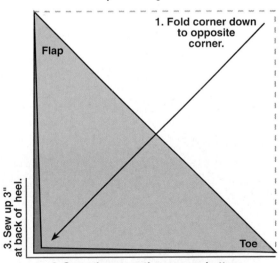

Flap

1. Fold corner down to opposite corner.

3. Sew up 3" at back of heel.

Toe

2. Sew edges together across bottom.

His Pullover

Designed by Donna Jones

Create this rugged pullover for your favorite guy using the Alternating Links stitch pattern.

MATERIALS: Wool-Ease® Art. 620 by Lion Brand® Yarn Company or worsted yarn: Amount Woods Print #232 needed for size; bobby pins or split stitch markers; tapestry needle; G and H crochet hooks *(or hooks needed to obtain gauges)*.

GAUGES: G hook; 12 ribbing sc = 2½"; 10 ribbing rows = 2". **H hook;** 14 sts in pattern = 4"; 16 rows in pattern = 4".

SIZES

Man's Small (34"–36" chest):
  Yarn: 29 oz.
  Garment chest: 40"
  Back length: 23"
Man's Medium (36"–40" chest):
  Yarn: 32 oz.
  Garment chest: 46"
  Back length: 25"
Man's Large (40"–44" chest):
  Yarn: 36 oz.
  Garment chest: 52"
  Back length: 27"
Man's X-Large (44"–48" chest):
  Yarn: 40 oz.
  Garment chest: 55"
  Back length: 29"

NOTE

Instructions are for size **Small; changes** for **Medium, Large** and **X-Large** are in [ ].

BACK
Ribbing

Row 1: With G hook, ch 13, sc in second ch from hook, sc in each ch across, turn. *(12 sc made)*

Rows 2–71 [2–81; 2–91; 2–95]: Working these rows in **back loops** *(see Crochet Stitch Guide on page 191)*, ch 1, sc in each st across, turn. At end of last row, **do not turn.**

Body

Row 1: *(Right side)* With H hook, working in ends of rows across Ribbing, ch 1, sc in first row, (skip next row, 2 sc in next row) across, turn. *(71 [81, 91, 95] sc made)*

Row 2: Ch 1; for **X-large only,** 2 sc in first st; for **all sizes,** sc in each st across, turn. *(71 [81, 91, 96] sc)*

*NOTE: Work each **long sc front post (lscfp,** see Stitch Guide) around designated st on row before last, pull up to height of row being worked. Always **skip one st** on last row behind each scfp.*

Row 3: Ch 1, sc in first 5 sts, **lscfp** *(see Note)* around st on row before last directly below next st, (sc in next 4 sts on last row; lscfp around st on row before last directly below next st) across to last 5 sts, sc in last 5 sts on last row, turn.

Row 4: Ch 1, sc in each st across, turn.

Row 5: Ch 1, sc in first 5 sts, (scfp around next fp on row before last, sc in next 4 sts on last row) across with sc in last st on last row, turn.

Row 6: Ch 1, sc in each st across, turn.

Row 7: Ch 1, sc in first 4 sts, lscfp around fifth st on row before last, sc in next st on last row, skip next st on row before last, lscfp around next st, sc in next 2 sts on last row, (skip 2 sts on row before last, lscfp around next st, sc in next st on last row, skip next st on row before last, lscfp around next st, sc in next 2 sts on last row) across with sc in last 2 sts, turn.

Row 8: Ch 1, sc in each st across, turn.

Row 9: Ch 1, sc in first 4 sts, (scfp around next fp on row before last, sc in next st on last row, lscfp around next st on row before last, sc in next 2 sts on last row) across with sc in last 2 sts, turn.

Row 10: Ch 1, sc in each st across, turn.

*NOTE: To **work in pattern,** repeat rows 3–10 consecutively—see "How To Work In*

Pattern" in Chapter 1 on page 16.

Next rows: Work in pattern until piece measures 22" [24", 26", 28"] from bottom edge of ribbing.

Use bobby pins or split stitch markers to mark each end of last row made for shoulder seam.

Next 4 rows: For **shoulder shaping,** sl st in first 5 [6, 7, 8] sts, work in pattern across to last 6 [7, 8, 8] sts, leaving remaining sts unworked. At end of last row, fasten off. *(27 [29, 31, 32] sc)*

Use bobby pins or split stitch markers to mark first and last remaining sts for shoulder seam at neck edge.

FRONT
Ribbing and Body

Work Ribbing same as Back Ribbing; work Body same as Back Body until piece measures 18" [19½", 21½", 23"] from bottom edge of ribbing, ending after a wrong side row.

Left Side Neck Shaping

Row 1: Ch 1, work in pattern across first 25 [29, 33, 35] sts leaving remaining sts unworked, turn.

Row 2: Ch 1, skip first st, sc next 2 sts tog, work in pattern across, turn. *(23 [27, 31, 33] sc made)*

Row 3: Ch 1, work in pattern across to last 3 sts, sc next 2 sts tog leaving last st unworked, turn. *(21 [25, 29, 31] sc)*

Row 4: Ch 1, skip first st, work in pattern across, turn. *(20 [24, 28, 30] sc)*

Next rows: Work in pattern until side measures 22" [24", 26", 28"] from bottom edge of ribbing, ending at side edge.

Use bobby pin or split stitch marker to mark last st of last row for shoulder seam.

Next row: For **shoulder shaping,** sl st in first 5 [6, 7, 7] sts, work in pattern across, turn. *(15 [18, 21, 23] sc)*

Next row: Work in pattern across leaving last 5 [6, 7, 7] sts unworked, turn. *(10 [12, 14, 16] sc)*

Next row: Sl st in first 5 [6, 7, 7] sts, work in pattern across. Fasten off. *(5 [6, 7, 9] sc)*

Use bobby pin or split stitch marker to mark last st at neck edge for shoulder seam.

Right Side Neck Shaping

Row 1: With wrong side of last row on Body facing, skip next 21 [23, 25, 26] sts for center front neck edge, join with sc in

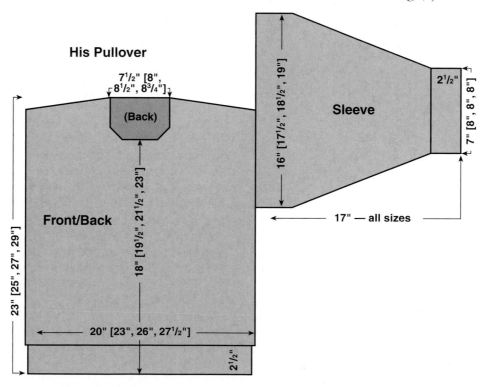

His Pullover

7½" [8", 8½", 8¾"]

(Back)

Front/Back

18" [19½", 21½", 23"]

23" [25", 27", 29"]

20" [23", 26", 27½"]

2½"

Sleeve

2½"

16" [17½", 18½", 19"]

7" [8", 8", 8"]

17" — all sizes

next st, work in pattern across, turn. *(25 [29, 33, 35] sc made)*

Row 2: Ch 1, work in pattern across to last 3 sts, sc next 2 sts tog leaving last st unworked, turn. *(23 [27, 31, 33] sc)*

Row 3: Ch 1, skip first st, sc next 2 sts tog, work in pattern across, turn. *(21 [25, 29, 31] sc)*

Row 4: Ch 1, work in pattern across to last 2 sts, sc last 2 sts tog, turn. *(20 [24, 28, 30] sc)*

Next rows: Work in pattern until side measures 22" [24", 26", 28"] from bottom edge of ribbing, ending at neck edge.

Use bobby pin or split stitch marker to mark first st of last row for shoulder seam.

Next row: For **shoulder shaping,** work in pattern across leaving last 5 [6, 7, 7] sts unworked, turn. *(15 [18, 21, 23] sc)*

Next row: Sl st in first 5 [6, 7, 7] sts, work in pattern across, turn. *(10 [12, 14, 16] sc)*

Next row: Work in pattern across leaving last 5 [6, 7, 9] sts unworked. Fasten off.

Use bobby pin or split stitch marker to mark first st at neck edge for shoulder seam.

SLEEVE (make 2)
Ribbing

Row 1: With G hook, ch 13, sc in second ch from hook, sc in each ch across, turn. *(12 sc made)*

Rows 2–35 [2–40; 2–40; 2–40]: Working these rows in **back loops,** ch 1, sc in each st across, turn. At end of last row, **do not turn.**

Arm Stitch Pattern (use with instructions for Arm)

Row 1: Sc in next st, lscfp around sc on row before last directly below next st, (sc in next 4 sts on last row, lscfp around sc on row before last directly below next st) across to one st before marker, sc in next st.

Row 2: Sc in next st, lscfp around first fp on row before last, (sc in next 4 sts on last row, lscfp around next fp on row before last) across to one st before marker, sc in next st.

Row 3: Lscfp around sc on row before last directly below next st, sc in next st on last row, lscfp around sc on row before last directly below next st, (sc in next 2 sts on last row, lscfp around sc on row before last directly below next st, sc in next st on last row, lscfp around sc on row before last directly below next st) across to marker.

Row 4: Lscfp around fp on row before last directly below next st, sc in next st on last row, lscfp around next fp on row before last, (sc in next 2 sts on last row, lscfp around next fp on row before last, sc in next st on last row, lscfp around next fp on row before last) across to marker.

Arm

Row 1: *(Right side)* With H hook, working in ends of rows across Ribbing, ch 1, 2 sc in first row, (skip next row, 2 sc in next row) across, turn. *(36 [41, 41, 41] sc made)*

Row 2: Ch 1, sc in each st across, turn.

Row 3: Ch 1, sc in first 4 sts, **mark** sc just made, sc in next st, lscfp around sc on row before last directly below next st, (sc in next 4 sts on last row, lscfp around sc on row before last directly below next st) 5 [6, 6, 6] times, sc in next 2 sts, **mark** sc just made, sc in last 3 sts, turn.

NOTE: When working into marked st, remove marker, work st, mark st just made.

Row 4: Ch 1, 2 sc in first st, sc in each st across with 2 sc in last st, turn. *(38 [43, 43, 43] sc)*

Row 5: Ch 1, sc in each st across to marker, sc in marked st, work row 2 of Arm Stitch Pattern, sc in each st across, turn.

Row 6: Ch 1, sc in each st across, turn.

Row 7: Ch 1, sc in each st across to marker, sc in marked st, work row 3 of Arm Stitch Pattern, sc in each st across, turn.

Row 8: Repeat row 4. *(40 [45, 45, 45] sc)*

Row 9: Ch 1, sc in each st across to marker, sc in marked st, work row 4 of Arm Stitch Pattern, sc in each st across, turn.

Row 10: Ch 1, sc in each st across, turn.

Row 11: Ch 1, sc in first 2 sts, lscfp around sc on row before last directly below next st, (sc in next 4 sts on last row, lscfp around sc on row before last directly below next st) across to last 2 sts, sc in last 2 sts, turn.

Row 12: Repeat row 4. *(42 [47, 47, 47] sc)*

Move markers to **second** sc and **next to last** sc of row.

Row 13: Ch 1, sc in each st across to marker, sc in marked st, work row 2 of Arm Stitch Pattern, sc in each st across, turn.

Row 14: Ch 1, sc in each st across, turn.

Row 15: Ch 1, sc in each st across to marker, sc in marked st, work row 3 of Arm Stitch Pattern, sc in each st across, turn.

Row 16: Repeat row 4. *(44 [49, 49, 49] sc)*

Row 17: Ch 1, sc in each st across to marker, sc in marked st, work row 4 of Arm Stitch Pattern, sc in each st across, turn.

Row 18: Ch 1, sc in each st across, turn

Row 19: Ch 1, sc in each st across to marker, sc in marked st, work row 1 of Arm Stitch Pattern, sc in each st across, turn.

Row 20: Repeat row 4. *(46 [51, 51, 51] sc)*

Rows 21–28: Repeat rows 13–20. At end of last row, *(50 [55, 55, 55] sts).*

Rows 29–32: Repeat rows 13–16. At end of last row *(52 [57, 57, 57] sts).*

Move markers to **second** sc and **next to last** sc of row.

Rows 33–36: Repeat rows 17–20. At end of last row *(54 [59, 59, 59] sts).*

Rows 37–40 [37–40, 37–48, 37–52]: Repeat rows 13–16 [13–16, 13–20, 13–20] consecutively, ending with row 16 [16, 16, 20]. At end of last row *(56 [61, 65, 67] sts).*

Row 41 [41, 49, 53]: Ch 1, sc in each st across to marker, sc in marked st; continuing in pattern as established, work next row of Arm Stitch Pattern, sc in each st across, turn.

Next rows: Repeat row 41 [41, 49, 53] until piece measures 17" from bottom edge of ribbing *(this is for all sizes—the body ease provides extra length)*, or **to desired Sleeve length**. At end of last row, fasten off.

ASSEMBLY AND FINISHING

1: Matching markers, sew Front to Back across each shoulder leaving neck edge sts unsewn.

2: On each side, matching center of Sleeve to shoulder seam and taking care not to stretch or gather either piece, sew last row on one Sleeve to ends of rows on Front and Back.

3: On each side, lapping last ribbing row over starting ch of Ribbing sections, matching sts and ends of rows, sew Sleeve and side seams.

NECK BAND

Row 1: With G hook, join with sl st in right shoulder seam, ch 9, sc in second ch from hook, sc in each ch across, sl st in next 2 sts on back neck edge, turn. *(Sl sts are not worked into or counted as sts; 10 sc made)*

Row 2: Working these rows in **back lps**, ch 1, sc in each st across, turn.

Row 3: Ch 1, sc in each st across, sl st in next 2 sts or rows on neck edge, turn.

Next rows: Working in sts and in ends of rows, repeat rows 2 and 3 alternately around neck edge, ending after a repeat of row 2. At end of last row, leaving end for sewing, fasten off.

Lap last row over starting ch of row 1; sew together forming ridge to match ribbing. ●

*W*hen stitching a pullover or cardigan, sometimes it helps to stitch both sleeves/fronts at once on the same size hooks with two balls of yarn. This ensures that each is made with an equal number of rows, and that increases and decreases are made at even intervals.

Mitered Corners Stitch Pattern

*F*our tiny multi-colored squares worked in garter stitch are used to create this unique pattern with each of the last three squares worked onto the previous square(s).

The crochet version uses single crochet stitches worked in both loops of the previous row to achieve the garter stitch effect.

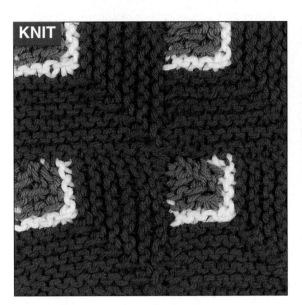

Afghan Square: ## Mitered Corners

READ BEFORE STARTING

Refer to **Chapter 2** for instructions for using Squares to make either Knit or Crochet Version of Large Afghan or Baby Afghan.

For comparison, each Square has instructions for **Knit Version** in blue type, and instructions for **Crochet Version** in black type.

KNIT VERSION

First Section

With medium needles and color B, cast on 23.

Row 1: *(Wrong side)* K 10; for **s2kp,** slip next 2 sts as if to knit, K 1, pass 2 slipped sts over K st and off needle *(s2kp completed);* K 10. *(21 sts on needles)*

CROCHET VERSION

With medium hook and color B, ch 49. Fasten off.

NOTE: *For one-color afghan, do not fasten off after rows 6 and 8; begin rows 7 and 9 with ch 1, sc in first st.*

First Section

Row 1: Skip first 12 chs for Second

Row 2: Slip 1, K 20.

Row 3: Slip 1, K 8, s2kp, K 9. *(19 sts)*

Row 4: Slip 1, K 18.

Row 5: Slip 1, K 7, s2kp, K 8. *(17 sts)*

Row 6: Slip 1, K 16.

Row 7: Slip 1, K 6, s2kp, K 7. *(15 sts)*

Row 8: Slip 1, K 14.

Row 9: Slip 1, K 5, s2kp, K 6. *(13 sts)*

Row 10: Slip 1, K 12.

Row 11: Slip 1, K 4, s2kp, K 5. *(11 sts)*
Leaving end to hide, cut yarn.

Row 12: With white, slip 1, K 10.

Row 13: Slip 1, K 3, s2kp, K 4. *(9 sts)*
Leaving end to hide, cut yarn.

Row 14: With color A, slip 1, K 8.

Row 15: Slip 1, K 2, s2kp, K 3. *(7 sts)*

Row 16: Slip 1, K 6.

Row 17: Slip 1, K 1, s2kp, K 2. *(5 sts)*

Row 18: Slip 1, K 4.

Row 19: Slip 1, s2kp, K 1. *(3 sts)*

Row 20: S2kp. Leaving end to hide, cut yarn; remove loop from needle, pull cut end through loop, pull tight. Hide all ends.

Section, join color B with sc in 13th ch from end, sc in next 10 chs; for **corner st,** sc next 3 chs tog; sc in next 11 chs, leaving remaining 12 chs unworked for Third Section, turn. *(23 sc made)*

Rows 2–6: Ch 1, sc in each st across to one st before corner st; for **corner st,** sc next 3 sts tog; sc in each st across, turn. At end of last row *(13 sts)*. Fasten off.

Row 7: Join white with sc in first st, sc in each st across to one st before corner st; for **corner st,** sc next 3 sts tog; sc in each st across, turn. *(11)*

Row 8: Repeat row 2. Fasten off. *(9)*

Row 9: With color A repeat row 7. *(7)*

Rows 10–11: Repeat row 2. *(5, 3)*

Row 12: Ch 1, sc 3 sts tog. Fasten off.

Second Section

Row 1: With right side of row 1 on First Section facing, join color B with sc in end ch at right of First Section, sc in next 10 chs; for **corner st,** sc next ch and next worked ch and end of row 1 on First Section tog; sc in end of each row across First Section, turn *(see Mitered Corners illustration)*. *(23 sts)*

Rows 2–12: Repeat rows 2–12 of First Section.

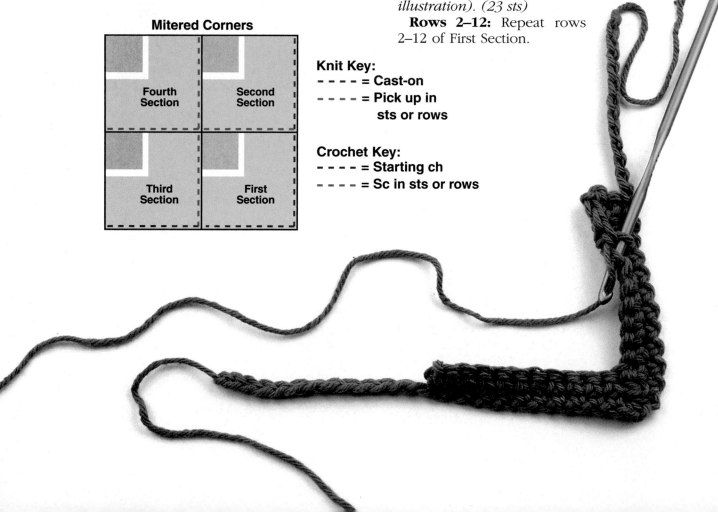

Mitered Corners

Fourth Section	Second Section
Third Section	First Section

Knit Key:

- - - - = Cast-on

- - - - = Pick up in sts or rows

Crochet Key:

- - - - = Starting ch

- - - - = Sc in sts or rows

Second Section

With right side of First Section facing, with color B, cast on 12, pick up and K 11 evenly spaced in ends of rows across First Section *(see Mitered Corners illustration)*. *(23 sts)*

Rows 1–20: Repeat rows 1–20 of First Section.

Third Section

With right side of First Section facing, with color B, pick up and K in end of row 20 on First Section, pick up and K 11 evenly spaced in ends of rows across First Section, cast on 11 *(see Mitered Corners illustration)*. *(23 sts)*

Rows 1–20: Repeat rows 1–20 of First Section.

Fourth Section

Row 1: With right side of First Section facing, with color B, spacing sts evenly, pick up and K 11 in ends of rows across left side of Second Section, pick up and K 1 in corner of First Section, pick up and K 11 in ends of rows across Third Section. *(23 sts)*

Rows 1–20: Repeat rows 1–20 of First Section.

Piece should measure same as gauge.

Work Edging in Basic Finishing on page 28.

Third Section

Row 1: With right side of row 1 on First Section facing, join color B with sc in end of row 12 on First Section, sc in end of each row across to row 1; for **corner st,** sc end of row 1 and last worked ch and next unworked ch of ch-49 tog; sc in last 11 chs, turn *(see Mitered Corners illustration)*. *(23 sts)*

Rows 2–12: Repeat rows 2–12 of First Section.

Fourth Section

Row 1: With right side of Sections facing, join color B with sc in end of row 12 on Second Section, sc in end of each row across to row 1; for **corner st,** sc row 1 and last stitch of First Section and row 1 of Third Section tog; sc in each row across Third Section, turn. *(23)*

Rows 2–12: Repeat rows 2–12 of First Section.

Piece should measure same as gauge.

Work Edging in Basic Finishing on page 28.

Mitered Corners Pot Holder

Designed by Donna Jones

Use the Mitered Corners stitch pattern to create a kitchen accessory that's a joy to use.

FINISHED SIZE: 6¼" square, plus Hanger.

MATERIALS: Kitchen Cotton Art. 760 by Lion Brand® Yarn Company or cotton worsted yarn: 2 oz. Cinnamon #135, 2 oz. Sage #181, 1 oz. Maize #186; tapestry needle; F crochet hook *(or hook needed to obtain gauge).*

GAUGE: 9 sc = 2"; 9 sc rows = 2".

FRONT
With cinnamon, ch 49. Fasten off.

First Section
Row 1: Skip first 12 chs for Second Section, join cinnamon with sc in 13th ch from end, sc in next 10 chs; for **corner st,** sc next 3 chs tog; sc in next 11 chs, leaving remaining 12 chs unworked for Third Section, turn. *(23 sc made)*

Rows 2–6: Ch 1, sc in each st across to one st before corner st; for **corner st,** sc next 3 sts tog; sc in each st across, turn. At end of last row *(13 sts).* Fasten off.

Row 7: Join maize with sc in first st, sc in each st across to one st before corner st; for **corner st,** sc next 3 sts tog; sc in each st across, turn. *(11)*

Row 8: Repeat row 2. Fasten off. *(9)*
Row 9: With sage, repeat row 7. *(7)*
Rows 10–11: Repeat row 2. *(5, 3)*
Row 12: Ch 1, sc 3 sts tog. Fasten off.

Second Section
Row 1: With right side of row 1 on First Section facing and row 12 at top, join cinnamon with sc in end ch at right of First Section, sc in next 10 chs; for **corner st,** sc last unworked ch and next worked ch and end of row 1 on First Section tog; sc in end of each row across First Section, turn *(see Mitered*

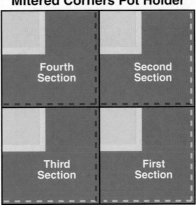

Mitered Corners Pot Holder

Fourth Section	Second Section
Third Section	First Section

Key:
- - - - = **Starting ch**
- - - - = **Sc in sts or rows**

Corners Pot Holder illustration). (23 sts)

Rows 2–12: Repeat rows 2–12 of First Section.

Third Section
Row 1: With right side of row 1 on First Section facing, join cinnamon with sc in end of row 12 on First Section, sc in end of each row across to row 2; for **corner st,** sc ends of rows 1 and 2 and next unworked ch of ch-49 tog; sc in last 11 chs, turn. *(23 sts)*

Rows 2–12: Repeat rows 2–12 of First Section.

Fourth Section
Row 1: With right side of Sections facing, join cinnamon with sc in end of row 12 on Second Section, sc in end of each row across to row 1; for **corner st,** sc row 1 and last stitch of First Section and row 1 of Third Section tog; sc in each row across Third Section, turn. *(23)*

Rows 2–12: Repeat rows 2–12 of First Section.

Border
Working around outer edge, with right side of Sections facing, join cinnamon with

Continued on page 70

Mitered Corners Mini Bag

Designed by Darla Sims

Make a clever little bag to give as a gift using the traditional Mitered Corners stitch pattern.

FINISHED SIZE: 8" high x 9½" wide, plus Straps.

MATERIALS: Kitchen Cotton Art. 760 by Lion Brand® Yarn Company or cotton worsted yarn: 4 oz. White #100, 3 oz. Fern Green #131, 2 oz. Maize #186; tapestry needle; F and G crochet hooks *(or hook needed to obtain G hook gauge).*

GAUGE: G hook, 16 sts = 4"; 20 rows = 4".

SIDE (Make 2)
Bottom Panel
Row 1: For **First Section,** with G hook and green, loosely ch 51, sc in second ch from hook, sc in next 8 chs; skip next 2 chs at **corner,** sc in next 9 chs leaving last 30 chs unworked, turn. *(18 sc made)*

Rows 2–4: Ch 1, sc in each st across to one st before corner, skip next 2 sts at **corner,** sc in each st across, turn. At end of last row *(12 sts).* Fasten off.

Row 5: Join white with sc in first st, sc in next 4 sts, skip next 2 sts at **corner,** sc in last 5 sts, turn. *(10)*

Row 6: Repeat row 2. Fasten off. *(8)*

Row 7: Join maize with sc in first st, sc in next 2 sts, skip next 2 sts at **corner,** sc in last 3 sts, turn. *(6)*

Row 8: Repeat row 2. *(4)*

Row 9: Ch 1, sc in first st, skip next 2 sts at **corner,** sc in last st, turn. *(2)*

Row 10: Ch 1, sc 2 sts tog. Fasten off.

Row 1: For **Second Section,** with right side of previous Section facing and row 10 at upper right, join green with sc in end of row 10, sc in next 8 rows, skip last row and first unworked ch on starting ch, sc in next 9 chs leaving last 20 chs unworked, turn. *(18 sts)*

Rows 2–10: Repeat rows 2–10 of First Section.

Row 1: For **Third Section,** working in ends of row on Second Section and in next 10 chs of starting ch, repeat row 1 of Second Section, leaving last 10 chs unworked. *(18 sts)*

Rows 2–10: Repeat rows 2–10 of First Section.

Row 1: For **Fourth Section,** working in ends of row on Third Section and in last 10 chs of starting ch, repeat row 1 of Second Section. *(18 sts)*

Rows 2–10: Repeat rows 2–10 of First Section.

Center Panel
Row 1: Working in ends of rows, with G hook, join white with sc in end of row 1 on First Section, evenly space 34 more sc across all four Sections with last sc in end of row 10 on Fourth Section, turn. *(35 sc made)*

Row 2: Ch 1, sc in each st across, turn.

*NOTE: Work each **long sc front post (lscfp,** see Crochet Stitch Guide on page 191) around st on row before last, pull up to height of row being worked. Always **skip one st** on last row behind each fp st.*

Row 3: Ch 1, sc in first st, (lscfp—*see Note*—around st on row before last directly below next st, sc in next st on this row) across, turn.

Rows 4–19: Repeat rows 2 and 3 alternately. At end of last row, fasten off.

Matching sts and ends of rows; with matching colors, sew Sides wrong sides together on three edges leaving row 19 open.

Top Panel
Rnd 1: With F hook, join maize with sc in first st past either seam, sc in each st around assembled Sides, join with sl st in first sc.

Rnds 2–4: Ch 1, sc in each st around, join. At end of last rnd, fasten off.

STRAP (make 2)

Row 1: With F hook and green, ch 11, sc in second ch from hook, sc in each ch across, turn. *(10 sc made)*

Rows 2–4: Ch 1, sc first 2 sts tog, sc in each st across to last 2 sts, sc last 2 sts tog, turn. *(8, 6, 4)*

Rows 5–47: Ch 1, sc in each st across, turn.

Rows 48–50: Ch 1, 2 sc in first st, sc in each st across with 2 sc in last st, turn. At end of last row, fasten off. *(6, 8, 10)*

On each Side, sew ends of one Strap to Top Panel centered 3" apart. ●

Mitered Corners Pot Holder

Continued from page 67

sc in corner st on last row of Fourth Section, sc in same st, sc in end of each row across to next corner, 3 sc in corner; working on opposite side of starting ch, (sc in each ch across to corner, 3 sc in corner ch) 2 times, sc in each row across to corner, sc in same st as joining sc, join with sl st in first sc. Fasten off.

BACK

With sage, ch 49. Fasten off.

First Section

Row 1: Skip first 12 chs for Second Section, join sage with sc in 13th ch from end, sc in next 10 chs; for **corner st,** sc next 3 chs tog; sc in next 11 chs, leaving remaining 12 chs unworked for Third Section, turn. *(23 sc made)*

Rows 2–6: Ch 1, sc in each st across to one st before corner st; for **corner st,** sc next 3 sts tog; sc in each st across, turn. At end of last row *(13 sts),* fasten off.

Row 7: Join maize with sc in first st, sc in each st across to one st before corner st; for **corner st,** sc next 3 sts tog; sc in each st across, turn. *(11)*

Row 8: Repeat row 2. Fasten off. *(9)*

Row 9: With cinnamon, repeat row 7. *(7)*

Rows 10–11: Repeat row 2. *(5, 3)*

Row 12: Ch 1, sc 3 sts tog. Fasten off.

Second Section

Row 1: With right side of row 1 on First Section facing, join sage with sc in end ch at right of First Section, sc in next 10 chs; for corner st, sc next 2 chs and end of row 1 on First Section tog; sc in end of each row across First Section, turn. *(23 sts)*

Rows 2–12: Repeat rows 2–12 of First Section.

Third Section

Row 1: With right side of row 1 on First Section facing, join sage with sc in end of row 12 on First Section, sc in end of each row across to row 2; for **corner st,** sc ends of rows 1 and 2 and next unworked ch of ch-49 tog; sc in last 11 chs, turn. *(23 sts)*

Rows 2–12: Repeat rows 2–12 of First Section.

Fourth Section

Row 1: With right side of Sections facing, join sage with sc in end of row 12 on Second Section, sc in end of each row across to row 1; for **corner st,** sc row 1 and last stitch of First Section and row 1 of Third Section tog; sc in each row across Third Section, turn. *(23)*

Rows 2–12: Repeat rows 2–12 of First Section.

Border

With sage, repeat Front Border.

Assembly and Hanger

Hold Front and Back wrong sides together, matching stitches; working through both layers as one, join maize with sl st in any center corner st; working from left to right, **reverse sc** *(see Crochet Stitch Guide on page 191)* in next st and in each st around, sl st in joining sl st, **turn;** for **Hanger,** ch 8, sl st in first reverse sc to form ring, **turn,** 16 sc in ring, sl st in last reverse sc. Fasten off. ●

Dash
Stitch Pattern

*K*nitted dash stitch is easily adapted to crochet; in this instance, single crochet *stitches are used to resemble the reverse stockinette stitch background, and front post stitches form the alternating raised vertical "dash" design.*

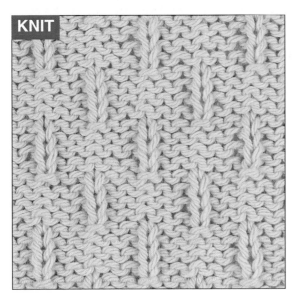

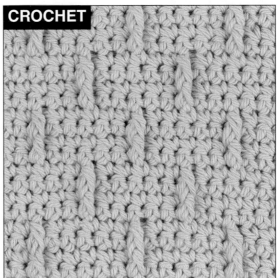

Afghan Square: Dash Stitch

READ BEFORE STARTING

Refer to **Chapter 2** for instructions for using Squares to make either Knit or Crochet Version of Large Afghan or Baby Afghan.

For comparison, each Square has instructions for **Knit Version** in blue type, and instructions for **Crochet Version** in black type.

KNIT VERSION

With medium needles and color B, cast on 25.

Row 1: *(Right side)* P 3, K 1, (P 5, K 1) 3 times, P 3.

Row 2: K 3, P 1, (K 5, P 1) 3 times, K 3.

Rows 3–4: Repeat rows 1 and 2.

Row 5: P 6, K 1, (P 5, K 1) 2 times, P 6.

Row 6: K 6, P 1, (K 5, P 1) 2 times, K 6.

Rows 7–8: Repeat rows 5 and 6.

CROCHET VERSION

Row 1: With medium hook and color B, ch 26, sc in second ch from hook, sc in each ch across, turn. *(25 sc made)*

Row 2: Ch 1, sc in each st across, turn.

NOTE: *Work **all sc sts** into sts of **last row**.*

Row 3: Ch 1, sc in first 3 sc, **hdcfp** *(see Special Stitch on page 24)* around third st on row before last, (sc in next 5 sc, hdcfp around st on row before last directly

Rows 9–24: Repeat rows 1–8 consecutively.

Rows 25–28: Repeat rows 1–4.
Piece should measure same as gauge.
Bind off purlwise.
Work Edging in Basic Finishing on page 28.

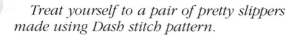

below next st) 3 times, sc in last 3 sc, turn.

Row 4: Ch 1, sc in each st across, turn.

Rows 5–6: Repeat rows 3–4.

Row 7: Ch 1, sc in first 6 sc, hdcfp around st on row before last directly below next st, (sc in next 5 sc, hdcfp around st on row before last directly below next st) 2 times, sc in last 6 sc, turn.

Row 8: Ch 1, sc in each st across, turn.

Rows 9-10: Repeat rows 7–8.

Rows 11–29: Repeat rows 3–10 consecutively, ending with row 5. At end of last row, fasten off.

Piece should measure same as gauge.
Work Edging in Basic Finishing on page 28.

Beaded Slippers

Designed by Donna Jones

Treat yourself to a pair of pretty slippers made using Dash stitch pattern.

FINISHED SIZES: Small fits up to 8½"-long foot. **Medium** fits 9½"-long foot. **Large** fits up to 10½"-long foot.

MATERIALS: 4 oz. Seaspray #123 Wool-Ease® Art. 620 by Lion Brand® Yarn Company or worsted yarn; stitch markers; 20 assorted-color pony beads; tapestry needle; crochet hook needed to obtain gauge for size.

GAUGES

Small: E hook; 5 sc = 1"; 5 rows = 1".
Medium: F hook; 9 sc = 2"; 9 rows = 2".
Large: G hook; 4 sc = 1"; 4 rows = 1".

SLIPPER (make 2)
Sole

Rnd 1: With hook and gauge for size, ch 25, 3 sc in second ch from hook, sc in next 22 chs, 3 sc in end ch; working on opposite side of ch, sc in next 22 chs, join with sl st in first sc, **turn.** *(50 sc made)*

Rnd 2: Ch 1, sc in first st, (mark sc just made, sc in next 21 sts, mark sc just made, 2 sc in each of next 3 sts), sc in next st; repeat between ( ), join, **turn.** *(56)*

NOTE: *When working into marked st, remove marker, work st, place marker in st just made.*

Rnd 3: Ch 1, 2 sc in each of next 6 sts, sc in next 22 sts, 2 sc in each of next 6 sts, sc in next 10 sts, sl st in next st, **turn,** ch 1, skip sl st, sc in next 32 sts, sl st in next st, **turn,** ch 1, skip sl st, sc in each st and in each ch around, join, **turn.** *(Sc and ch-1 sps are worked into and counted as sts; sl sts are not worked into or counted—68 sts made)*

Rnd 4: Ch 1, sc in each st around to next marker, sc in marked st, 2 sc in each st around to next marker, sc in marked st, sc in each st around, join, **turn.** *(80)*

Rnd 5: Ch 1, sc in first 3 sts, 2 sc in each of next 6 sts, (sc in each st across to next marker) 2 times, sc in marked st, sc in next 18 sts, sl st in next st, **turn,** ch 1, skip sl st, sc in next 12 sts, sl st in next st, **turn,** ch 1, skip sl st, sc in each st around, join, **turn.** *(86)*

Rnd 6: Ch 1, sc in first 32 sts, 2 sc in each st of next 4 sts, sc in each st around, join, **turn.** *(90)*

Rnd 7: Removing markers as you go, ch 1, sc in each st around, join. Fasten off.

Sides

Wind 15 yds. yarn into small ball and lay aside for Instep.

Rnd 1: With right side of rnd 7 facing, working this rnd in **back posts** *(bp; see Crochet Stitch Guide on page 191)*, skip first 7 sts, join remaining yarn from skein with scbp around next st, scbp around each st on rnd 7, join with sl st in first st, **turn.** *(90 scbp made)*

Rnd 2: Ch 1, sc in each st around, join, **turn.**

*NOTES: For **hdc front post** (hdcfp, see Crochet Stitch Guide), hdc around st on rnd before last and pull up to height of row being worked. **Skip one st** on last rnd for each fp worked into previous rnd unless otherwise stated.*

Work all sc sts into sts of last rnd.

Rnd 3: Ch 1, sc in first 3 sts, skip first 3 sts on rnd before last, **hdcfp** *(see Note above)* around next st, (sc in next 5 sts, skip next 5 sts on rnd before last, hdcfp around next st) around to last 2 sts, sc in last 2 sts, join, **turn.**

Rnd 4: Ch 1, sc in each st around, join, **turn.**

Rnd 5: Ch 1, sc in first 3 sts, (hdcfp around next fp on rnd before last, sc in next 5 sts) 14 times, hdcfp around next fp on rnd before last, sc in last 2 sts, join, **turn.**

Pull up long loop and remove hook.

Instep

Row 1: With wrong side facing and small ball of yarn, join with sl st in 39th st from joining on rnd 5 of Sides, skip next st, 2 sc in next st, sc in next 7 sts, 2 sc in next st, skip next unworked st on rnd 5, sl st in next 2 sts leaving last 38 sts unworked, turn. *(Sl sts are not worked into or counted as sts—11 sc made)*

Row 2: Sc in first 2 sts, hdcfp around st on row before last directly below next st, sc in next 5 sts, hdcfp around st on row before last directly below next st, sc in last 2 sts, sl st in next 2 unworked sts on rnd 5, turn.

Row 3: Sc in each st across, sl st in next 2 unworked sts on rnd 5, turn.

Row 4: Sc in first 2 sts, hdcfp around next fp on row before last, sc in next 5 sts, hdcfp around next fp on row before last, sc in last 2 sts, sl st in next 2 unworked sts on rnd 5, turn.

Row 5: Sc in each st across, sl st in next 2 unworked sts on rnd 5, turn.

Row 6: Hdcfp around first st on row before last; without skipping a st, sc in first 5 sts, hdcfp around st on row before last directly below next st, sc in last 5 sts, hdcfp around last st on row before last, sl st in next 2 unworked sts on rnd 5, turn. *(13)*

Row 7: Sc in each st across, sl st in next 2 unworked sts on rnd 5, turn.

Row 8: Hdcfp around first fp on row before last, skip first st on last row, sc in next 5 sts, hdcfp around next fp on row before last, sc in next 5 sts, hdcfp around last fp on row before last, skip last st on last row, sl st in next 2 unworked sts on rnd 5, turn.

Row 9: Sc in each st across, sl st in next 2 unworked sts on rnd 5, turn.

Row 10: Sc in first 3 sts, hdcfp around st on row before last directly below next st, sc in next 5 sts, hdcfp around st on row before last directly below next st, sc in last 3 sts, sl st in next 2 unworked sts on rnd 5, turn.

Row 11: Sc in each st across, sl st in next 2 unworked sts on rnd 5, turn.

Row 12: Sc in first 3 sts, hdcfp around next fp on row before last, sc in next 5 sts, hdcfp around next fp on row before last, sc in last 3 sts, sl st in next 2 unworked sts on rnd 5, turn.

Row 13: Sc in each st across, sl st in next 2 unworked sts on rnd 5, turn.

Row 14: Hdcfp around first st on row before last, skip first st on last row, sc in next 5 sts, hdcfp around st on row before last directly below next st, sc in next 5 sts, hdcfp around last st on row before last, skip last st on last row, sl st in next 2 unworked sts on rnd 5, turn.

Row 15: Sc in each st across, sl st in next 2 unworked sts on rnd 5, turn.

Row 16: Hdcfp around first fp on row before last, skip first st on last row, sc in next 5 sts, hdcfp around next fp on row before last, sc in next 5 sts, hdcfp around last fp on row before last, skip last st on last row, sl st in next 2 unworked sts on rnd 5, turn.

Rows 17–20: Repeat rows 9–12. At end of last row, sl st in only one st. Fasten off. *(13 sts on Instep)*

Sides (continued)

Return long loop on Sides to hook.

Rnd 6: With wrong side of rnd 5 facing, ch 1, sc in first 18 sts, sc next st and first unworked st on Instep tog, sc in next 11 sts, sc next st and next unworked st on rnd 5 tog, sc in last 19 sts, join with sl st in first st, **turn.** *(50 sts made)*

Rnd 7: Ch 1, hdcfp around first st on row before last, (sc in next 5 sts, hdcfp around st on rnd before last directly below next st) 3 times, sc next 2 sts tog, sc in next 4 sts, hdcfp around next st on rnd before last, sc in next 4 sts, sc next 2 sts tog, hdcfp around st on rnd 5 on Sides directly below next st, sc in next 5 sts, (hdcfp around st on rnd before last directly below next st, sc in next 5 sts) 2 times, join, **turn.** *(48)*

Rnd 8: Ch 1, sc in each st around, join, **turn.**

Rnd 9: Ch 1, hdcfp around first st on rnd before last, sc in next 5 sts, (hdcfp around st on rnd before last directly below next st, sc in next 5 sts) 7 times, join, **turn.** *(48)*

Rnds 10–11: Ch 1, sc in each st around, join, **turn.**

Rnd 12: For **beading rnd,** ch 1, sc in first st, ch 1, skip next st, (sc in next st, ch 1, skip next st) around, join. Fasten off.

Cuff

Thread eight pony beads onto yarn.

Row 1: With right side of rnd 12 on Sides facing and working toward ends of row, join with sc in sc directly above last fp at center of Instep, sc in each st and in each ch sp around, turn; **do not join.** *(48 sc made)*

Row 2: For **fold row,** ch 1, sc in top of first sc, scbp around same st, scbp around each st across to center back of heel, 2 scbp around center back st, scbp around each st across with scbp around last st, sc in top of last st, turn. *(51)*

Row 3: Ch 1, sc in each st across, turn.

Row 4: Ch 1, sc in first st, hdcfp around st on row before last directly below next st, (sc in next 5 sts, hdcfp around st on row before last directly below next st) across

with sc in last st, turn.

Row 5: Ch 1, sc in each st across, turn.

Row 6: Ch 1, sc in first st, hdcfp around next fp on row before last, (sc in next 5 sts, hdcfp around next fp on row before last) across with sc in last st, turn.

Row 7: Ch 1, sc first 2 sts tog, sc in each st across to last 2 sts, sc last 2 sts tog, turn. *(49)*

Row 8: Ch 1, sc first 2 sts tog, sc in next st, hdcfp around st on row before last directly below next st, (sc in next 5 sts, hdcfp around st on row before last directly below next st) across to last 3 sts, sc in next st, sc last 2 sts tog, turn. *(47)*

Row 9: Repeat row 7. *(45)*

Row 10: Sl st in first st, ch 1, hdcfp around next fp on row before last, ch 1, pull up a bead snug against hook, ch 1, sl st in top of fp just made, (sc in next 5 sts, hdcfp around next fp on row before last, ch 1, pull up a bead snug against hook, ch 1, sl st in top of fp just made) across, ch 1, sl st in last st. Fasten off.

Tie

Thread two pony beads onto yarn.

For **drawstring,** leaving 8" end, ch 1, pull up a bead snug against hook, ch to measure 16", pull up a bead snug against hook, ch 1; leaving 8" end, fasten off.

Beginning at center front between ends of Cuff, weave drawstring through beading rnd.

For each **Tassel** *(make on each end of drawstring),* wrap yarn five times around three fingers to form ring; remove ring from fingers, run 8" end of drawstring through center of ring and tie tightly to end of ch. Thread 8" end into tapestry needle. Hold 8" end tightly against side of ring forming a small loop about ½" below knot, wrap 8" end very tightly four or five times around ring over loop; use tapestry needle to secure end through loop. Hide end in center of ring. Cut loops and yarn ends at opposite end 1¼" from knot at end of drawstring.

Pull drawstring to desired length and tie in bow. ●

Eyeglasses Case
and Cell Phone Case

Designed by Darla Sims

Quick-and-easy accessories for those must-have companions.

FINISHED SIZES: Eyeglasses Case is 3½" wide x 6½" long.

Cell Phone Case is 3½" wide x 6¼" long, plus belt loop.

MATERIALS FOR EYEGLASSES CASE:
MicroSpun Art. 910 by Lion Brand® Yarn Company or sport yarn: 1¼ oz. desired color *(Mango #186 shown);* desired novelty button *(sunglasses shown);* tapestry needle; F and G crochet hooks *(or hook needed to obtain G hook gauge).*

MATERIALS FOR CELL PHONE CASE:
MicroSpun Art. 910 by Lion Brand® Yarn Company or sport yarn: 1¼ oz. desired color *(Lime #194 shown);* desired novelty button *(sunglasses shown);* tapestry needle; F and G crochet hooks *(or hook needed to obtain G hook gauge).*

GAUGE: G hook, 9 sts = 2"; 9 rows = 2".

EYEGLASSES CASE
Side (make 2)

Row 1: With G hook, ch 14, sc in second ch from hook, sc in each ch across, turn. *(13 sc made)*

Row 2: Ch 1, sc in each st across, turn.

*NOTE: For **hdc front post (hdcfp,** see Crochet Stitch Guide on page 191), hdc around designated st and pull up to height of row being worked. **Skip one st** on last row for each fp worked into previous row unless otherwise stated.*

Row 3: Ch 1, sc in first 3 sts, **hdcfp** *(see Note above)* around st on row before last directly below next st, sc in next 5 sts, hdcfp around st on row before last directly below next st, sc in last 3 sts, turn.

Row 4: Ch 1, sc in each st across, turn.

Row 5: Ch 1, sc in first 3 sts, hdcfp around next fp on row before last, sc in next 5 sts, hdcfp around next fp on row before last, sc in last 3 sts, turn.

Row 6: Ch 1, sc in each st across, turn.

Row 7: Ch 1, sc in first 6 sts, hdcfp around st on row before last directly below next st, sc in last 6 sts, turn.

Row 8: Ch 1, sc in each st across, turn.

Row 9: Ch 1, sc in first 6 sts, hdcfp around next fp on row before last, sc in last 6 sts, turn.

Rows 10–29: Repeat rows 2–9 consecutively, ending with row 5. At end of last row, fasten off.

Assembly and Finishing

1: To **join Sides,** with wrong sides together, matching stitches and ends of rows, working through both layers as one, with F hook, join with sc in end of row 29 on one long edge, complete as follows:

A: Sc in each row across to corner, 3 sc in corner;

B: Working across opposite side of starting ch, sc in each ch across with 3 sc in corner,

C: Sc in each row across, leaving other short edge open at top. Fasten off.

2: For **top trim,** join with sc in seventh st on one side *(this is back side of Case),* sc in each st and in each seam around, sc in same st as joining sc; for **button loop,** ch to length needed to fit around novelty button, join with sl st in first sc. Fasten off.

3: Position button on front side of case to fit button loop; sew in place.

CELL PHONE CASE
Front

Rows 1–9: Work same as rows 1–9 of Eyeglasses Case.

Rows 10–25: Repeat rows 2–9 of

Eyeglasses Case consecutively. At end of last row, fasten off.

Back

Rows 1–9: Work same as rows 1–9 of Eyeglasses Case.

Rows 10–33: Repeat rows 2–9 of Eyeglasses Case consecutively. At end of last row, fasten off. *(Rows 25–33 form Flap.)*

Assembly and Finishing

1: For **joining rnd,** with wrong sides together and Front facing you, matching stitches and ends of rows 1–25, working through both layers as one, with F hook, join with sc in end of row 25 on one long edge, complete as follows:

    A: Sc in end of each row across to corner of row 1, 3 sc in corner;

    B: Working across opposite side of starting ch, sc in each ch across with 3 sc in corner;

    C: Sc in each row across to opposite end of row 25;

    D: Working across flap on Back only, sc in end of each row across to corner, 3 sc in corner;

    E: Sc in next 7 sts on last row of Back; for **button loop,** ch to length needed to fit around novelty button, sc in same st as last sc, sc in next 6 sts, 3 sc in corner;

    F: Sc in end of each row across, join with sl st in first sc, **turn.**

    G: For **belt loop,** ch 25, sc in second ch from hook, sc in each ch across, sl st in last sc of step F. Leaving strand for sewing, fasten off.

    H: Fold belt loop to Front; sew end to first and last sts of joining rnd.

2: Position button on Front of case to match button loop; sew in place. ●

Parallel Lines
Stitch Pattern

*T*he long raised stitches in this knitted pattern are created by placing a yarn-over next to the stitch that will be raised. On the next row, the raised stitch is slipped and the yarn-over is dropped; this gives added length so the slipped stitch will lay flat as it is slipped on each of the next two rows.

In the crochet version, single crochet stitches mimic the stockinette stitch background while long single crochet front post stitches are used to create the raised ridges.

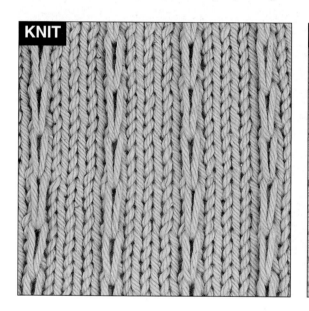

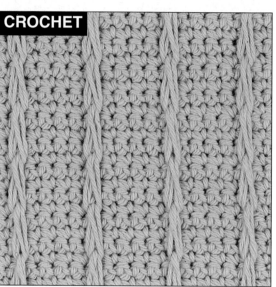

Afghan Square: Parallel Lines

READ BEFORE STARTING

Refer to **Chapter 2** for instructions for using Squares to make either Knit or Crochet Version of Large Afghan or Baby Afghan.

For comparison, each Square has instructions for **Knit Version** in blue type, and instructions for **Crochet Version** in black type.

<table>
<tr><td>

KNIT VERSION

With large needles and color B, cast on 26.

Row 1: *(Right side)* (K 5, yo) 4 times, K 6. *(30 sts on needles)*

Row 2: P 5, (slip 1 purlwise, drop yo, P 4) 4 times, P 1. *(26 sts)*

Row 3: K 5, (slip 1 purlwise, K 4) 4 times, K 1.

</td><td>

CROCHET VERSION

Row 1: With small hook and color B, ch 27, sc in second ch from hook, sc in each ch across, turn. *(26 sc made)*

Rows 2–3: Ch 1, sc in each st across, turn. *NOTE: Work **all sc sts** into sts of **last row**.*

Row 4: Ch 1, sc in first 5 sts, (**scfp**—*see*

</td></tr>
</table>

Row 4: P 5, (slip 1 purlwise, P 4) 4 times, P 1.

Row 5: K 5, (yo, K slipped st, K 4) 4 times, K 1. *(30 sts)*

Next rows: Repeat rows 2–5 consecutively until piece measures same as gauge, ending after a repeat of row 4.

Bind off.

Work Edging in Basic Finishing on page 28.

Special Stitch on page 24—around sc on row before last directly below next st, sc in next 4 sc—*see Note*) 4 times, sc in last sc, turn.

Rows 5–7: Ch 1, sc in each st across, turn.

Row 8: Ch 1, sc in first 5 sts, (scfp around next fp on fourth row before, sc in next 4 sc) 4 times, sc in last sc, turn.

Next rows: Repeat rows 5–8 consecutively until piece measures same as gauge, ending with row 8. At end of last row, fasten off.

Work Edging in Basic Finishing on page 28.

Cleaning and Storage of Knit and Crochet Items

*K*nit and crochet items should be cared for in basically the same way, but be sure to read the label on the yarn before deciding to wash them, as dry cleaning is occasionally required. Knitted items may sometimes be machine washed if they are lightweight and closely knit, but crochet should be hand washed.

Use a mild shampoo or a wool detergent for washing wool, angora or mohair. Stronger detergents can be used on synthetics or cotton, but avoid using a wool detergent to wash cotton, as it may cause the cotton yarn to fade. Don't worry if the water becomes discolored, just use enough water so the item can move freely, and rinse well. In hard water, two tablespoons of white vinegar per quart of rinse water will restore softness to the yarn and brighten colors.

Natural fibers should be washed in cold water or they may shrink or fade. Take care to support the piece well when you lift it from the water so the weight of the water does not stretch it out of shape. Press out as much water as possible, but do not wring or twist; then roll it in a heavy towel and press it to absorb excess water.

Lay the piece flat on another towel, pat it into shape and allow to dry; if the piece has layers with multiple colors, place another towel between the layers to prevent colors from bleeding.

For items made of fluffy yarns, after they have dried, brush them lightly to bring the fluff back to the yarn.

To prevent mildew, be sure the item is thoroughly dry before putting it away; then store it with baking soda and/or activated charcoal.

A knit or crochet item should be stored in a drawer or on a shelf, rather than hung. To prevent discoloration, any item that is stored in a drawer or box should be protected from the acid in the wood or cardboard by wrapping it in white cotton muslin or acid-free tissue paper. If the item is made of a wool-type yarn, store it in a special garment bag made for protecting against moths and carpet beetles.

With the proper care, you can look forward to enjoying your knit and crochet handiwork for years to come.

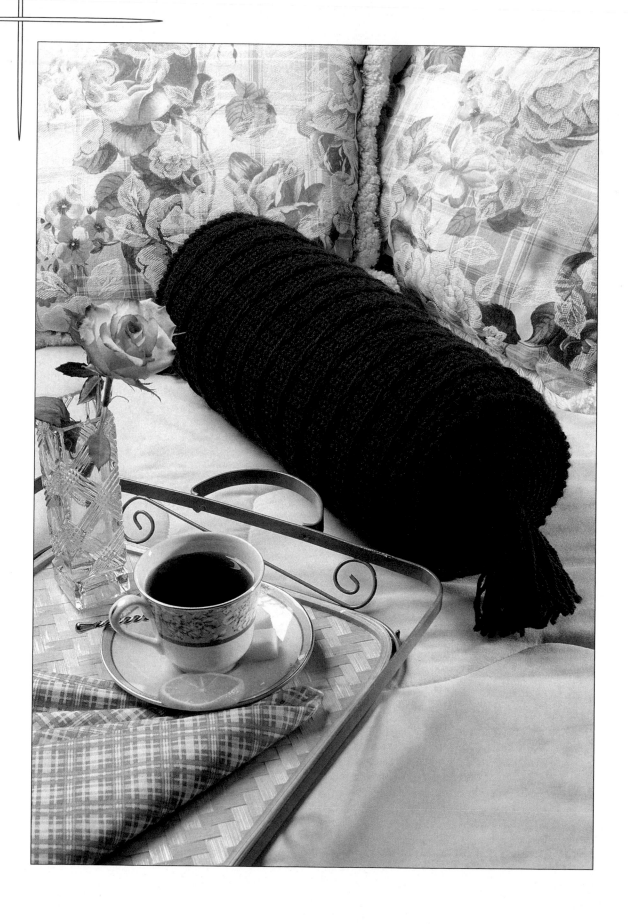

Bolster Pillow

Designed by Donna Jones

Using the Parallel Lines stitch pattern is one way to bolster your home decor.

FINISHED SIZE: 5" across x 14" long, plus tassels.

MATERIALS: 7 oz. Navy #111 Wool-Ease® Art. 620 by Lion Brand® Yarn Company or worsted yarn; 5" x 14" neck-roll or bolster pillow form; bobby pins or stitch markers; 4" square of cardboard; tapestry needle; F crochet hook *(or hook needed to obtain gauge)*.

GAUGE: 9 sc = 2"; 9 sc rows = 2".

SIDE

Row 1: Ch 62, sc in second ch from hook, sc in each ch across, turn. *(61 sc made)*

Rows 2–3: Ch 1, sc in each st across, turn. *NOTE: Work each **long sc front post (lscfp**, see Stitch Guide) around designated st on row before last, pull up to height of row being worked. Always **skip one st** on last row behind each scfp.*

Row 4: Ch 1, sc in first 5 sts; pulling all fp sts up to height of row being worked and skipping one st on last row behind each fp, *****lscfp** *(see Note)* around corresponding sc on row before last, sc in next 4 sts on this row; repeat from * across with sc in last st, turn.

Rows 5–7: Ch 1, sc in each st across, turn.

Row 8: Ch 1, sc in first 5 sts, (lscfp around next fp on previous row, sc in next 4 sts on this row) across with sc in last st, turn.

Next rows: Repeat rows 5–8 consecutively until piece measures 18½", or as needed to fit around pillow form, ending last repeat with row 5. At end of last row, fasten off.

END (make 2)

Rnd 1: Ch 4, sl st in first ch to form ring, ch 1, 8 sc in ring. *(8 sc made)* Work in continuous rnds; do not join. Mark first st of each rnd.

Rnd 2: 2 sc in each st around. *(16)*

Rnd 3: (Sc in next st, 2 sc in next st) around. *(24)*

Rnd 4: (Sc in next st, 2 sc in next st, sc in next st) around. *(32)*

Rnd 5: (2 sc in next st, sc in next 3 sts) around. *(40)*

Rnd 6: Sc in each st around.

Rnd 7: (Sc in next 3 sts, 2 sc in next st) around. *(50)*

Rnd 8: (Sc in next 2 sts, 2 sc in next st, sc in next 2 sts) around. *(60)*

Rnds 9–10: Sc in each st around.

Rnd 11: (Sc in next 4 sts, 2 sc in next st) around, sl st in next st. *(72)*

Rnd 12: Working from left to right, **reverse sc** *(see Crochet Stitch Guide)* in each st around, join with sl st in first reverse sc. Fasten off.

ASSEMBLY

1: With right side out, matching sts, lap last row of Side over starting ch of row 1 to form a tube; sew together across 1" at each end. Leave 12" opening at center.

2: With right side out, sew the base of rnd 12 on End pieces to ends of rows on each end of Side tube. Place pillow form inside tube, sew opening closed.

3: For each **tassel** *(make 2),* wrap yarn 40 times around 4" cardboard. Remove cardboard, tie separate 8" strand yarn through center of loops. Wrap separate 10" strand several times around all loops 1" below 8" tie. Cut loops at opposite end; trim ends even.

4: Sew tassels to center of Ends. ●

Parallel Lines Summer Shell

Designed by Darla Sims

Parallel Lines stitch pattern adds a touch of distinction to an elegant warm-weather top.

MATERIALS: MicroSpun Art. 910 by Lion Brand® Yarn Company or sport yarn: Amount needed for size—*Mango #186 is shown;* bobby pins or split stitch markers; tapestry needle; E and G crochet hooks *(or hook needed to obtain G hook gauge).*

GAUGE: G hook; 18 sts in pattern = 4"; 22 rows in pattern = 4".

SIZES
Lady's Small (30"–32" chest):
  Yarn: 14 oz.
  Garment chest: 33"
  Back length: 17½"
Lady's Medium (32"–36" chest):
  Yarn: 15 oz.
  Garment chest: 37½"
  Back length: 18"
Lady's Large (36"–40" chest):
  Yarn: 17 oz.
  Garment chest: 42"
  Back length: 18½"
Lady's X-Large (40"–44" chest):
  Yarn: 19 oz.
  Garment chest: 47"
  Back length: 19"

NOTE
Instructions are for size **Small;** changes for **Medium, Large** and **X-Large** are in [ ].

BACK
Row 1: Ch 76 [86, 96, 106], sc in second ch from hook, sc in each ch across, turn. *(75 [85, 95, 105] sc made)*

*NOTE: Work each **long sc front post (lscfp,** see Stitch Guide) around designated st on row before last, pull up to height of row being worked. Always **skip one st** on last row behind each fp st.*

Row 2: Ch 1, sc in each st across, turn.

Row 3: *(Right side)* Ch 1, sc in first 2 sts, **lscfp** *(see Note)* around sc on row before last directly below next st, (sc in next 4 sts on this row, lscfp around sc on row before last directly below next st) across with sc in last 2 sts, turn.

Rows 4–6: Ch 1, sc in each st across, turn.

Row 7: Ch 1, sc in first 2 sts, lscfp around next fp on previous row, (sc in next 4 sts on this row, lscfp around next fp on previous row) across with sc in last 2 sts, turn.

***NOTE:** To **work in pattern,** repeat rows 4–7 consecutively—see "How to Work in Pattern" in Chapter 1 on page 16.*

Next rows: Work in pattern *(see Note)* until piece measures 10" or desired length to 2" below underarm, ending with row 6. At end of last row, fasten off.

Armhole Shaping
Row 1: With wrong side of work facing, skip first 5 [7, 9, 11] sts, join with sc in next st, work in pattern across leaving last 5 [7, 9, 11] sts unworked, turn. *(65 [71, 77, 83] sc)*

Row 2: Ch 1, sc first 2 sts tog, work in pattern across to last 2 sts, sc last 2 sts tog, turn. *(63 [69, 75, 81] sc)*

Row 3: Work in pattern.

Row 4: Repeat row 2. *(61 [67, 73, 79] sc)*

Row 5: Work in pattern.

Row 6: Repeat row 2. *(59 [65, 71, 77] sc)*

Next rows: Work in pattern until Armhole Shaping measures 6½" [7", 7½", 8"], ending after a right-side row.

Shoulders
Row 1: For **first shoulder,** work in pattern across first 18 [20, 22, 24] sts leaving remaining sts unworked, turn.

Row 2: Ch 1, sc first 2 sts tog, work in pattern across, turn. *(17 [19, 21, 23] sc)*

Row 3: Work in pattern.

Row 4: Ch 1, sc first 2 sts tog, work in pattern across. Fasten off. *(16 [18, 20, 22] sc)*

Row 1: For **second shoulder,** with wrong side of last row on Armhole Shaping facing, skip next 23 [25, 27, 29] sts for neck edge, join with sc in next st, work in pattern across, turn. *(18 [20, 22, 24] sts)*

Row 2: Ch 1, work in pattern across to last 2 sts, sc last 2 sts tog. *(17 [19, 21, 23] sc)*

Row 3: Work in pattern.

Row 4: Ch 1, work in pattern across to last 2 sts, sc last 2 sts tog. Fasten off. *(16 [18, 20, 22] sc)*

FRONT

Work same as Back until piece measures 12½" [13", 13½", 14"] from beginning, ending with a right side row. Do not cut yarn.

Neck Shaping

Row 1: For **first side,** work in pattern across first 29 [32, 35, 38] sts leaving remaining sts unworked, turn.

Rows 2–9: Work in pattern, ending last row at neck edge. At end of last row, fasten off.

Row 10: For **shoulder,** with right side of last row facing, skip first 10 [11, 12, 13] sts for neck edge, join with sc in next st, work in pattern across, turn. *(19 [21, 23, 25] sc)*

Row 11: Ch 1, work in pattern across to last 2 sts, sc last 2 sts tog. *(18 [20, 22, 24] sc)*

Row 12: Ch 1, sc first 2 sts tog, work in pattern across, turn. *(17 [19, 21, 23] sc)*

Row 13: Ch 1, work in pattern across to last 2 sts, sc last 2 sts tog. *(16 [18, 20, 22] sc)*

Next rows: Work in pattern until piece measures same as Back Shoulder. Fasten off.

Row 1: For **second side,** with wrong side of last row on Front Armhole Shaping facing, skip next unworked st, join with sc in next st, work in pattern across, turn. *(29 [32, 35, 38] sts)*

Rows 2–9: Work in pattern.

Row 10: For **shoulder,** work in pattern across first 19 [21, 23, 25] sts, leaving last 10 [11, 12, 13] sts unworked for neck edge, turn.

Row 11: Ch 1, sc first 2 sts tog, work in pattern across, turn. *(18 [20, 22, 24] sc)*

Row 12: Ch 1, work in pattern across to last 2 sts, sc last 2 sts tog. *(17 [19, 21, 23] sc)*

Row 13: Ch 1, work in pattern across to last 2 sts, sc last 2 sts tog. *(16 [18, 20, 22] sc)*

Next rows: Work in pattern until piece measures same as Back Shoulder. Fasten off.

Assembly

Matching stitches, sew last rows on Front and Back Shoulders together.

On each side, matching ends of rows, sew Front and Back together from row 1 to Armhole Shaping.

Neck Trim

With E hook and right side of work facing, join with sc in shoulder seam; spacing sts so edge lays flat, sc in sts and in ends of rows around neck opening with 3 sc in same place at each front corner, join with sl st in first sc. Fasten off.

Armhole Trim (make on each armhole)

With E hook and right side of work facing, join with sc in top of side seam; spacing sts so edge lays flat, sc in sts and in ends of rows around armhole opening, join with sl st in first sc. Fasten off.

Bottom Trim

Rnd 1: With E hook and right side of bottom edge facing, working on opposite side of starting ch on row 1, join with sc in first ch past side seam, (sc in each ch around bottom edge to next side seam; for **small, medium and large only,** sc in side seam) 2 times, join with sl st in first sc; **do not turn.** *(152 [172, 192, 212] sts made)*

Rnd 2: Ch 1, sc in each st around, join.

Rnd 3: Ch 7, dc in fourth ch from hook, dc in same st on rnd 2 as ch-7, skip next 3 sts, *(dc, ch 4, dc in fourth ch from hook, dc) in next st on rnd 2, skip next 3 sts; repeat from * around, join with sl st in third ch of ch-7. Fasten off. ●

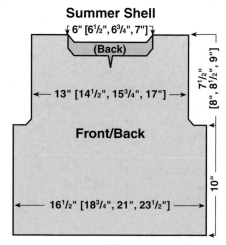

Summer Shell

6" [6½", 6¾", 7"]

(Back)

7½" [8", 8½", 9"]

13" [14½", 15¾", 17"]

Front/Back

10"

16½" [18¾", 21", 23½"]

Chapter Four

Diagonal Stitch Patterns

*I*nterest on the diagonal is the subject of this set of lessons. Patterns that run in a diagonal line have long been favorites of knitters. You'll see how to convert these to crochet with beautiful afghan squares and clever projects.

Diagonal Stitch Patterns

Knitted long stitches are usually formed by slipping stitches from the previous row. For longer slipped sts, one, two or three yarn-overs may be placed beside the stitch to be slipped, then the yarn-overs are dropped on the following rows to provide enough yarn length for the stitch to be slipped on multiple rows.

In this chapter we demonstrate how these vertical and diagonal long stitches, some of which are crossed, can be converted to crochet to produce a look similar to their knitted counterparts.

This is normally achieved by crocheting front post stitches into previous rows, pulling the post stitches up to the same height as the row being worked. Any desired stitch—single, half-double, double or treble crochet stitches—can be used for this purpose.

Hourglass

KNIT

long slipped stitches

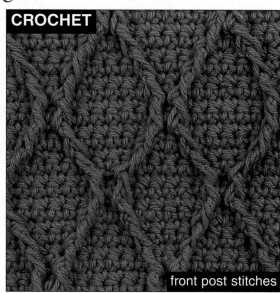

CROCHET

front post stitches

"V" design

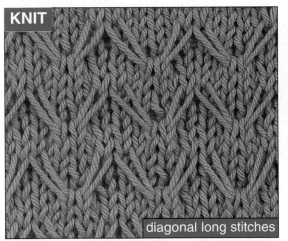

KNIT

diagonal long stitches

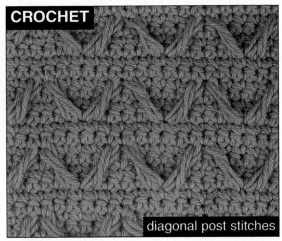

CROCHET

diagonal post stitches

Diagonal Ribbing

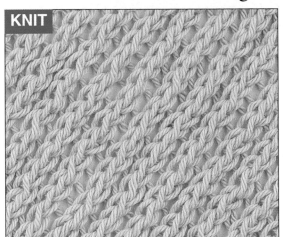

KNIT

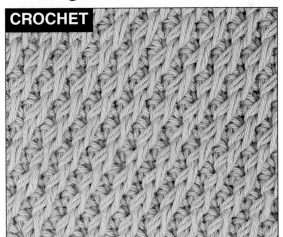

CROCHET

Diamonds

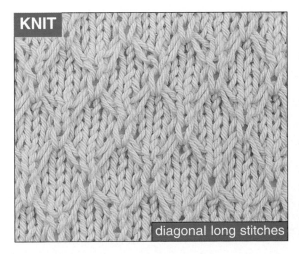

KNIT

diagonal long stitches

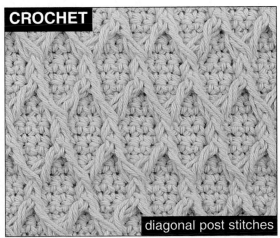

CROCHET

diagonal post stitches

Zigzag Stitch Pattern

K̲nitted diagonal stitches formed by slipping and crossing stitches in alternating directions on a stockinette stitch background create this interesting stitch design. To duplicate this look in crochet, work a single crochet background with long single crochet front post stitches to create the zigzag pattern.

KNIT

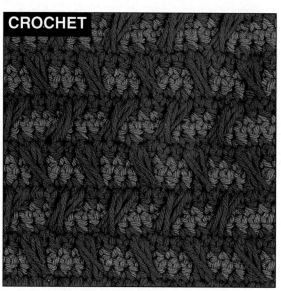

CROCHET

Afghan Square: Zigzags

READ BEFORE STARTING

Refer to **Chapter 2** for instructions for using Squares to make either Knit or Crochet Version of Large Afghan or Baby Afghan.

For comparison, each Square has instructions for **Knit Version** in blue type, and instructions for **Crochet Version** in black type.

KNIT VERSION

With medium needles and color B, cast on 29.
NOTES: *Always slip sts as if to purl.*
Carry dropped yarn loosely along ends of rows; pick up again when needed.
Row 1: *(Right side)* With color B, K across.
Row 2: P across. Drop color B, do not cut.
Row 3: With color A, K across.
Row 4: P 3, (yo, P 4) across to last 2 sts, P 2.

CROCHET VERSION

Row 1: With small hook and color B, ch 30, sc in second ch from hook, sc in each ch across, turn. *(29 sc made)*
Row 2: Ch 1, sc in each st across, changing to color A in last st *(see Crochet Stitch Guide on page 191),* turn.
NOTES: *Drop unused color; do not cut, pick up again when needed.*

Drop color A, do not cut. *(35 sts on needles)*

Row 5: With color B, K 5, (slip 1, drop yo, K 3) across. *(29 sts)*

Row 6: (P 3, slip 1) across to last 5 sts, P 5. Drop color B, do not cut.

Row 7: With color A, K 3, (slip next 2 sts to right needle, drop long loop of slipped st to front of work, slip same 2 slipped sts back to left needle, return dropped loop to left needle, K 4) across to last 2 sts, K 2.

Row 8: P 3, (yo, P 4) across to last 2 sts, yo, P 2. Drop color A, do not cut. *(36 sts)*

Row 9: With color B, K 1, (slip 1, drop yo, K 3) across. *(29 sts)*

Row 10: (P 3, slip 1) across to last st, P 1. Drop color B, do not cut.

Row 11: With color A, K 1, (drop long loop of slipped st to front of work, slip next 2 sts to right needle, return dropped loop to left needle, slip same 2 slipped sts back to left needle; K 4) across.

Next rows: Repeat rows 4–11 consecutively until length of piece measures about one-half inch less than width of piece, ending after a repeat of row 6 or row 10; at end of last row, do not drop color B.

Next row: With color B, work next row of repeat (row 7 or row 11).

Last row: P across.

Bind off.

Piece should measure same as gauge.

Work Edging in Basic Finishing on page 28.

*Work **all sc sts** into sts of **last row.***

Rows 3–4: With color A, ch 1, sc in each st across, turn, changing to color B in last st of last row.

Row 5: With color B, ch 1, sc in each st across, turn.

Row 6: Ch 1, sc in each st across changing to color A in last st, turn.

Row 7: Ch 1, sc in first 3 sc *(see Notes);* skip first 5 sts on fourth row below, **scfp** *(see Stitch Guide on page 191)* around sixth st on fourth row below, (sc in next 3 sc; counting from last fp, skip next 3 sts on fourth row below, scfp around next st) 5 times, sc in last 5 sc, turn.

Row 8: Ch 1, sc in each st across changing to color B in last st, turn.

Row 9: With color B, ch 1, sc in each st across, turn.

Row 10: Ch 1, sc in each st across changing to color A in last st, turn.

Row 11: Ch 1, sc in first 3 sc, scfp around second st on fourth row below, (sc in next 3 sc; counting from last fp, skip next 3 sts on fourth row below, scfp around next st) 6 times, sc in last sc, turn.

Row 12: Ch 1, sc in each st across, changing to color B in last st, turn.

Rows 13–34: Repeat rows 5–12 consecutively, ending with row 10. At end of last row, do not change colors. Fasten off.

Piece should measure same as gauge.

Work Edging in Basic Finishing on page 28.

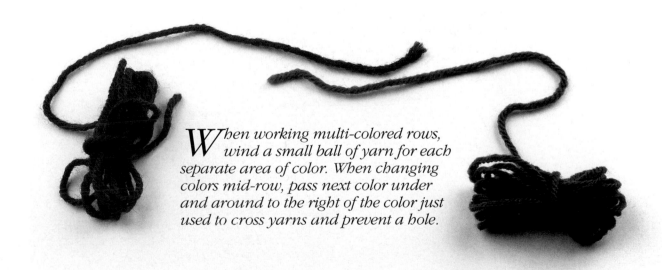

*W*hen working multi-colored rows, wind a small ball of yarn for each separate area of color. When changing colors mid-row, pass next color under and around to the right of the color just used to cross yarns and prevent a hole.

"Turtleneck" Tissue Cover

Designed by Donna Jones

Add an extra touch of warmth to winter with a tissue cover made with the Zigzag stitch pattern.

FINISHED SIZE: Fits standard boutique tissue box.

MATERIALS: 3 oz. Hunter Green #132 Wool-Ease® Art. 620 by Lion Brand® Yarn Company or worsted yarn; tapestry needle; F crochet hook *(or hook needed to obtain gauge)*.

GAUGE: 9 sc = 2"; 9 sc rows = 2".

COVER

Rnd 1: Ch 68, join with sl st in first ch to form a ring, ch 1, skip first ch, (3 sc in next ch for **corner,** sc in next 16 chs) 3 times, 3 sc in next ch, sc in last 15 chs, sc in first ch, join with sl st in first sc, **turn.** *(76 sc made)*

Rnds 2–6: Ch 1, sc in each st around, join with sl st in first sc, **turn.**

NOTES: *Work each **sc front post (scfp,** see Crochet Stitch Guide on page 191) around designated st on row before last, pull up to height of row being worked; always **skip one st on last row behind each fp.***

*Work **all sc sts** into sts of **last row.***

Rnd 7: Ch 1, sc in first 3 sts; skip first 5 sts on previous rnd 4 rnds below, **scfp** *(see Notes)* around next st on previous rnd, (sc in next 3 sts on last rnd; counting from last fp on previous rnd, skip next 3 sts, scfp around next st) around to last 4 sts on last rnd, sc in next 3 sts, skip first st on previous rnd, scfp around next st, join, **turn.** *(57 sc, 19 fp)*

Rnds 8–10: Ch 1, sc in each st around, join, **turn.** *(76 sc)*

Rnd 11: Ch 1, sc in first 3 sts; skip first st on previous rnd 4 rnds below, scfp around next st on previous rnd, (sc in next 3 sts on last rnd; counting from last fp on previous rnd, skip next 3 sts, scfp around next st) around, join, **turn.** *(57 sc, 19 fp)*

Rnds 12–14: Ch 1, sc in each st around, join, **turn.** *(76 sc)*

Rnds 15–28: Repeat rnds 7–14 consecutively, ending with rnd 12.

Rnd 29: Ch 1, sc first 3 sts tog, sc in next 16 sts, (sc next 3 sts tog, sc in next 16 sts) 3 times, join, **turn.** *(68)*

Rnd 30: Ch 1, sc in each st around, join, **turn.**

Rnd 31: Ch 1, sc first 3 sts tog, sc in next 14 sts, (sc next 3 sts tog, sc in next 14 sts) 3 times, join, **turn.** *(60)*

Rnd 32: Ch 1, sc in each st around, join, **turn.**

Rnd 33: Ch 1, sc first 3 sts tog, sc in next 12 sts, (sc next 3 sts tog, sc in next 12 sts) 3 times, join, **turn.** *(52)*

Rnd 34: Ch 1, sc in each st around, join, **turn. Do not fasten off.**

Turtleneck Opening Trim

Row 1: Ch 21; working in **back lps** *(see Stitch Guide)*, sc in second ch from hook, sc in each ch across, sl st in **both lps** of first 2 sc on rnd 34, turn. *(20 sc, 2 sl sts made)*

Row 2: Skip sl sts; sc in **back lp** of each sc across, turn. *(20 sc)*

Row 3: Ch 1, sc in **back lp** of each sc across, sl st in **both lps** of next 2 sc on rnd 34, turn. *(20 sc, 2 sl sts)*

Next rows: Repeat rows 2 and 3 alternately around rnd 34, ending with row 2. At end of last row, leaving end for sewing, fasten off.

Sew **back lps** of last row over starting ch of row 1 to form rib.

Matching corners, place Cover over tissue box; fold Turtleneck Opening Trim to outside *(see photo)*. ●

Zigzag Stitch Dishcloth
Designed by Darla Sims

Make dishwashing a pleasant task using a cloth made of Zigzag stitch pattern.

FINISHED SIZE: 11" square.

MATERIALS: Kitchen Cotton Art. 760 by Lion Brand® Yarn Company or cotton worsted yarn: 3 oz. Cinnamon #135; 2 oz. Maize #186; F and G crochet hooks *(or hook needed to obtain G hook gauge).*

GAUGE: G hook, 16 sts = 4"; 18 rows in pattern = 4".

DISHCLOTH

Row 1: With G hook and cinnamon, ch 38, sc in second ch from hook, sc in each ch across, turn. *(37 sc made)*

Row 2: Ch 1, sc in each st across, turn. Drop loop from hook; **do not cut.**

Row 3: Join maize with sc in first st, sc in each st across, turn.

Row 4: Ch 1, sc in each st across, turn.

Drop loop from hook; **do not cut.**

Row 5: Place dropped cinnamon loop on hook, ch 3 *(up to height of this row),* sc in each st across, turn.

Row 6: Ch 1, sc in each st across, turn. Drop loop from hook; **do not cut.**

NOTES: *Work each* **long sc front post (lscfp,** *see Crochet Stitch Guide on page 191) around designated st on row before last, pull up to height of row being worked; always* **skip one st** *on last row behind each fp.*

Work **all sc sts** *into sts of* **last** *row.*

Row 7: Place dropped maize loop on hook, ch 3, sc in first st, **lscfp** *(see Notes)* around fifth st on last maize row, (sc in next 3 sts on last row; skip 3 sts from last fp on last maize row, scfp around next st) across to last 3 sts on last row, sc in last 3 sts, turn.

Row 8: Ch 1, sc in each st across, turn. Drop loop from hook; **do not cut.**

Row 9: Place dropped cinnamon loop on hook, ch 3, sc in each st across, turn.

Row 10: Ch 1, sc in each st across, turn. Drop loop from hook; **do not cut.**

Row 11: Place dropped maize loop on hook, ch 3, sc in first 5 sts, lscfp around fifth st on last maize row, (sc in next 3 sts on last row; skip 3 sts from last fp on last maize row, scfp around next st) across to last 3 sts on last row, sc in last 3 sts, turn.

Row 12: Ch 1, sc in each st across, turn. Drop loop from hook; **do not cut.**

Rows 13–42: Repeat rows 5–12 consecutively, ending with row 10. At end of last row, fasten off cinnamon.

Rnd 43: Place dropped maize loop on **F hook;** working around outer edge, ch 3, 3 sc in first st, sc in each st, across to last st, 3 sc in last st, evenly space 37 sc in ends of rows across; working in starting ch on opposite side of row 1, 3 sc in first ch, sc in each ch across to last ch, 3 sc in last ch, evenly space 37 sc in ends of rows across, join with sl st in first sc. *(156 sts)*

Rnd 44: Ch 1, sc in first 3 sts, ch 3, (sc in next 3 sts, ch 3) around, join. Fasten off. ●

Flying Geese Stitch Pattern

*L*ong slipped stitches knitted diagonally into a stockinette stitch background are combined to resemble a flight of geese for a pleasing stitch design.

To crochet this design, use a single crochet background and work long half-double crochet stitches diagonally into the fourth row below.

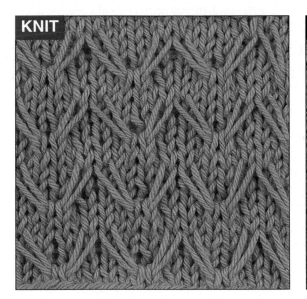

KNIT

CROCHET

Afghan Square: Flying Geese

READ BEFORE STARTING

Refer to **Chapter 2** for instructions for using Squares to make either Knit or Crochet Version of Large Afghan or Baby Afghan.

For comparison, each Square has instructions for **Knit Version** in blue type, and instructions for **Crochet Version** in black type.

KNIT VERSION

With medium needles and color A, cast on 26.

NOTES: *For* **long st,** *insert right needle into next st as if to P, wrap yarn 2 times around needle and pull both wraps through st at same time as if to P (2 wraps count as one st).*

Always slip sts as if to purl.

Row 1: *(Wrong side)* P 1, **long st** *(see Note),* P 4, (long st 2 times, P 4) 3 times, long st, P 1.

CROCHET VERSION

Row 1: With small hook and color A, ch 27, sc in second ch from hook, sc in each ch across, turn. *(26 sc made)*

Rows 2–5: Ch 1, sc in each st across, turn.

NOTE: *Work* **all sc sts** *into sts of* **last row.**

Row 6: Ch 1, sc in first 3 sc *(see Note),* skip first st on fourth row below, **hdcfp** *(see Special Stitch on page 24)* around

Row 2: K 1, slip first wrap of long st, drop next wrap, K 4, *(slip first wrap of long st, drop next wrap) 2 times, K 4; repeat from * across to last 2 sts, slip first wrap of long st, drop next wrap, K 1.

Row 3: P 1, slip 1, P 4, (slip 2, P 4) across to last 2 sts, slip 1, P 1.

Row 4: K 1, slip 1, K 4, (slip 2, K 4) across to last 2 sts, slip 1, K 1.

Row 5: Repeat row 3.

Row 6: K 1, (drop next long st from needle, K 2, return dropped st to left needle, K 1, slip next 2 sts to right needle, drop next long st from needle, slip same 2 sts back to left needle, return dropped long st to left needle, K 3) 4 times, K 1.

Next rows: Repeat rows 1–6 consecutively until piece measures same as gauge, ending after a repeat of row 6.

Bind off purlwise.

Work Edging in Basic Finishing on page 28.

next st on fourth row below; counting from last fp, skip next 4 sts on fourth row below, hdcfp around next st, (sc in next 4 sc, hdcfp around next st on fourth row below, skip next 4 sts on fourth row below, hdcfp around next st) 3 times, sc in last 3 sc, turn.

Rows 7–11: Ch 1, sc in each st across, turn.

Rows 12–30: Repeat rows 5-10 consecutively, ending with row 5.

Rows 31–32: Ch 1, sc in each st across, turn. At end of last row, fasten off.

Piece should measure same as gauge.

Work Edging in Basic Finishing on page 28.

Bread Cozy

Designed by Donna Jones

Keep your freshly-baked muffins and biscuits warm in this cozy cover made with Flying Geese stitch pattern.

FINISHED SIZE: Fits 10" plate.

MATERIALS: Kitchen Cotton Art. 760 by Lion Brand® Yarn Company or cotton worsted yarn: 8 oz. Sage #181, 2 oz. White #100; straight pins; 14" x 14" dinner napkin; 10" dinner plate *(or bowl or basket with same-size bottom as 10" plate)*; tapestry needle; I crochet hook *(or hook needed to obtain gauge)*.

GAUGE: 12 sc = 4"; 12 sc rows = 4".

SIDE (make 4)
Center

Row 1: Beginning at outer edge and working toward center, with sage, ch 27, sc in second ch from hook, sc in each ch across, turn. *(26 sc made)*

Row 2: Ch 1, sc in first 2 sts, sc next 2 sts tog, (sc in next 8 sts, sc next 2 sts tog) 2 times, sc in last 2 sts, turn. *(23)*

Row 3: Ch 1, sc in each st across, turn.

Rows 4–5: Ch 1, sc in first st, (sc in next 5 sts, sc next 2 sts tog) 2 times, sc in each st across, turn. *(21, 19)*

Rows 6–8: Repeat rows 3–5. *(17, 15)*

Row 9: Ch 1, sc in each st across, turn.

Rows 10–11: Ch 1, sc in first st, (sc in next 3 sts, sc next 2 sts tog) 2 times, sc in each st across, turn. *(13, 11)*

Rows 12–13: Ch 1, sc in first st, sc next 2 sts tog, sc in each st across to last 3 sts, sc next 2 sts tog, sc in last st, turn. *(9, 7)*

Row 14: Ch 1, sc in each st across, turn.

Row 15: Ch 1, sc in first st, sc next 2 sts tog, sc in next st, sc next 2 sts tog, sc in last st, turn. *(5)*

Row 16: Ch 1, sc in each st across, turn.

Row 17: Ch 1, sc in first st, sc next 3 sts tog, sc in last st, turn. *(3)*

Row 18: Ch 1, sc 3 sts tog. Fasten off. *(1)*

Cover

Row 1: With right side of row 1 on Center facing, working in starting ch on opposite side of row 1, join sage with sc in first ch, sc in each ch across, turn. *(26 sc made)*

Rows 2–5: Ch 1, sc in each st across, turn.

Row 6: Ch 1, sc in first st; skip first 3 sts on row before last, **hdcfp** *(see Special Stitch on page 24)* around next st on row before last, skip next st on last row behind fp st, sc in next 4 sts on last row, *hdcfp around next st on row before last, skip next 4 sts on row before last, hdcfp around next st, skip 2 sts on last row behind fp sts, sc in next 4 sts on last row; repeat from * across to last 2 sts, hdcfp around next st on row before last, sc in last st on last row, turn. *Row 6 is now right side of work.*

Rows 7–9: Ch 1, sc first 2 sts tog, sc in each st across to last 2 sts, sc last 2 sts tog, turn. *(24, 22, 20)*

Row 10: Placing first hdcfp around **fifth** st on row before last, repeat row 6.

Rows 11–13: Repeat rows 7–9. *(18, 16, 14)*

Row 14: Ch 1, sc in first st, hdcfp around **fifth** st on row before last, skip next st on last row behind fp st, sc in next 4 sts on last row, hdcfp around next st on row before last, skip next 4 sts on row before last, hdcfp around next st, skip 2 sts on last row behind fp sts, sc in next 4 sts on last row, hdcfp around next st on row before last, sc in last st on last row, turn.

Rows 15–17: Ch 1, sc first 2 sts tog, sc in each st across to last 2 sts, sc last 2 sts tog, turn. *(12, 10, 8)*

Row 18: Ch 1, sc in first st, hdcfp around **fifth** st on row before last, skip next st on last row behind fp st, sc in next 4 sts on last row, hdcfp around next st on row before last, skip next st on last row behind fp st, sc in last st on last row, turn.

Rows 19–20: Ch 1, sc first 2 sts tog, sc in each st across with sc last 2 sts tog, turn. *(6, 4)*

Row 21: Ch 1, skip first st, sc in next 2 sts ch 1, sl st in last st. Fasten off.

Row 22: For **border,** with right side of Cover facing, join sage with sc in end of row 1, sc in end of each row across to row 21, 2 sc in ch-1 on row 21, sc in next 2 sts, 2 sc in ch-1, sc in end of each row across to other end of row 1, **do not turn.** Fasten off. *(46 sc)*

Row 23: With right side of row 22 facing, holding white behind work, insert hook through first st and pull loop to front *(for joining sl st),* sl st in each st across, **do not turn.** Fasten off. *(46 sl sts)*

Row 24: With right side of row 22 facing, working this row in **back loops** *(see Crochet Stitch Guide on page 191)* of sl sts and in **both lps** of sc on row 22, join sage with sc in first st, sc in each st across with 3 sc in each corner, turn. *(50)*

Row 25: Ch 1, sc in each st across with 3 sc in each center corner st, turn. *(54)*

Row 26: Sl st in first st; (for **side scallop,** skip next st, 2 dc in each of next 2 sts, skip next st, sl st in next st—*side scallop made)* 4 times; for **corner scallop,** dc in next st, 3 dc in next st, dc in next st, sl st in next st *(corner scallop made);* work side scallop, work corner scallop, work side scallop 4 times. Fasten off.

FINISHING

1: Sew ends of rows on Centers together to form a circle, leaving Cover sections loose.

2: Lay assembled Bread Cozy in plate, spread dinner napkin inside.

3: Place hot bread in center of napkin, fold corners of napkin over bread; fold Cover sections of Bread Cozy over top. ●

Diagonal Rib Stitch Pattern

*K*nitted decreases each with an adjacent yarn-over forms a uniquely slanted diagonal rib pattern.

To duplicate the look in crochet, use single crochet stitches for the background and long single crochet front post stitches to create the ribs.

This stitch pattern can be adapted to slant in either direction.

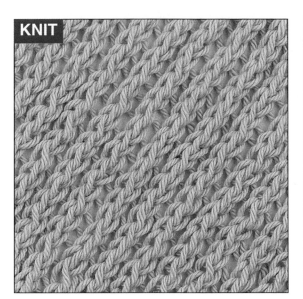

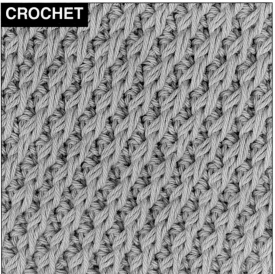

Afghan Square: Diagonal Rib

READ BEFORE STARTING

Refer to **Chapter 2** for instructions for using Squares to make either Knit or Crochet Version of Large Afghan or Baby Afghan.

For comparison, each Square has instructions for **Knit Version** in blue type, and instructions for **Crochet Version** in black type.

KNIT VERSION

With small needles and white, cast on 26.
Row 1: K across.
Row 2: P 1, (yo, P 2 tog) across to last st, P 1.
Row 3: K 2, (yo, K 2 tog) across.
Row 4: P 2, (yo, P 2 tog) across.
Row 5: K 1, (yo, K 2 tog) across to last

CROCHET VERSION

Row 1: With white and medium hook, ch 27, sc in second ch from hook, sc in each ch across, turn. *(26 sts made)*
Row 2: Ch 1, sc in each st across, turn.
NOTE: *Work **all sc sts** into sts of **last row.***
Row 3: Ch 1, sc in first sc, **scfp** *(see Special Stitch on page 24)* around third st

st, K 1.

Next rows: Repeat rows 2–5 consecutively until piece measures same as gauge, ending after row 3 or 5.

Last row: P across.

Bind off.

Work Edging in Basic Finishing on page 28.

Makeup Bag

Designed by Darla Sims

Keep cosmetics corralled with a stylish bag made with Diagonal Rib stitch pattern.

FINISHED SIZE: 4½" x 7½".

MATERIALS: 2 oz. Sherbet Swirl #298 Kitchen Cotton Art. 760 by Lion Brand® Yarn Company or cotton worsted yarn; 4 white ⅜" shank buttons; sewing needle and thread; tapestry needle; G and I crochet hooks *(or hook needed to obtain I hook gauge).*

GAUGE: I hook, 12 sts = 4"; 18 rows = 4".

BAG

Row 1: With I hook, loosely ch 28, sc in second ch from hook, sc in each ch across, turn. *(27 sc made)*

Row 2: Ch 1, sc in each st across, turn.

NOTES: *Work each* **sc front post (scfp,** *see Crochet Stitch Guide on page 191) around designated st on row*

on row 1, (sc in next sc—*see Note,* skip one st on row 1, scfp around next st) across with sc in last 2 sc, turn.

Row 4: Ch 1, sc in each st across, turn.

Row 5: Ch 1, scfp around first fp on row before last, sc in next sc, (scfp around next fp, sc in next sc) across to last 2 sc, scfp around last st on row before last, sc in last sc, turn.

Row 6: Ch 1, sc in each st across, turn.

Row 7: Ch 1, sc in first sc, (scfp around next fp, sc in next sc) across to last sc, sc in last sc, turn.

Next rows: Repeat rows 4–7 consecutively until piece measures same as gauge, ending with row 5 or 7. At end of last row, fasten off.

Work Edging in Basic Finishing on page 28.

before last, pull up to height of row being worked; always **skip one st** *on last row behind each fp.*

Work **all sc sts** *into sts of* **last** *row.*

Row 3: Ch 1, sc in first st, **scfp** *(see Notes)* around second st on row 1, (sc in next st on last row, skip one st on row 1, scfp around next st) across to last st, sc in last st, turn.

Row 4: Ch 1, sc in each st across, turn.

Row 5: Ch 1, sc in first 2 sts, scfp around first fp on row before last, (sc in next st, scfp around next fp) across, turn.

Row 6: Ch 1, sc in each st across, turn.

Row 7: Ch 1, sc in first st, scfp around first st on row before last, sc in next st, (scfp around next fp, sc in next st) across, turn.

Rows 8–31: Repeat rows 4–7 consecutively. At end of last row, fasten off.

Rnd 32: With right side of sts facing and G hook, join with sc in end of row 1, evenly space 31 sc across ends of rows, *(32 sc in ends of rows),* work 2 more sc in same row as last sc, working in starting ch on opposite side of row 1, sc in each ch across, 3 sc in end of row

31, evenly space 31 more sc across, work 2 more sc in same row as last sc, sc in each st across, 2 sc in same ch as first sc, join with sl st in first sc.

Row 33: For **button loops,** ch 1, sc in first 4 sts, ch 3, (sc in next 3 sts, sc next 2 sts tog, sc in next 3 sts, ch 3) 3 times, sc in next 4 sts, sl st in next st leaving remaining sts unworked. Fasten off.

Pull piece slightly in direction of natural slant to make the slant more pronounced and to pull the diagonal post stitches into a more upright position.

Fold Bag as shown in illustration, align top and bottom edges. Using tapestry needle with yarn, match folded edges and sew all layers together across each end leaving center open.

Using sewing needle and thread, sew buttons on opposite side to match button loops. ●

Makeup Bag

1: Fold right side 1" at top, 3" at bottom.
2: Fold left side to cover right edge.

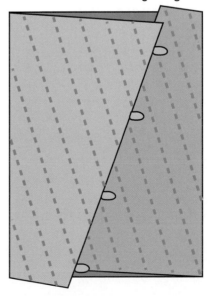

Bare Branches
Stitch Pattern

Twisted knit stitches combined with vertical rib stitches on a reversed stockinette stitch background create the illusion of bare winter branches after the leaves have dropped.

To duplicate the look in crochet, we've used long single crochet stitches worked in front posts to represent the vertical twigs and diagonal branches with single crochet stitches to represent the reversed stockinette stitch background.

KNIT

CROCHET

Afghan Square: Bare Branches

READ BEFORE STARTING

*Refer to **Chapter 2** for instructions for using Squares to make either Knit or Crochet Version of Large Afghan or Baby Afghan.*

*For comparison, each Square has instructions for **Knit Version** in blue type, and instructions for **Crochet Version** in black type.*

KNIT VERSION

With large needles and white, cast on 27.

NOTES: For **right twist (RT),** *insert right needle into next 2 sts at same time as if to K tog and transfer to left needle, slip same 2 sts one at a time back to left needle, K 1 **through back loop,** P 1.*

CROCHET VERSION

Row 1: With small hook and white, ch 28, sc in second ch from hook, sc in each ch across, turn. *(27 sc made)*

Row 2: Ch 1, sc in each st across, turn.

NOTE: *Work **all sc sts** into sts of **last row.***

Row 3: Ch 1, sc in first sc *(see Note),*

*For **left twist, (LT)**, slip next 2 sts one at a time as if to K, insert left needle right to left through same 2 sts at same time and transfer back to left needle, P 1, K 1.*

Row 1: *(Wrong side)* P 2, (K 4, P 3, K 4, P 1) 2 times, P 1.

Row 2: K 2, (P 3, **RT**—*see Notes*, K 1, **LT**—*see Notes*, P 3, K 1) 2 times, K 1.

Row 3: P 2, K 3, P 1, (K 1, P 1) 2 times, (K 3, P 1) 2 times, (K 1, P 1) 2 times, K 3, P 2.

Row 4: K 2, (P 2, RT, P 1, K 1, P 1, LT, P 2, K 1) 2 times, K 1.

Row 5: P 2, (K 2, P 1) across to last st, P 1.

Row 6: K 2, (P 1, RT, P 2, K 1, P 2, LT, P 1, K 1) 2 times, K 1.

Row 7: P 2, K 1, P 1, (K 3, P 1) 2 times, (K 1, P 1) 2 times, (K 3, P 1) 2 times, K 1, P 2.

Row 8: K 2, (RT, P 3, K 1, P 3, LT, K 1) 2 times, K 1.

Next rows: Repeat rows 1–8 consecutively until piece measures same as gauge. Bind off purlwise.

Work Edging in Basic Finishing on page 28.

*scfp *(see Special Stitch on page 24)* around st on row before last directly below next st, sc in next 3 sc; counting from last fp, skip next 4 sts on row before last, scfp around next st, (sc in next sc, scfp around next st on row before last) 2 times, sc in next 3 sc; repeat from *, scfp around st on row before last directly below next st, sc in last sc, turn.

Row 4: Ch 1, sc in each st across, turn.

Row 5: Ch 1, sc in first sc, scfp around next fp on row before last, (sc in next 2 sc, scfp around next fp on row before last) across with sc in last sc, turn.

Row 6: Ch 1, sc in each st across, turn.

Row 7: Ch 1, sc in first sc, scfp around first fp on row before last, *sc in next sc, scfp around next fp, (sc in next 3 sc, scfp around next fp) 2 times, sc in next sc, scfp around next fp; repeat from *, sc in last sc, turn.

Row 8: Ch 1, sc in each st across, turn.

Row 9: Ch 1, sc in first sc, *scfp around each of next 2 fp, (sc in next 4 sc, scfp around next fp) 2 times; repeat from *, scfp around next fp, sc in last sc, turn.

Row 10: Ch 1, sc in each st across, turn.

Row 11: Ch 1, sc in first sc, scfp around next fp, (sc in next 3 sc; counting from last fp on row before last, scfp around fourth sc on row before last, sc in next sc, scfp around next fp, sc in next sc, scfp around next sc on row before last, sc in next 3 sc, skip next fp, scfp around next fp) 2 times, sc in last sc, turn.

Rows 12–33: Repeat rows 4–11 consecutively, ending with row 9. At end of last row, fasten off.

Piece should measure same as gauge.

Work Edging in Basic Finishing on page 28.

*P*urchase sufficient yarn in the same dye lot to finish a large project. Subtle color variations can show dramatically on finished work.

Hat and Scarf

Designed by Donna Jones

Create an elegant hat and scarf set with textural interest using the Bare Branches stitch pattern.

FINISHED SIZES: Hat fits head up to 23½" around. Scarf is 9¾" x 60", plus fringe.

MATERIALS: 18 oz. Loden #177 Wool-Ease® Art. 620 by Lion Brand® Yarn Company or worsted yarn; thread elastic *(optional)*; stitch markers; tapestry needle; G crochet hook *(or hook needed to obtain gauge)*.

GAUGE: 16 sts in pattern = 4"; 20 rows in pattern = 4".

HAT

Rnd 1: Beginning at top, ch 2, 8 sc in second ch from hook, join with sl st in first sc, **turn.** *(8 sc made)*

Rnd 2: Ch 1, 2 sc in each st around, join, **turn.** *(16)*

NOTE: *Work each* **sc front post (scfp,** *see Crochet Stitch Guide on page 191) around designated st on row before last, pull up to height of row being worked.*

Rnd 3: Ch 1, sc in first st, **scfp** *(see Note)* around first st on rnd 1; without skipping sts behind fp, sc in next st on last rnd, scfp around same st on rnd 1 as last fp, (sc in next st on last rnd, scfp around next st on rnd 1, sc in next st on last rnd, scfp around same st on rnd 1 as last fp) around, join, **turn.** *(32)*

Rnd 4: Ch 1, sc in each st around, join, **turn.**

Rnd 5: Ch 1, sc in first st, scfp around first fp on previous rnd, skip next st on last rnd, (sc in next st on last rnd, scfp around next fp on previous rnd, skip next st on last rnd) around, join, **turn.**

Rnd 6: Ch 1, sc in each st around, join, **turn.**

Rnd 7: Ch 1, sc in first 2 sts, scfp around first fp on previous rnd; (without skipping sts, sc in next 2 sts on last rnd, scfp around next fp on previous rnd) around, join, **turn.** *(48)*

Rnd 8: Ch 1, sc in each st around, join, **turn.**

Rnd 9: Ch 1, sc in first 2 sts, scfp around first fp on previous rnd, skip next st on last rnd, (sc in next 2 sts on last rnd, scfp around next fp on previous rnd, skip next st on last rnd) around, join, **turn.**

Rnd 10: Ch 1, sc in each st around, join, **turn.**

Rnd 11: Ch 1, sc in first 3 sts, scfp around first fp on previous rnd; (without skipping sts, sc in next 3 sts on last rnd, scfp around next fp on previous rnd) around, join, **turn.** *(64)*

Rnd 12: Ch 1, sc in each st around, join, **turn.**

Rnd 13: Ch 1, sc in first 3 sts, scfp around first fp on previous rnd, skip next st on last rnd, (sc in next 3 sts on last rnd, scfp around next fp on previous rnd, skip next st on last rnd) around, join, **turn.**

Rnd 14: Ch 1, sc in each st around, join, **turn.**

Rnd 15: Ch 1, sc in first st 4 sts, scfp around first fp on previous rnd; (without skipping sts, sc in next 4 sts on last rnd, scfp around next fp on previous rnd) around, join, **turn.** *(80)*

Rnd 16: Ch 1, sc in each st around, join, **turn.**

Rnd 17: Ch 1, sc in first 4 sts, scfp around first fp on previous rnd, skip next st on last rnd, (sc in next 4 sts on last rnd, scfp around next fp on previous rnd, skip next st on last rnd) around, join, **turn.**

Rnd 18: Ch 1, sc in each st around, join, **turn.**

Rnd 19: Ch 1, sc in first 5 sts, scfp around first fp on previous rnd; (without skipping sts, sc in next 5 sts on last rnd, scfp around next fp on previous rnd) around, join, **turn.** *(96)*

Rnd 20: Ch 1, sc in each st around, join, **turn.**

Rnd 21: Ch 1, sc in first 5 sts, scfp around first fp on previous rnd, skip next st on last rnd, (sc in next 5 sts on last rnd, scfp around next fp on previous rnd, skip next st on last rnd) around, join, **turn.**

Rnds 22–31: Repeat rnds 20 and 21 alternately.

Rnd 32: Ch 1, sc in first 10 sts, (sc next 2 sts tog, sc in next 10 sts) around to last 2 sts, sc last 2 sts tog, join, **turn.** *(88)*

Rnd 33: Ch 1, sc in first 4 sts, scfp around next fp on previous rnd, skip next st on last rnd, (sc in next 5 sts on last rnd, scfp around next fp on previous rnd, skip next st on last rnd, sc in next 4 sts, scfp around next fp on previous rnd, skip next st on last rnd) 7 times, sc in next 5 sts, scfp around last fp on previous rnd, skip last st on last rnd, join, **turn.**

Rnd 34: Ch 1, sc in each st around, join, **turn.**

Rnd 35: Repeat rnd 33.

Rnd 36: Ch 1, sc in each st around, join, **do not turn.**

Rnd 37: For **fold,** ch 1; working this rnd in **back posts** *(see Crochet Stitch Guide),* sc around each of first 10 sts, (2 sc around next st, sc around each of next 10 sts) around with 2 sc around last st, join, **turn.** *(96)*

Cuff

Rnd 1: For **fold,** ch 1; working this rnd in **front posts** *(see Stitch Guide),* sc around each st around, join, **do not turn.**

Rnd 2: Ch 1, sc in each st around, join, **turn.**

*NOTE: **Always** skip one st on last rnd behind each fp worked into previous rnd.*

Rnd 3: Ch 1, scfp around first st on rnd before last; skip first st and st behind each remaining fp *(see Note),* *[sc in next 3 sts on last rnd; counting from last fp, scfp around fifth st on rnd before last, (sc in next st on last rnd, scfp around next st on rnd before last) 2 times, sc in next 3 sts on last rnd]; counting from last fp, scfp around fifth st on rnd before last; repeat from * 6 more times; repeat between [ ], join, **turn.**

Rnd 4: Ch 1, sc in each st around, join, **turn.**

Rnd 5: Ch 1, scfp around first fp on rnd before last, (sc in next 2 sts on last rnd, scfp around next fp on rnd before last) around with sc in last 2 sts on last rnd, join, **turn.**

Rnd 6: Ch 1, sc in each st around, join, **turn.**

Rnd 7: Ch 1, scfp around first fp on rnd before last, *[sc in next st on last rnd, scfp around next fp on rnd before last, (sc in next 3 sts on last rnd, scfp around next fp on rnd before last) 2 times, sc in next st on last rnd], scfp around next fp on rnd before last; repeat from * 6 more times; repeat between [ ]. join, **turn.**

Rnd 8: Ch 1, sc in each st around, join, **turn.**

Rnd 9: Ch 1, (scfp around next fp on rnd before last) 2 times, skip 2 sts on last rnd, sc in next 4 sts, scfp around next fp on rnd before last, skip one st on last rnd, sc in next 4 sts, *(scfp around next fp on rnd before last) 3 times, skip 3 sts on last rnd, sc in next 4 sts, scfp around next fp on rnd before last, skip one st on last rnd, sc in next 4 sts on last rnd; repeat from * around to last st, scfp around last fp on rnd before last, skip last st on last rnd, join, **do not turn.**

Rnd 10: Ch 1, sc in first st, ch 3, sl st in sc just made, (sc in next 6 sts, ch 3, sl st in sc just made) around with sc in last 5 sts, join. Fasten off.

If needed for Hat to fit, thread tapestry needle with thread elastic and run through rnd 37 *(fold row)* on Hat, pull to desired size and secure; hide ends.

Button

Cut a 28" strand of yarn and lay aside.

Rnd 1: Ch 2, 6 sc in second ch from hook.

*NOTE: Work in continuous rnds; do not join. **Mark** first st of each rnd.*

Rnd 2: 2 sc in each st around. *(12 sc made)*

Rnd 3: Sc in each st around.

Rnd 4: (Sc next 2 sts tog) around. Sl st in next st. Leaving 8" end, fasten off. *(6)*

Wrap 28" yarn around index finger to form a ring; remove from finger and stuff ring inside rnds 1–4.

Thread tapestry needle with 8" end, sew opening closed. (Run yarn through center to outside of rnd 1, then back through center to outside of rnd 4; pull tight to flatten Button) 2 times. Secure.

Sew Button to rnd 1 on outside of Hat.

Fold Cuff up over outside of crown, tack in place.

SCARF

Border row: Ch 40, sc in second ch from hook, sc in next ch, ch 3, sl st in last sc made, (sc in next 6 chs, ch 3, sl st in last sc made) across with (sc, ch 1, sl st) in last ch.

Row 1: Continuing on opposite side of ch, ch 1, sc in each ch across, turn. *(39 sc made)*

Row 2: Ch 1, sc in first 39 sts leaving remaining sts on Border Row unworked, turn.

Row 3: Ch 1, sc in first st, *scfp around st on row before last directly below next st; skipping st on last row behind each fp throughout, sc in next 3 sts on last row; counting from last fp, scfp around seventh st on row before last, (sc in next st on last row, scfp around next st on row before last) 2 times, sc in next 3 sts on last row; repeat from * 2 more times, scfp around st on row before last directly below next st, sc in last st on last row, turn. *(39 sts)*

Row 4: Ch 1, sc in each st across, turn.

Row 5: Ch 1, sc in first st, scfp around next fp on row before last, (sc in next 2 sts on last row, scfp around next fp on row before last) across with sc in last st on last row, turn.

Row 6: Ch 1, sc in each st across, turn.

Row 7: Ch 1, sc in first st, scfp around first fp on row before last, *sc in next st on last row, scfp around next fp on row before last, (sc in next 3 sts on last row, scfp around next fp on row before last) 2 times, sc in next st on last row, scfp around next fp on row before last; repeat from * across with sc in last st on last row, turn.

Row 8: Ch 1, sc in each st across, turn.

Row 9: Ch 1, sc in first st, *(scfp around next fp on row before last) 2 times, skip 2 sts on last row, (sc in next 4 sts on last row, scfp around next fp on row before last) 2 times; repeat from * across to last 2 sts, scfp around next fp, sc in last st on last row, turn.

Row 10: Ch 1, sc in each st across, turn.

Row 11: Ch 1, sc in first st, *scfp around next fp on row before last, sc in next 3 sts, skip next fp and next 4 sts on row before last, scfp around next st on row before last, sc in next st on last row, scfp around next fp, sc in next st, scfp around next st on row before last, sc in next 3 sts; repeat from * across to last 2 sts, sc fp around next fp, sc in last st, turn.

Next rows: Repeat rows 4–11 consecutively until piece measures about 60", ending with row 9.

Border row: Ch 1, sc in first 2 sts, ch 3, sl st in last sc made, (sc in next 6 sts, ch 3, sl st in last sc made) across with sc in last st. Fasten off.

For each **fringe,** cut six 20"-long pieces yarn; holding all pieces together as one, fold in half; insert hook from back to front through ch-3 loop on Border, pull fold through ch-3 loop, pull ends through fold, pull tight.

Fringe in each ch-3 loop of Border row on each end of Scarf.

Trim fringe ends even. ●

Bare Branches Tasseled Rug
Designed by Darla Sims

Use the Bare Branches stitch pattern for a floor covering to suit any decor.

FINISHED SIZE: 19" x 25", plus tassel trim.

MATERIALS: Cotton Thick & Quick® Art. 720 by Lion Brand® Yarn Company or cotton chunky yarn: 22 oz. Natural #098; 1¼ yds. of 2"-wide tassel trim; brush-on rug backing *(optional for non-carpeted floors);* sewing needle and thread; G and H crochet hooks *(or hook needed to obtain H book gauge).*

GAUGE: H hook; 14 sts in pattern = 4"; 10 rows = 4".

RUG
Row 1: With H hook, ch 74, sc in second ch from hook, sc in each ch across, turn. *(73 sc made)*

Row 2: Ch 1, sc in each st across, turn.

*NOTES: Work each **sc front post (scfp,** see Crochet Stitch Guide on page 191) around designated st on row before last, pull up to height of row being worked; always **skip one st** on last row behind each fp.*

*Work **all regular sc sts** into sts of **last** row.*

Row 3: *(Right side)* Ch 1, sc in first 4 sts, **scfp** *(see Note above)* around sixth st on row before last, (sc in next st, scfp around next st on row before last) 2 times, sc in next 3 sts on row before last; complete row as follows:

A: Scfp around st on row before last directly below next st, sc in next 3 sts on last row;

B: Counting from last fp, scfp around fourth st on row before last, (sc in next st on last row, scfp around next st on row before last) 2 times, sc in next 3 sts on last row;

C: Repeat steps A and B 4 more times, sc in last st on last row, turn.

Row 4: Ch 1, sc in each st across, turn.

Row 5: Ch 1, sc in first 3 sts, (scfp around next fp on row before last, sc in next 2 sts) across to last st, sc in last st, turn.

Row 6: Ch 1, sc in each st across, turn.

Row 7: Ch 1, sc in first 2 sts, (scfp around next fp, sc in next 3 sts) 2 times, *(scfp around next fp, sc in next st) 2 times, (scfp around next fp, sc in next 3 sts) 2 times; repeat from * 4 more times, scfp around next fp, sc in last 2 sts, turn.

Row 8: Ch 1, sc in each st across, turn.

Row 9: Ch 1, sc in first st, (scfp around next fp, sc in next 4 sts) 2 times, (scfp around each of next 3 fp, sc in next 4 sts, scfp around next fp, sc in next 4 sts) 5 times, scfp around next fp, sc in last st, turn.

Row 10: Ch 1, sc in each st across, turn.

Row 11: Ch 1, sc in first 4 sts, scfp around sixth st on row before last, sc in next st, scfp around next fp, sc in next st, scfp around next st on row before last, sc in next 3 sts on row before last; complete row as follows:

A: Scfp around next fp, sc in next 3 sts on last row;

B: Counting from last fp on row before last, scfp around fifth st, sc in next st on last row, scfp around next fp, sc in next st, scfp around next st on row before last, sc in next 3 sts on last row;

C: Repeat steps A and B 4 more times, sc in last st on last row, turn.

Next rows: Repeat rows 4–11 consecutively until piece measures about 25" long, ending with row 9. At end of last row, **do not turn.**

Last rnd: With G hook and right side of work facing, working around outer edge, sc in end of each row and in each st around with 3 sc in each corner, join with sl st in last st. Fasten off.

On each short end of Rug, cut a piece of tassel trim to fit across end plus 1" extra. Fold each cut edge of trim ½" to wrong side and sew in place. Sew back of trim to front of Rug across short end. If desired, apply rug backing to back of rug; let dry. ●

Hourglass
Stitch Pattern

*K*nitted right cross, left cross and slipped stitches create the raised design on a
reversed stockinette stitch background in this hourglass design.
   *To achieve the same effect in crochet, use single crochet stitches for the
background and work double crochet post stitches to create the raised design.*

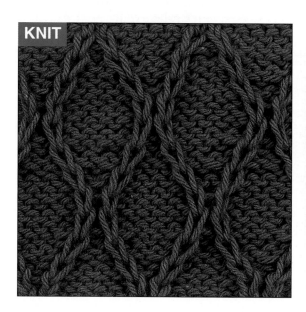

KNIT

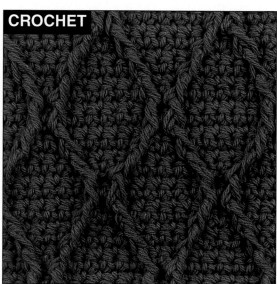

CROCHET

Afghan Square: Hourglass

READ BEFORE STARTING

   *Refer to **Chapter 2** for instructions for using Squares to make either
Knit or Crochet Version of Large Afghan or Baby Afghan.*
   *For comparison, each Square has instructions for **Knit Version** in blue
type, and instructions for **Crochet Version** in black type.*

KNIT VERSION

   NOTES: *For **yarn front (yf),** and **yarn
back (yb),** bring yarn **between** needles to
other side of work.*

   *For **Right Cross (RC),** insert right needle from left to right through front loops of
next 2 sts at same time (as if to knit tog)
and slip to right needle, causing sts to
cross, insert left needle through fronts of*

CROCHET VERSION

   Row 1: With small hook and color A,
ch 29, sc in second ch from hook, sc in
each ch across, turn. *(28 sts made)*
   Row 2: Ch 1, sc in each st across, turn.
   NOTE: *Work **all sc sts** into sts of **last row.***
   Row 3: Ch 1, sc in first 5 sc *(see Note),*
(dcfp—*see Special Stitch on page 24*—
around st on row before last directly below

same 2 sts and slip back to left needle; yb, insert right needle from left to right through back loop of next st and slip to right needle (do not work the st); yf, P 1.

For **Left Cross (LC)**, slip next 2 sts one at a time as if to K, insert left needle from right to left through fronts of same 2 sts at same time and slip both to left needle, causing sts to cross, P 1; yb, slip 1 as if to P (do not work the st).

With large needles and color A, cast on 28.

Row 1: P 5, K 2, (P 6, K 2) 2 times, P 5.

Row 2 and all even-numbered rows: K each K st and P each P st and each slipped st.

Row 3: P 4, (RC, LC, P 4) across.

Row 5: P 3, (RC, P 2, LC, P 2) 3 times, P 1.

Row 7: P 2, (RC, P 4, LC) 3 times, P 2.

Row 9: P 2, yb, slip 1 purlwise, (yf, P 6, yb, slip 2 purlwise) 2 times, yf, P 6, yb, slip 1 purlwise, yf, P 2.

Row 11: P 2, (LC, P 4, RC) 3 times, P 2.

Row 13: P 3, (LC, P 2, RC, P 2) 3 times, P 1.

Row 15: P 4, (LC, RC, P 4) across.

Row 17: P 5, yb, slip 2 purlwise, (P 6, yb, slip 2 purlwise) 2 times, P 5.

Next rows: Repeat rows 2–16; piece should measure same as gauge.

Bind off.

Work Edging in Basic Finishing on page 28.

next st) 2 times, *sc in next 6 sc, (dcfp around st on row before last directly below next st) 2 times; repeat from *, sc in last 5 sc, turn.

Row 4: Ch 1, sc in each st across, turn.

Row 5: Ch 1, sc in first 3 sc, (dcfp around next fp, sc in next 4 sc, dcfp around next fp, sc in next 2 sc) across with sc in last st, turn.

Row 6: Ch 1, sc in each st across, turn.

Row 7: Ch 1, sc in first 2 sc, (dcfp around next fp, sc in next 6 sc, dcfp around next fp) 3 times, sc in last 2 sc, turn.

Rows 8–9: Repeat rows 6–7.

Row 10: Ch 1, sc in each st across, turn.

Row 11: Ch 1, sc in first 3 sc, (dcfp around next fp, sc in next 4 sc, dcfp around next fp, sc in next 2 sc) across with sc in last st, turn.

Row 12: Ch 1, sc in each st across, turn.

Row 13: Ch 1, sc in first 4 sc, (dcfp around next fp, sc in next 2 sc, dcfp around next fp, sc in next 4 sc) 2 times, (dcfp around next fp, sc in next 2 sc) 2 times, sc in last 2 sc, turn.

Row 14: Ch 1, sc in each st across, turn.

Row 15: Ch 1, sc in first 5 sc, dcfp around next 2 fp, (sc in next 6 sc, dcfp around next 2 fp) 2 times, sc in last 5 sc, turn.

Rows 16–17: Repeat rows 14–15.

Rows 18–29: Repeat rows 4–15. At end of last row, fasten off.

Piece should measure same as gauge.

Work Edging in Basic Finishing on page 28.

When working with scrap yarns, strand a thin yarn with a thick yarn to achieve desired tension and create custom colors and textures. When making an item from scraps, use yarns of similar weight and tension to ensure a smooth-finished fabric. Make sure to check that washing requirements are similar for all yarns used.

Hourglass Accent Pillow

Designed by Donna Jones

Stitch soothing patterns on an accent pillow with Hourglass stitch pattern.

FINISHED SIZE: 14" square.

MATERIALS: 10 oz. Cranberry #138 Wool-Ease® Art. 620 by Lion Brand® Yarn Company or worsted yarn; 14" square pillow form; 4" x 8" cardboard; masking tape; tapestry needle; F crochet hook *(or hook needed to obtain gauge).*

GAUGE: 9 sc = 2"; 9 sc rows = 2".

SIDE (make 2)

Row 1: Ch 57, sc in second ch from hook, sc in each ch across, turn. *(56 sts made)*

Row 2: Ch 1, sc in each st across, turn.

*NOTES: Work each **dc front post (dcfp,** see Crochet Stitch Guide on page 191) around designated st on row before last, pull up to height of row being worked; always **skip one st** on last row behind each fp.*

*Work **all sc sts** into sts of **last** row.*

Row 3: Ch 1, sc in first 7 sts, skip first 7 sts on row before last; pulling all fp sts up to height of row being worked, **dcfp** *(see Notes)* around each of next 2 sts on row before last, (sc in next 6 sts, skip next 6 sts on row before last, dcfp around next 2 sts on row before last) 5 times, sc in last 7 sts, turn.

Row 4: Ch 1, sc in each st across, turn.

Row 5: Ch 1, sc in first 5 sts, (dcfp around next fp, sc in next 4 sts on last row, dcfp around next fp, sc in next 2 sts on last row) 6 times, sc in last 3 sts, turn.

Row 6: Ch 1, sc in each st across, turn.

Row 7: Ch 1, sc in first 4 sts, (dcfp around next fp, sc in next 6 sts on last row, dcfp around next fp) 6 times, sc in last 4 sts on last row, turn.

Rows 8–9: Repeat rows 6–7.

Row 10: Ch 1, sc in each st across, turn.

Row 11: Ch 1, sc in first 5 sts, (dcfp around next fp, sc in next 4 sts on last row, dcfp around next fp, sc in next 2 sts on last row) 6 times, sc in last 3 sts, turn.

Row 12: Ch 1, sc in each st across, turn.

Row 13: Ch 1, sc in first 6 sts, (dcfp around next fp, sc in next 2 sts on last row, dcfp around next fp, sc in next 4 sts on last row) 5 times, (dcfp around next fp, sc in next 2 sts on last row) 2 times, sc in last 4 sts, turn.

Row 14: Ch 1, sc in each st across, turn.

Row 15: Ch 1, sc in first 7 sts, dcfp around each of next 2 fp, (sc in next 6 sts on last row, dcfp around each of next 2 fp) 5 times, sc in last 7 sts, turn.

Row 16: Ch 1, sc in each st across, turn.

Row 17: Ch 1, sc in first 7 sts, dcfp around each of next 2 fp, (sc in next 6 sts on last row, dcfp around each of next 2 fp) 5 times, sc in last 7 sts, turn.

Row 18: Ch 1, sc in each st across, turn.

Row 19: Ch 1, sc in first 6 sts, (dcfp around next fp, sc in next 2 sts on last row, dcfp around next fp, sc in next 4 sts on last row) 5 times, (dcfp around next fp, sc in next 2 sts on last row) 2 times, sc in last 4 sts, turn.

Rows 20–33: Repeat rows 4–17.

Rows 34–49: Repeat rows 4–19.

Rows 50–61: Repeat rows 4–15. At end of last row, **do not turn.**

Rnd 62: Working around outer edge, with right side of piece facing, ch 1, 2 sc in corner st, (sc in each st or in end of each row across to next corner, 3 sc in corner st) 3 times, sc in each st or in each row across to first corner, sc in same st as joining sc, join with sl st in first sc.

Rnds 63–64: Ch 1, 2 sc in first st, sc in each st around with 3 sc in each center corner st, sc in same st as joining sc. On **first Side only,** fasten off at end of last rnd; **do not fasten off** second Side.

ASSEMBLY

Hold Sides wrong sides together, matching stitches; working through both layers as one, ch 1, sc in each st around, inserting pillow form before closing last side, join with sl st in first sc. Fasten off.

TASSEL (make 4)

For each **Tassel,** fold a 24" strand of yarn in half to form one 12"-long double strand; tape double strand lengthwise across one long edge of 4" x 8" cardboard leaving ends loose.

Wrap yarn 50 times around 4" cardboard. Remove tape and tie ends of double strand very tightly around all wraps. Remove cardboard. Wrap separate 18" strand several times around all wraps 1" below first knot; tie securely and run ends to inside to hide. Cut loops of wraps opposite first knot; trim ends even.

Using ends of double strand, sew one Tassel to each corner of Pillow. ●

Crossed Stripes Stitch Pattern

This knitted geometric design is formed by slipped stitches worked over contrasting color stockinette stitch rows to create the raised design.

A comparable look can be achieved in crochet by working a single crochet background in contrasting colors with double crochet front post stitches worked diagonally to create the design.

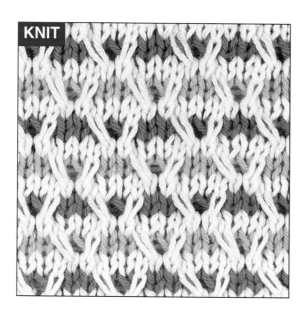

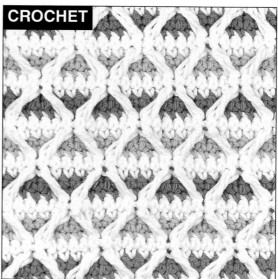

Afghan Square: Crossed Stripes

READ BEFORE STARTING

*Refer to **Chapter 2** for instructions for using Squares to make either Knit or Crochet Version of Large Afghan or Baby Afghan.*

*For comparison, each Square has instructions for **Knit Version** in blue type, and instructions for **Crochet Version** in black type.*

KNIT VERSION

With medium needles and white, cast on 30.

NOTES: *Always slip sts as if to purl.*

Carry dropped yarn loosely along ends of rows; pick up again when needed.

*For **right cross (RC)**, skip first st on left needle; working in front of skipped st, K in*

CROCHET VERSION

NOTES: *When **changing colors** (see Crochet Stitch Guide on page 191), do not cut unused color. Carry unused color along ends of rows; pick up again when needed.*

*Work **all sc sts** into sts of **last row**.*

Row 1: With small hook and white, ch 31, sc in second ch from hook, sc in

front loop of second st and leave on needle, K in back loop of skipped st and drop both from left needle at same time.

*For **left cross (LC),** skip first st on left needle, working in back of skipped st, K in back loop of second st and leave on needle, K in front loop of skipped st and drop both from left needle at same time.*

Row 1: P 3, (yo, P 6) across to last 3 sts, yo, P 3. *(35 sts on needles)* Drop white, do not cut.

Row 2: With color A, K 2, slip 1 *(see Notes),* drop yo, slip 1, (K 4, slip 1, drop yo, slip 1) across to last 2 sts, K 2. *(30 sts)*

Row 3: P 2, slip 2, (P 4, slip 2) across to last 2 sts, P 2. Drop color A, do not cut.

Row 4: With white, K 1, **RC** *(see Notes),* **LC** *(see Notes),* (K 2, RC, LC) across to last st, K 1.

Row 5: P 6, (yo, P 6) across. *(34 sts)* Drop white, do not cut.

Row 6: With color B, K 5, (slip 1, drop yo, slip 1, K 4) across to last st, K 1. *(30 sts)*

Row 7: P 5, (slip 2, P 4) across to last st, P 1. Drop color B, do not cut.

Row 8: With white, K 4, (RC, LC, K 2) across to last 2 sts, K 2.

Row 9: P 3, (yo, P 6) across to last 3 sts, yo, P 3. *(35 sts on needles)* Drop white, do not cut.

Next rows: Repeat rows 2–9 consecutively until piece measures same as gauge, ending last repeat with row 4 or 8. Cut colors A and B.

Bind off purlwise with white.

Work Edging in Basic Finishing on page 28.

each ch across, changing to color A in last st *(see Notes),* turn. *(30 sc made)*

Row 2: With color A, ch 1, sc in each st across, turn.

Row 3: Ch 1, sc in each st across changing to white in last st, turn.

Row 4: With white, ch 1, sc in first 2 sc, skip first 4 sts on third row below, **dcfp** *(see Special Stitch on page 24)* around next st on third row below, (sc in next 4 sc, dcfp around next st on third row below; counting from last fp, skip next 4 sts on third row below, dcfp around next st) 4 times, sc in last 3 sc, turn.

Row 5: Ch 1, sc in each st across changing to color B in last st, turn.

Row 6: With color B, ch 1, sc in each st across, turn.

Row 7: Ch 1, sc in each st across changing to white in last st, turn.

Row 8: With white, ch 1, sc in first 4 sc, skip first 2 sts on third row below, (dcfp around next st on third row below, skip next 4 sts on third row below, dcfp around next st, sc in next 4 sc) 4 times, dcfp around next st on third row below, sc in last sc, turn.

Row 9: Ch 1, sc in each st across changing to color A in last st, turn.

Rows 10–32: Repeat rows 2–9 consecutively, ending with row 8. At end of last row, fasten off.

Piece should measure same as gauge.

Work Edging in Basic Finishing on page 28.

*W*hen sewing buttons onto a thick cardigan, use shank buttons or make thread shank that accommodates thickness of sweater front to avoid tight or puckered buttonholes.

Fringed Winter Scarf
Designed by Darla Sims

Look at the interesting difference in the back and front of the Crossed Stripes stitch pattern.

FINISHED SIZE: 6½" wide x 50" long, plus Fringe.

MATERIALS: MicroSpun Art. 910 by Lion Brand® Yarn Company or sport yarn: 6½ oz. Turquoise #148, 1½ oz each Coral #103, White #100, Lime #194 and Buttercup #158; F crochet hook *(or hook needed to obtain gauge).*

GAUGE: 20 sts = 4"; 20 rows = 4".

SCARF

Row 1: With turquoise, ch 33, sc in second ch from hook, sc in each ch across, turn. *(32 sc made)*

Row 2: Ch 1, sc in each st across, turn. Drop loop from hook; **do not cut.**

Row 3: Join coral with sc in first st, sc in each st across, turn.

Row 4: Ch 1, sc in each st across, turn. Fasten off coral.

NOTES: *Work each **dc front post (dcfp,** see Crochet Stitch Guide on page 191) around designated st on last turquoise row below, pull up to height of row being worked; always **skip one st** on last row behind each fp.*

*Work **all sc sts** into sts of **last** row.*

Row 5: Return dropped turquoise loop to hook, ch 3 *(up to height of this row),* sc in first st, **dcfp** *(see Note)* around fourth st on last turquoise row, sc in next 4 sc; (working on last turquoise row, dcfp around next st, skip 4 sts past last fp, dcfp around next st, sc in next 4 sts on last row) across to last 2 sts, dcfp around next st on last turquoise row, sc in last st, turn.

Row 6: Ch 1, sc in each st across, turn. Drop loop from hook; **do not cut.**

Row 7: Join white with sc in first st, sc in each st across, turn.

Row 8: Ch 1, sc in each st across, turn. Fasten off white.

Row 9: Return dropped turquoise loop to hook, ch 3, sc in first 3 sts, dcfp around second st on last turquoise row, (working around sts on last turquoise row, skip 4 sts past last fp, dcfp around next st, sc in next 4 sts, dcfp around next st on last turquoise row) across to last 4 sts, dcfp around next-to-last st on last turquoise row, sc in last 3 sts, turn.

Row 10: Ch 1, sc in each st across, turn. Drop loop from hook; **do not cut.**

Row 11: Join lime with sc in first st, sc in each st across, turn.

Row 12: Ch 1, sc in each st across, turn. Fasten off lime.

Rows 13–14: Repeat rows 5 and 6.

Row 15: Join buttercup with sc in first st, sc in each st across, turn.

Row 16: Ch 1, sc in each st across, turn. Fasten off buttercup.

Rows 17–18: Repeat rows 9 and 10.

Next rows: Repeat rows 3–18 consecutively until piece measures about 50" or desired length, ending after a repeat of row 6 or 10.

Last rnd: Working around outer edge, with turquoise and right side of work facing, ch 1, sc in each st and in end of each row around with 3 sc in each corner, join with sl st in first sc. Fasten off.

Fringe

For each **Fringe,** cut three strands turquoise each 12" long. Holding three strands together as one, fold in half; from back, insert hook through stitch, pull fold through, pull ends through fold, pull snug.

Fringe in every other st across both short ends of Scarf. ●

Diamond Stitch Pattern

Three stitches are slipped on two separate front-side rows while carrying the yarn across the front side of the work; then the two loose strands are pulled up and knitted together on the next front-side row to create raised diamonds on a stockinette stitch background.

To achieve the same effect in crochet, use single crochet stitches for the background and work double crochet post stitches to create the raised design.

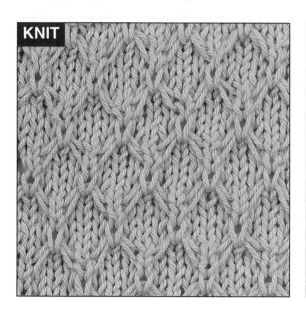

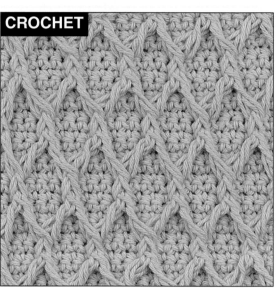

Afghan Square: Diamonds

READ BEFORE STARTING

Refer to **Chapter 2** for instructions for using Squares to make either Knit or Crochet Version of Large Afghan or Baby Afghan.

For comparison, each Square has instructions for **Knit Version** in blue type, and instructions for **Crochet Version** in black type.

KNIT VERSION

With medium needles and color B, cast on 27.

Row 1: *(Wrong side)* P across.

NOTE: *Slip all sts as if to purl and carry yarn **very loosely** across **knit** side of work.*

Row 2: K 2, **(yarn front—yf,** slip 3— *see Note,* **yarn back—yb,** K 1) across to

CROCHET VERSION

Row 1: With small hook and color B, ch 28, sc in second ch from hook, sc in each ch across, turn. *(27 sc made)*

Row 2: Ch 1, sc in each st across, turn.

Row 3: Ch 1, sc in first 3 sc, *****long scfp (lscfp, see Special Stitch on page 24)**

last st, K1.

Row 3: P across.

Row 4: K 2, (yf, slip 3, yb, K 1) across to last st, K 1.

Row 5: P across.

Row 6: K 3; for **K loose strands into next st,** insert right needle under 2 loose strands from previous rows then into next st on this row and K all tog *(K loose strands into next st completed),* (K 3, K loose strands into next st) across to last 3 sts, K 3.

Row 7: P across.

Row 8: K 4, (yf, slip 3, yb, K 1) across to last 3 sts, K 3.

Row 9: P across.

Row 10: K 4, (yf, slip 3, yb, K 1) across to last 3 sts, K 3.

Row 11: P across.

Row 12: K 5, K loose strands into next st, (K 3, K loose strands into next st) across to last 5, K 5.

Row 13: P across.

Next rows: Repeat rows 2–13 consecutively until piece measures same as gauge, ending with row 7.

Bind off.

Work Edging in Basic Finishing on page 28.

around st on row 1 directly below next st, sc in next 3 sc; repeat from * across, turn.

Rows 4–6: Ch 1, sc in each st across, turn.

***NOTES:** For **dcfp-2-tog,** dc two fp sts tog; skip one st on last row behind dcfp-2-tog.*

Work **all sc sts** into sts of **last row.**

Row 7: Ch 1, sc in first sc *(see Note),* lscfp around next fp below, sc in next 3 sc; **(dcfp-2-tog**—*see Note*—around last worked fp and next fp, sc in next 3 sc) 5 times, lscfp again around last worked fp, sc in last sc, turn.

Row 8: Ch 1, sc in each st across, turn.

Row 9: Ch 1, sc in first sc, lscfp around next fp, sc in next 3 sc, (lscfp around next dcfp-2-tog, sc in next 3 sc) 5 times, lscfp around last fp, sc in last sc, turn.

Rows 10–12: Ch 1, sc in each st across, turn.

Row 13: Ch 1, sc in first 3 sc, dcfp-2-tog around first 2 fp, sc in next 3 sc (dcfp-2-tog around last worked fp and next fp, sc in next 3 sc) across, turn.

Row 14: Ch 1, sc in each st across, turn.

Row 15: Ch 1, sc in first 3 sc, (lscfp around next fp, sc in next 3 sc) across, turn.

Next rows: Repeat rows 4–15 consecutively until piece measures same as gauge. At end of last row, fasten off.

Work Edging in Basic Finishing on page 28.

*M*ake your own shoulder pads for a garment. Use swatches or leftover yarn to make two squares, each approximately 5"-wide. Fold each in half diagonally and stitch open edges together. (If a thicker pad is desired, you can fill pad with triangle of thin foam or quilt batting before stitching edges together.) With fold at shoulder edge at top of arm, stitch in place.

Woman's Tunic

Designed by Donna Jones

A fashion statement is fun to make using Diamonds stitch pattern.

MATERIALS: Wool-Ease® Art. 620 by Lion Brand® Yarn Company or worsted yarn: amount Navy #111 needed for size, 6 oz. Navy Sprinkles #110 *(sprinkles);* split stitch markers; tapestry needle; H and I crochet hooks *(or hooks needed to obtain gauges).*

GAUGES: H hook; 16 Border sts = 4"; 3 dc rows and 3 sc rows = 2¼". **I hook;** 16 sts in pattern = 4"; 18 rows in pattern = 4".

SIZES

Lady's Small (30"–32" chest):
  Yarn: 29 oz. navy
  Garment chest: 34"
  Back length: 26"

Lady's Medium (32"–38" chest):
  Yarn: 35 oz. navy
  Garment chest: 42"
  Back length: 28"

Lady's Large (38"–42" chest):
  Yarn: 39 oz. navy
  Garment chest: 46"
  Back length: 28"

Lady's X-Large (42"–48" chest):
  Yarn: 45 oz. navy
  Garment chest: 54"
  Back length: 29"

NOTE

Instructions are for size **Small;** changes for **Medium, Large** and **X-Large** are in [ ].

BACK
Border

Row 1: With H hook and sprinkles, ch 70 [86, 94, 110], dc in third ch from hook, (skip next ch, dc in next ch; working behind last dc, dc into skipped ch) across to last ch, dc in last ch, turn. *(ch-2 at beginning of row is not worked or counted as a st; 68 [84, 92, 108] sts made)*

Row 2: Ch 1, sc in each st across, turn.

Row 3: For **first dc,** (sc, ch 2) in first st; for **cross stitch,** (skip next st, dc in next st; working behind last dc, dc into skipped st—*cross st made*) across to last st, dc in last st, turn.

Rows 4–6: Repeat rows 2, 3, 2. At end of last row, fasten off.

Body

Rows 1–2: With I hook, join navy with sc in first st, sc next 2 sts tog, sc in each st across, turn. *(67 [83, 91, 107] sts made)*

NOTE: *Work each **front post (fp)** or **back post (bp,** see Crochet Stitch Guide on page 191) around designated st on row before last, pull up to height of row being worked; always **skip one st** on last row behind each post st.*

*Work **all sc sts** into sts of **last** row.*

Row 3: *(Right side)* Ch 1, sc in first 3 sts; *long sc front post (lscfp—see Note)* around sc on row 1 directly below next st, sc in next 3 sts on last row; repeat from * across, turn.

Rows 4–6: Ch 1, sc in each st across, turn.

NOTE: *For **dcfp-2-tog,** pulling each dc st up to same height as this row, working around front post of sts, dc two fp tog; skip one st on last row behind dcfp-2-tog.*

Row 7: Ch 1, sc in first st; working around posts of sts on fourth row below, dcfp around next fp, sc in next 3 sts on last row; **(dcfp-2-tog**—*see Note*—around last worked fp and next fp, sc in next 3 sts on last row) across to last 2 sts, dcfp again around last worked fp, sc in last st on this row, turn.

Row 8: Ch 1, sc in each st across, turn.

Row 9: Ch 1, sc in first st, lscfp around next fp, sc in next 3 sts on last row, (lscfp around next dcfp-2-tog, sc in next 3 sts on last row) across to last 2 sts, scfp around last fp, sc in last st on this row, turn.

Rows 10–12: Ch 1, sc in each st across, turn.

Row 13: Ch 1, sc in first 3 sts, dcfp-2 tog around first 2 fp, sc in next 3 sts on last row, (dcfp-2-tog around last worked fp and next fp, sc in next 3 sts on last row) across, turn.

Rows 14: Ch 1, sc in each st across, turn.

Row 15: Ch 1, sc in first 3 sts, (lscfp around next fp on previous row, sc in next 3 sts on last row) across, turn.

To **work in pattern,** repeat rows 4–15 consecutively *(see "How To Work In Pattern", Chapter 1, page 16).*

Next rows: Work in pattern until piece measures about 26" [28", 28", 29"] from beginning of Border, ending after a repeat of row 9 or 15.

Last row: Ch 1, sc in each st across. Fasten off.

FRONT
Border and Body

Work Border same as Back Border; work Body same as Back Body until piece measures about 19" [20", 20", 21"] from beginning of Border, ending after a repeat of row 9 or 15.

First Shoulder

Row 1: Ch 1, work in pattern across first 24 [28, 32, 40] sts leaving remaining sts unworked, turn.

Next rows: Work in pattern until piece measures same as Back, ending after a repeat of row 9 or 15.

Last row: Ch 1, sc in each st across. Fasten off.

Second Shoulder

Row 1: Skip next 19 [27, 27, 27] sts on Front for **center front neck edge,** join navy with sc in next st, work in pattern across last 23 [27, 31, 39] sts, turn.

Next rows: Work in pattern until piece measures same as Back, ending after a repeat of row 9 or 15.

Last row: Ch 1, sc in each st across. Fasten off.

SLEEVE (make 2)
Border

Row 1: With H hook and sprinkles, ch 46 [54, 54, 62], dc in third ch from hook, (skip next ch, dc in next ch; working

behind last dc, dc into skipped ch) across to last st, dc in last st, turn. *(ch-2 at beginning of row is not worked or counted as a st; 44 [52, 52, 60] sts made)*

Rows 2–6: Repeat rows 2–6 of Back Border.

Arm

Row 1: With I hook, join navy with sc in first st, sc next 2 sts tog, sc in each st across, turn. *(43 [51, 51, 59] sts)*

Row 2: Ch 1, sc in each st across, turn.

Row 3: *(Right side)* Ch 1, sc in first 3 sts, (lscfp around sc on row before last directly below next st, sc in next 3 sts on last row) across, turn.

Row 4: Ch 1, 2 sc in first st, sc in each st across with 2 sc in last st, turn. *(45 [53, 53, 61] sts)*

Rows 5–6: Ch 1, sc in each st across, turn.

Row 7: Ch 1, sc in first 2 sts, dcfp around first fp, sc in next 3 sts, (dcfp-2-tog around last worked fp and next fp, sc in next 3 sts) across to last 3 sts, dcfp again around last worked fp, sc in last 2 sts, turn.

Row 8: Ch 1, 2 sc in first st, sc in each st across with 2 sc in last st, turn. *(47 [55, 55, 63] sts)*

Row 9: Ch 1, sc in first 3 sts, lscfp around first fp, sc in next 3 sts, (lscfp around next dcfp-2-tog, sc in next 3 sts) across to last 4 sts, scfp around last fp, sc in last 3 sts, turn.

Row 10: Ch 1, 2 sc in first st, sc in each st across with 2 sc in last st, turn. *(49 [57, 57, 65] sts)*

Rows 11–12: Ch 1, sc in each st across, turn.

Row 13: Ch 1, sc in first 2 sts, dcfp around first fp, sc in next 3 sts, (dcfp-2-tog around last worked fp and next fp, sc in next 3 sts) across to last 3 sts, dcfp again around last worked fp, sc in last 2 sts, turn.

Row 14: Ch 1, sc in each st across, turn.

Row 15: Ch 1, sc in first 2 sts, lscfp around first fp, (sc in next 3 sts, lscfp around next fp) across to last 2 sts, sc in last 2 sts, turn.

Row 16: Ch 1, 2 sc in first st, sc in each st across with 2 sc in last st, turn. *(51 [59, 59, 67] sts)*

Rows 17–18: Ch 1, sc in each st across, turn.

Row 19: Ch 1, sc in first st, dcfp around first fp, sc in next 3 sts, (dcfp-2-tog around last worked fp and next fp, sc in next 3 sts) across to last 2 sts, dcfp again around last worked fp, sc in last st, turn.

Row 20: Ch 1, sc in each st across, turn.

Row 21: Ch 1, sc in first st, lscfp around first fp, sc in next 3 sts, (lscfp around next dcfp-2-tog, sc in next 3 sts) across to last 2 sts, lscfp again around last fp, sc in last st, turn.

Row 22: Ch 1, 2 sc in first st, sc in each st across with 2 sc in last st, turn. *(53 [61, 61, 69] sts)*

Rows 23–24: Ch 1, sc in each st across, turn.

Row 25: Ch 1, sc in first 4 sts, dcfp-2 tog around first 2 fp, sc in next 3 sts, (dcfp-2-tog around last worked fp and next fp, sc in next 3 sts) across with sc in last st, turn.

Row 26: Ch 1, sc in each st across, turn.

Row 27: Ch 1, sc in first 4 sts, (lscfp around next fp on previous row, sc in next 3 sts on last row) across with sc in last st turn.

Rows 28–30: Ch 1, sc in each st across, turn.

Row 31: Ch 1, sc in first 2 sts, dcfp around first fp, sc in next 3 sts, (dcfp-2-tog around last worked fp and next fp, sc in next 3 sts) across to last 3 sts, dcfp again around last worked fp, sc in last 2 sts, turn.

Row 32: Ch 1, sc in each st across, turn.

Row 33: Ch 1, sc in first 2 sts, lscfp around first fp, sc in next 3 sts, (lscfp around next dcfp-2-tog, sc in next 3 sts) across to last 3 sts, lscfp again around last fp, sc in last 2 sts, turn.

Rows 34–36: Ch 1, sc in each st across, turn.

Rows 37–51: Repeat rows 25–36 consecutively, ending with row 27.

Rows [52–55, 52–55, 52–55] for medium, large and X-large only: Repeat rows 28–31.

Rows [56–57, 56–57] for large and X-large only: Repeat rows 32–33.

Last row for all sizes: Ch 1, sc in each st across. Fasten off.

ASSEMBLY

1: Matching ends of rows at side edges, sew 24 [28, 32, 40] sts of each Front shoulder to matching sts at ends of last row on Back, leaving center 20 [28, 28, 28] sts open for Back neck edge.

2: On each side, match center of last row on one Sleeve to shoulder seam; taking care not to stretch or gather either piece, sew last row on Sleeve to ends of rows on Front and Back.

3: Sew underarm and side seams.

NECK BAND

Rnd 1: With right side of work facing, using H hook, work around neck edge as follows:

A: Join navy sprinkles with sc in first st past right shoulder seam, sc in next 19 [27, 27, 27] sts across back neck edge ending at left shoulder seam;

B: Working on Front, evenly space 27 [31, 31, 31] sc in ends of rows to sts across center front neck edge;

C: Skip first sc, sc in next 18 [26, 26, 26] sts across center front neck edge, skip last sc;

D: Evenly space 27 [31, 31, 31] sc in ends of rows across to right shoulder seam, join with sl st in first sc, **turn.** *(92 [116, 116, 116] sts made)*

Rnd 2: Ch 1, sc in each st around, join, **turn.**

Rnd 3: Ch 3, skip next st, cross st 22 [28, 28, 28] times, dc next 4 sts tog, cross st 7 [11, 11, 11] times, dc next 4 sts tog, cross st 12 [14, 14, 14] times, skip ch-3, dc in next skipped st, join with sl st in top of ch-3, **turn.** *(Cross st counts as 2 dc; 86 [110, 110, 110] dc made)*

Rnd 4: Ch 1, sc in first 25 [29, 29, 29] sts, sc next 2 sts tog, sc in next 12 [20, 20, 20] sts, sc next 2 sts tog, sc in each st around, join with sl st in first sc, **turn.**

Rnd 5: Sl st in each st around, join with sl st in first sl st. Fasten off. ●

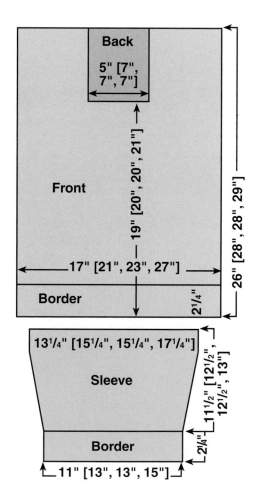

Chapter Five

Bobbles, Beads and Berry Stitches

Learn how to crochet your favorite berry stitches, bobbles and more to mimic beautiful knitted looks. These stitches will lend an exciting texture to your afghans, sweaters and other projects.

Bobbles, Beads and Berry Stitches

When combined with other stitches, knitted bobbles, beads, and berry sts, etc., can produce contrast, texture or whimsical personality to an otherwise plain item.

The smaller bead and berry stitches can be completed in as few as one or two rows, while larger variations may take as many as four to six rows to complete.

In this chapter, we explain four of these stitches and demonstrate how they can be converted to crochet to produce a look and feel similar to their knitted counterparts.

5-Stitch Bobble

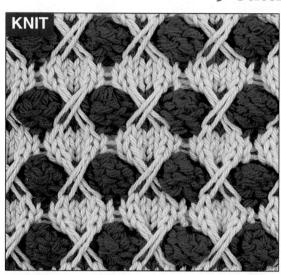
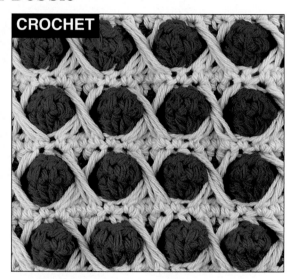

3-Stitch Bobble

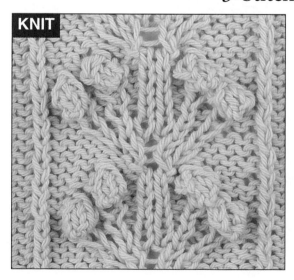

Bead Stitch

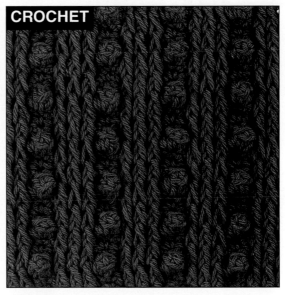

Berry Stitch

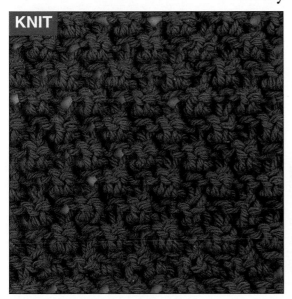

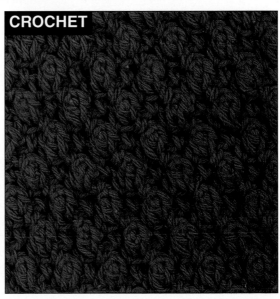

Gum Balls
Stitch Pattern

*T*wo knit stitch patterns—bobbles worked over four rows and long crossed stitches—
are combined to produce this uniquely textured design.

To achieve a similar look in crochet, half-double crochet front post stitches are used
for the crossed stitches; for the bobbles, five stitches are worked into one stitch on the right-
side row, then the first and last stitches of the bobble are pulled together on the next row.

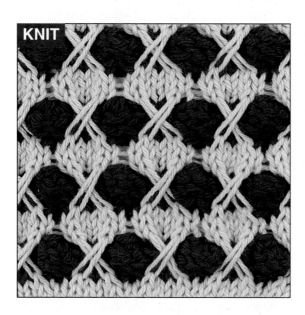

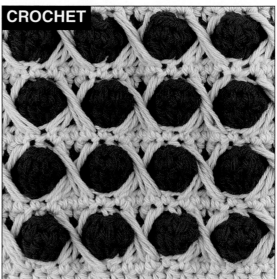

Afghan Square: Gum Balls

READ BEFORE STARTING

Refer to **Chapter 2** for instructions for using Squares to make either
Knit or Crochet Version of Large Afghan or Baby Afghan.

For comparison, each Square has instructions for **Knit Version** in blue
type, and instructions for **Crochet Version** in black type.

KNIT VERSION

With large needles and color B, cast on 26.
Row 1: *(Wrong side)* P across.
Rows 2: K across.
Row 3: *P 1; for **long st,** insert right needle into next st as if to P, wrap yarn 2 times
and pull both wraps through st at same time
(long st completed); P 2, long st; repeat from

CROCHET VERSION

Row 1: With medium hook and color B,
ch 27, hdc in second ch from hook, hdc in
each ch across, turn. *(26 hdc made)*
Rows 2–3: Ch 1, hdc in each st across,
turn. At end of last row, drop yarn, **do
not cut.**
Row 4: For **bobble row,** join color A

* across to last st, P 1. *(36 sts on needles)*

NOTE: *Drop last color; pick up when needed.*

Row 4: With color A, K 1, *slip next wrap of long st, drop next wrap, K 2, slip next wrap of long st, drop next wrap, (K 1, yo, K 1, yo, K 1) all in next st; repeat from * 3 more times, slip next wrap of long st, drop next wrap, K 2, slip next wrap of long st, drop next wrap, K 1. *(42 sts)*

Row 5: P 1, slip long st, P 2, slip long st, ***yarn back (yb),** K 5, **yarn front (yf),** slip long st, P 2, slip long st; repeat from * 3 more times, P 1.

Row 6: K 1, slip long st, K 2, slip long st, (yf, P 5, yb, slip long st, K 2, slip long st) 4 times, K 1.

Row 7: P 1, slip long st, P 2, slip long st, (yb, K 2 tog, K 3 tog, pass K-2-tog st over K-3-tog st and off needle, yf, slip long st, P 2, slip long st) 4 times, P 1. *(26 sts)*

NOTE: *To **cross long sts,** drop next long st from needle, slip next 2 color-A sts, drop next long st from needle; place first dropped long st on left needle, slip same 2 color-A sts back to left needle, place second dropped st on left needle.*

Row 8: With color B, K 1, **(cross long sts**—*see Note,* K 5) across.

Row 9: P across.

Row 10: K across.

Next rows: Repeat rows 3–10 consecutively 3 more times.

Piece should measure same as gauge. Bind off.

Work Edging in Basic Finishing on page 28.

with sl st in first st, ch 1, hdc in first 5 sts; *for **bobble variation** (bobble), 5 hdc in next st; hdc in next 4 sts; repeat from * 3 more times, sc in last st, turn.

Row 5: Ch 1, hdc in first 5 sts; (to **close top of bobble,** hdc in next 5 sts, remove loop from hook, insert hook back to front through first st of 5-hdc group, return loop to hook and pull loop through st, pull snug—*bobble closed;* hdc in next 4 sts) 4 times, hdc in last st, turn. Drop yarn, **do not cut;** pick up again when needed.

Row 6: Join dropped color B with sl st in first st, ch 1, hdc in first st, **hdcfp** *(see Special Stitch on page 24)* around fifth st on third row below, hdc in next 2 sts on last row; hdcfp around second st on third row below, (hdc in top of next bobble, skip next 4 sts on third row below, hdcfp around next st, hdc in next 2 sts on last row, hdcfp around second skipped st on third row below) 4 times, hdc in last st on last row, turn.

Row 7: Ch 1, hdc in each st across, turn. Drop yarn, **do not cut;** pick up again when needed.

Rows 8–19: Repeat rows 4–7 consecutively.

Row 20: Ch 1, hdc in each st across. Fasten off both colors.

Piece should measure same as gauge.

Work Edging in Basic Finishing on page 28.

M̲ake your own designer labels using 1"-wide satin ribbon and a fine-tip permanent marker or fabric paint in a fine-tip squeeze bottle, or embroider your labeling.

Christmas Tree Skirt

Designed by Donna Jones

Trim an easy-to-make tree skirt with textured stitches.

FINISHED SIZE: About 22" from center to outer point.

MATERIALS: Wool-Ease® Art. 620 by Lion Brand® Yarn Company or worsted yarn: 12 oz. Fisherman #99, 4 oz. Cranberry #138, 4 oz. Hunter Green #132; 22" x 22" piece of paper for pattern; 2½ yds. off-white fabric; sewing needle and thread; straight pins; tapestry needle; D and H crochet hooks *(or hook needed to obtain H hook gauge).*

GAUGE: H hook, 14 sts = 4"; 10 hdc rows = 4".

PANELS

1: For paper **pattern,** fold and cut the 22" x 22" piece of paper according to illustration 1, forming two triangles. Fold and cut each triangle according to illustrations 2–4.

2: Using the paper patterns, cut eight pieces from fabric according to Cutting Diagram.

3: To hem each fabric Panel, fold each edge under ⅛", then fold under again ¼"; sew in place.

Crochet Trim (work on each Panel)

Row 1: With D hook and fisherman, loosely ch 128 to measure 18" to fit bottom edge of Panel *(see red dotted line on illustration 4);* with H hook sc in second ch from hook, (ch 2, skip next ch, sc in next ch) across, turn. Sew starting chain in place over edge of Panel. *(63 ch sps, 64 sc made)*

Row 2: Ch 1, hdc in first sc, (hdc in next

Continued on page 133

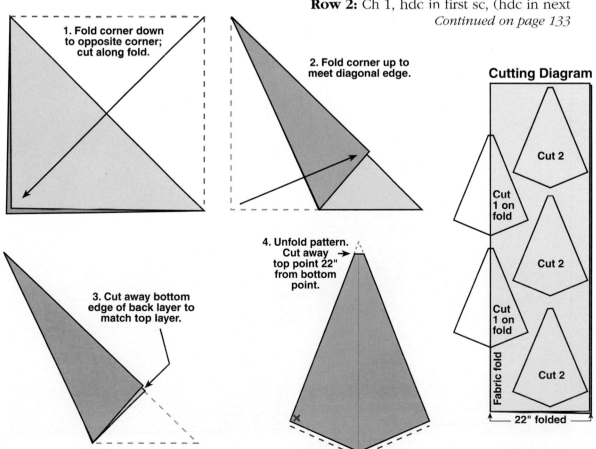

1. Fold corner down to opposite corner; cut along fold.

2. Fold corner up to meet diagonal edge.

3. Cut away bottom edge of back layer to match top layer.

4. Unfold pattern. Cut away top point 22" from bottom point.

Cutting Diagram

Cut 2

Cut 1 on fold

Cut 2

Cut 1 on fold

Cut 2

Fabric fold

— 22" folded —

Project Bag
Designed by Donna Jones

Make a handy tote for your needlework projects with the Gumball stitch pattern.

FINISHED SIZE: 12" high x 13" wide x 2¾" thick, plus Handle.

MATERIALS: Kitchen Cotton® Art. 760 by Lion Brand® Yarn Company or cotton worsted yarn: 10 oz. Navy #110, 4 oz. Poppy Red #112; ¾ yd. navy cotton fabric for lining; plastic canvas pieces: 2 Sides each 11" x 12", 2 Ends each 2" x 11", 2" x 12" Bottom; stitch markers; straight pins; sewing needle and navy thread; tapestry needle; G crochet hook *(or hook needed to obtain gauge)*.

GAUGE: 16 sts = 4"; 12 hdc rows = 4"; 16 sc rows = 4".

SIDE (make 2)
Row 1: Beginning at **bottom edge,** with navy, ch 50, hdc in second ch from hook, hdc in each ch across, turn. *(49 hdc made)*

Row 2: Ch 1, hdc in each st across, turn.

Row 3: Ch 1, hdc in each st across, turn. Fasten off.

Row 4: *(Right side)* Join red with sl st in first st, ch 1, hdc in first 4 sts; (for **bobble base,** 5 hdc in next st; hdc in next 4 sts) across, turn. *(9 bobble bases, 40 hdc)*

Row 5: Ch 1, hdc in first 4 sts; (to **close bobble,** hdc in next 5 sts, remove loop from hook, insert hook from back to front through first st of 5-hdc, return loop to hook and pull loop through st, pull snug to close, push to front side of work–*bobble closed;* hdc in next 4 sts) across, turn. Fasten off. *(49 sts)*

NOTES: *Work each **hdc front post** (**hdcfp,** see Crochet Stitch Guide on page 191) around designated st on previous row, pull up to height of row being worked. Always **skip one st** on last row behind each hdcfp.*

Work all sc sts into sts of last row.

Row 6: Join navy with sl st in first st, ch 1, hdc in same st, **hdcfp** *(see Notes)* around fourth st on last navy row, hdc in next st on last row; hdcfp around third st on last navy row, (hdc in top of bobble on last row, skip next 4 sts on last navy row, hdcfp around next st, hdc in next 2 sts on last row, hdcfp around third skipped st on last navy row) 8 times, hdc in top of bobble on last row, skip next 4 sts on last navy row, hdcfp around next st, hdc in next st on last row, hdcfp around third skipped st on last navy row, hdc in last st on last row, turn.

Rows 7–31: Ch 1, hdc in each st across, turn. At end of last row, drop loop from hook; **do not cut.**

Rows 32–34: Repeat rows 4–6.

Rows 35–36: Ch 1, hdc in each st across, turn. At end of last row, **do not turn.**

Rnd 37: With right side of work facing, working around outer edge, ch 1, sc in end of each row and in each st around with 3 sc in each corner, join with sl st in first sc. Fasten off.

BOTTOM
Row 1: With navy, ch 50, sc in second ch from hook, sc in each ch across, turn. *(49 sc made)*

Rows 2–9: Ch 1, sc in each st across, turn.

Rnd 10: Working around outer edge, ch 1, sc in each st and in end of each row around with 3 sc in each corner, join with sl st in first sc. Fasten off.

ENDS AND HANDLE
Row 1: For **First End,** beginning at bottom edge, with navy, ch 10, hdc in second ch from hook, hdc in each ch across, turn. *(9 hdc made)*

Row 2: Ch 1, hdc in each st across, turn.

Row 3: Ch 1, hdc in each st across, turn. Fasten off.

Row 4: *(Right side)* Join red with sl st in first st, ch 1, hdc in first 4 sts, work bobble base in next st, hdc in last 4 sts, turn. *(1 bobble base, 8 hdc)*

Row 5: Ch 1, hdc in first 4 sts, close bobble, hdc in last 4 sts, turn. Fasten off. *(9 sts)*

Row 6: Join navy with sl st in first st, ch 1, hdc in same st, hdcfp around fifth st on last navy row, hdc in next st on last row; hdcfp around third st on last navy row, hdc in top of bobble on last row, skip next 4 sts on last navy row, hdcfp around next st, hdc in next st on last row, hdcfp around third skipped st on last navy row, hdc in last st on last row, turn.

Rows 7–31: Ch 1, hdc in each st across, turn.

Rows 32–34: Repeat rows 4–6.

Rows 35–36: Ch 1, hdc in each st across, turn. **Mark each end** of row 36.

Rows 37–38: For **Handle**, ch 1, hdc in first st, skip next st, hdc in each st across to last 2 sts, skip next st, hdc in last st, turn. *(7, 5)*

Rows 39–70: Ch 1, hdc in each st across, turn. At end of last row, fasten off.

Rows 71–139: For **Second End and Handle,** repeat rows 1–69. At end of last row, fasten off.

With tops of stitches touching, sew last rows on First and Second Handles together.

Rnd 140: With right side of Ends and Handles facing, working around outer edge, join navy with sc in any corner, sc in each st and in end of each row around with 3 sc in each corner, join with sl st in first sc. Fasten off.

LINING

1: Using crocheted pieces as patterns, cut one piece of fabric to match each crocheted piece plus ⅛" extra fabric extended all around; if necessary for Ends and Handle Lining, cut 3"-wide strips of fabric and sew end to end to length needed, then cut out Lining from this piece.

2: With each Lining piece, press all outer edges ¼" to wrong side. With wrong sides together, **leaving tops of sts on last rnd of crocheted piece exposed** for assembly, center Lining over matching crocheted piece with appropriate plastic canvas piece between; pin Lining in place.

3: On each piece, using sewing needle and thread and taking care that stitches do not show on outside, sew each folded Lining edge in place. If necessary, using sewing needle and matching thread, tack all layers together here and there across center of piece to stabilize.

ASSEMBLY

1: With wrong sides together, matching stitches, using tapestry needle with navy yarn, sew one long edge of Bottom to stitches on bottom edge of one Side; repeat with other Side on opposite long edge of Bottom.

2: Sew short edges of Ends and Handle to short edge at each end of Bottom; at each corner, continue sewing long edges of Sides and Ends together up to stitches worked into marked rows at top of Ends.

3: Working on one edge of Handle, join red with sl st in first stitch past corner seam, sl st in each stitch around Handle and across top edge of Side, join with sl st in first sl st. Fasten off.

4: Repeat step 3 on remaining edge of Handle and other Side. ●

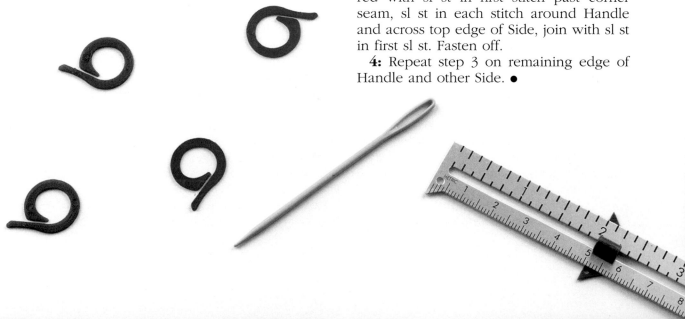

Christmas Tree Skirt
Continued from page 129

ch-2 sp) 31 times, 3 hdc in next st at center of Panel *(second st of 3-hdc group is* **point st);** (hdc in next ch-2 sp) 31 times, hdc in last sc, turn. *(67 hdc made)*

Row 3: Ch 1, hdc in each st across, turn.

Row 4: Ch 1, hdc in first 33 sts, 3 hdc in next point st, hdc in last 33 sts, turn. Fasten off. *(69)*

Row 5: Join hunter green with sl st in first st, ch 1, hdc in same st, hdc in each st across, **do not turn.** Fasten off.

Row 6: With right side facing you, join cranberry with sl st in first st, ch 1, hdc in same st, hdc in next 3 sts; (for **bobble, 5 hdc in next st;** hdc in next 4 sts) across, turn. *(13 bobbles, 56 hdc)*

Row 7: Ch 1, hdc in first 4 sts; (to **close bobble,** hdc in next 5 sts, remove loop from hook, insert hook from back to front through first st of 5-hdc group, return loop to hook and pull loop through st, pull snug to close, push to front side of work– *bobble closed;* hdc in next 4 sts) across, turn. Fasten off. *(69 sts)*

NOTE: Work each **hdc front post** *(***hdcfp,** *see Crochet Stitch Guide on page 191) around designated st on row before last, pull up to height of row being worked. Always* **skip one st** *on last row behind each hdcfp.*

Row 8: Join hunter green with sl st in first st, ch 1, hdc in same st, **hdcfp** *(see Note)* around fourth st on last hunter green row, hdc in next st on last row; hdcfp around second st on last hunter green row, complete row as follows:

A: (Hdc in top of bobble on last row, skip next 4 sts on last hunter green row, hdcfp around next st, hdc in next 2 sts on last row, hdcfp around second skipped st on last hunter green row) 6 times;

B: 3 hdc in top of next bobble at point on last row;

C: (Skip next 4 sts on last hunter green row, hdcfp around next st, hdc in next 2 sts on last row, hdcfp around second skipped st on last hunter green row, hdc in top of bobble on last row) 6 times;

D: Skip next 3 sts on last hunter green row, hdcfp around next st, hdc in next st on last row, hdcfp around second skipped st on last hunter green row, hdc in last st on last row, turn. Fasten off. *(71)*

Row 9: Join fisherman with sl st in first st, ch 1, hdc in each st across to point st, 3 hdc in point st, hdc in each st across, turn. *(73)* Remove loop from hook.

Row 10: For **border** around fabric, with H hook, join separate skein fisherman with sl st in end of starting chain on row 1, pinning loosely in place as you go, loosely ch to fit around remaining edges of Panel; carefully without twisting ch, sl st in other end of starting ch; **do not fasten off** *(As you complete row, chains can be added or removed, if needed.);* join separate skein fisherman with sc in first ch at beginning of row, evenly space 7 sc over every 2" across ch with 3 sc at each top corner, sl st in other end of row 1. Fasten off.

Rnd 11: Return dropped loop to hook; working across row 9, ch 1, 3 sc in first st, (skip next st, dc in next st; for **picot, ch 2, sl st in top of st just made;** ch 2, sl st in same st as last dc made) 17 times, dc in next st, picot, ch 2, sl st in same st as last dc made, (skip next st, dc in next st, picot, ch 2, sl st in same st as last dc made) 18 times, 3 sc in last st; working in ends of rows on Trim and in sts on border, sc in each row and in each st around with (sc, ch 1, sc) in center sc of 3-sc group at each top corner, join with sl st in first sc. Fasten off.

ASSEMBLY

Matching ch-1 sps at top corners and center sc of 3-sc group at bottom corners, using tapestry needle with fisherman yarn, sew long edges together to form a circle with seven seams, leaving remaining long edges unsewn for back opening. ●

Bobble Tree Stitch Pattern

*K*nitted ribs, crossed stitches and bobbles on a reversed stockinette stitch background are used to represent a tree.

Crochet post stitches and bobbles on a single crochet background can be used to achieve the same effect in crochet.

Afghan Square: Bobble Tree

READ BEFORE STARTING

Refer to **Chapter 2** for instructions for using Squares to make either Knit or Crochet Version of Large Afghan or Baby Afghan.

For comparison, each Square has instructions for **Knit Version** in blue type, and instructions for **Crochet Version** in black type.

KNIT VERSION

*NOTES: For **left cross (LC),** with yarn at back, skip first st on left needle; inserting needle from back, K in back loop of second st and leave on needle, K in front loop of skipped st and drop both sts from left needle.*

*For **right cross (RC),** skip first st on left needle; working in front of skipped st, K in front loop of second st and leave on needle,*

CROCHET VERSION

Row 1: With medium hook and white, ch 27, sc in second ch from hook, sc in each ch across, turn. *(26 sc made)*

Row 2: Ch 1, sc in each st across, turn.

*NOTE: Work **all sc sts** into sts of **last row.***

Row 3: Ch 1, sc in first 4 sc *(see Note),* **hdcfp** *(see Special Stitch on page 24)* around st on row before last directly below next st,

K in back loop of skipped st and drop both sts from left needle.

For **Left Twist (LT),** *slip next st onto cable needle and hold at front of work, P 1, K 1 from cable needle.*

For **Right Twist (RT),** *slip next st onto cable needle and hold at back of work, K 1, P 1 from cable needle.*

For **bobble,** *(K 1, P 1, K 1) all in next st,* **turn,** *P 3,* **turn,** *K 3,* **turn,** *P 3,* **turn,** *slip 1, K 2 tog, pass slipped st over K st and off needle (push to front of work).*

With large needles and white, cast on 26.

Row 1: *(Wrong side)* K 4, P 1, K 7, P 2, K 7, P 1, K 4.

Row 2: P 4, K 1-**through the back lp (-tbl),** P 6, **LC** *(see Notes),* **RC,** P 6, K 1-tbl, P 4.

Row 3: K 4, P 1, K 5, **LT** *(see Notes),* P 2, **RT** *(see Notes),* K 5, P 1, K 4.

Row 4: P 4, K 1-tbl, P 4, RT, RC, LC, LT, P 4, K1-tbl, P 4.

Row 5: K 4, P 1, K 3, LT, K 1, P 4, K 1, RT, K 3, P 1, K 4.

Row 6: P 4, K 1-tbl, P 2, RT, P 1, RT, K 2, LT, P 1, LT, P 2, K 1-tbl, P 4.

Row 7: K 4, (P 1, K 2) 2 times, P 1, K 1, P 2, K 1, P 1, (K 2, P 1) 2 times, K 4.

Row 8: P 4, K 1-tbl, P 2, **bobble** *(see Notes),* P 1, RT, P 1, K 2, P 1, LT, P 1, bobble, P 2, K 1-tbl, P 4.

Row 9: (K 4, P 1) 2 times, K 2, P 2, K 2, (P 1, K 4) 2 times.

Row 10: P 4, K 1-tbl, P 4, bobble, P 2, K 2, P 2, bobble, P 4, K 1-tbl, P 4.

Rows 11–30: Repeat rows 1–10 consecutively.

Piece should measure same as gauge. Bind off.

Work Edging in Basic Finishing on page 28.

sc in next 5 sc; counting from last fp on row before last, hdcfp around seventh st; working behind last row, **hdcbp** back around sixth skipped st; working in front of last row, hdcfp around next 2 sts, skip next st; working behind last row, hdcbp around next st; working in front of last row, hdcfp back around skipped st, sc in next 5 sc, hdcfp around st on row before last directly below next st, sc in last 4 sc, turn.

Row 4: Ch 1, sc in each st across, turn.

Row 5: Ch 1, sc in first 4 sc, hdcfp around next fp, sc in next 4 sc, hdcfp around each of next 2 post stitches, (sc in next sc, hdcfp around each of next 2 post stitches) 2 times, sc in next 4 sc, hdcfp around next fp, sc in last 4 sc, turn.

Row 6: Ch 1, sc in each st across, turn.

Row 7: Ch 1, sc in first 4 sc, hdcfp around next fp, sc in next 3 sc, hdcfp around each of next 2 fp, (sc in next 2 sc, hdcfp around each of next 2 fp) 2 times, sc in next 3 sc, hdcfp around next fp, sc in last 4 sc, turn.

NOTE: *For* **bobble variation** *(bobble), 3 dc in next st, remove loop from hook, insert hook from back to front through first dc made of 3-dc group, place dropped loop on hook, pull through.*

Row 8: Ch 1, sc in first 8 sts, **bobble** *(see Note),* sc in next 8 sts, bobble, sc in last 8 sts, turn.

Row 9: Ch 1, sc in first 4 sc; skipping each bobble and fp directly below each bobble, (hdcfp around next fp, sc in next 3 sc on last row) 2 times, hdcfp around each of next 2 fp, (sc in next 3 sc on last row, hdcfp around next fp) 2 times, sc in last 4 sc, turn.

Row 10: Repeat row 8.

Row 11: Ch 1, sc in first 4 sc, hdcfp around next fp, sc in next 7 sts, hdcfp around each of next 2 fp, sc in next 7 sts, hdcfp around next fp, sc in last 4 sc, turn.

Rows 12–21: Repeat rows 2–11.

Rows 22–25: Repeat rows 2–5.

Row 26: Repeat row 8.

Row 27: Ch 1, sc in first 4 sc, hdcfp around next fp, sc in next 3 sc on last row, skip bobble and next fp, hdcfp around next fp, sc in next 3 sc on last row, hdcfp around each of next 2 fp, sc in next 3 sc on last row, hdcfp around next fp, skip

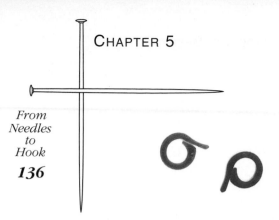

bobble and next fp, sc in next 3 sc, hdcfp around next fp, sc in last 4 sc, turn.

Row 28: Repeat row 8.

Row 29: Repeat row 11. Fasten off. Piece should measure same as gauge. Work Edging in Basic Finishing on page 28.

Christmas Stocking
Designed by Donna Jones

This heirloom stocking is made using the interesting Bobble Tree stitch pattern.

FINISHED SIZE: About 18" long from top edge to toe, plus hanging loop.

MATERIALS: Wool-Ease® Art. 620 by Lion Brand® Yarn Company or worsted yarn: 3½ oz. Fisherman #99, 2 oz. Cranberry #138, 1½ oz. Hunter Green #132; stitch markers; tapestry needle; F and G crochet hooks *(or hook needed to obtain G hook gauge).*

GAUGE: G hook, 16 sts = 4"; 16 sc rows = 4"; 12 hdc rows = 4".

TOE AND FOOT
Rnd 1: Beginning at **Toe,** with G hook and cranberry, ch 5, 5 hdc in second ch from hook, hdc in next 2 chs, 5 hdc in end ch; working on opposite side of ch, hdc in next 2 chs, join with sl st in top of first hdc, **turn.** *(14 sts made)*

Rnd 2: Ch 1, hdc in first 3 sts, 2 hdc in each of next 3 sts, hdc in next 4 sts, 2 hdc in each of next 3 sts, hdc in last st, join, **turn.** *(20)*

Rnd 3: Ch 1, hdc in first 2 sts, 2 hdc in each of next 4 sts, hdc in next 6 sts, 2 hdc in each of next 4 sts, hdc in last 4 sts, join, **turn.** *(28)*

Rnd 4: Ch 1, hdc in first 6 sts, 2 hdc in each of next 4 sts, hdc in next 10 sts, 2 hdc in each of next 4 sts, hdc in last 4 sts, join, **turn.** *(36)*

Rnd 5: Ch 1, hdc in each st around, join, **turn.**

Rnd 6: Ch 1, hdc in first 9 sts, 2 hdc in each of next 4 sts, hdc in next 14 sts, 2 hdc in each of next 4 sts, hdc in last 5 sts, join, **turn.** *(44)*

Rnd 7: Ch 1, hdc in each st around, join, **turn.**

Rnd 8: Ch 1, hdc in first 11 sts, 2 hdc in each of next 4 sts, hdc in next 18 sts, 2 hdc in each of next 4 sts, hdc in last 7 sts, join, **turn.** Fasten off. *(52)*

Rnd 9: For **Foot,** join fisherman with sl st in first st, ch 1, sc in same st, sc in each st around, join, **turn.** *(52 sc)*

Rnds 10–24: Ch 1, sc in each st around, join, **turn.**

*NOTES: Work each **hdc front post (hdcfp,** see Crochet Stitch Guide on page 191) or **hdc back post (hdcbp)** around designated st on previous row or rnd, pull up to height of row or rnd being worked. Always **skip one st** on last row or rnd for each hdcfp or hdcbp.*

Work all sc sts into sts of last row.

*To **change colors** (see Crochet Stitch Guide), carry dropped color loosely across wrong side of work; pick up again when needed.*

*For **bobble variation (bobble),** with cranberry, 5 dc in next st changing to fisherman in last st, remove loop from hook, insert hook from back to front through top loop of first dc of 5-dc group, return loop to hook and pull through st on hook.*

Rnd 25: Ch 1, sc in first 23 sts; complete rnd as follows:

A: Skip first 25 sts on rnd before last; with green *(see Notes),* **hdcfp** *(see Notes)* around next st on rnd before last; with fisherman, sc in next st on last rnd;

with green, hdcfp around same st on rnd before last as last fp;

B: Hdcfp around next st; with fisherman, sc in next st on last rnd; with green, hdcfp around same st on rnd before last as last fp; with fisherman, sc in last 23 sts, join, **turn.**

Rnd 26: Ch 1, sc in first 22 sts; with cranberry, **bobble** *(see Notes);* with fisherman, sc in next 6 sts; with cranberry, bobble; with fisherman, sc in last 22 sts, join, **turn.**

Rnd 27: Ch 1, sc in first 25 sts; with green, hdcfp around each of next 2 fp; with fisherman, sc in last 25 sts, join, **turn.**

Rnd 28: Ch 1, sc in first 25 sts; with cranberry, bobble in each of next 2 sts; with fisherman, sc in last 25 sts, join, **turn.** Fasten off green and cranberry.

Rnds 29–34: Ch 1, sc in each st around, join, **turn.** At end of last rnd, pull up long loop and remove hook; **do not cut yarn.**

Heel

Row 1: With back side of last rnd facing, skip first 2 sts, join cranberry with sl st in next st, ch 1, hdc in same st as sl st, hdc in next 21 sts leaving last 28 sts unworked, turn. *(22 hdc made)*

Rows 2–5: Ch 1, **mark** ch-1 just made; for **hdc dec,** yo, (insert hook in next st, yo, pull through st) 2 times, yo, pull through all 4 lps on hook *(hdc dec made),* hdc in each st across to last 2 sts, hdc dec, turn. At end of last row, **do not turn;** sl st in top of st at end of row 4, turn. *(14)*

Row 6: Skip sl st, 2 hdc in first hdc, hdc in each st across with 2 hdc in last st, skip last row, sl st in next marked ch-1 at end of row 5, turn. *(16 hdc) Remove marker as each ch-1 is worked.*

Row 7: Repeat row 6 with last sl st in row 4, turn. *(18 hdc)*

Row 8: Repeat row 6 with last sl st in row 3, turn. *(20 hdc)*

Row 9: Repeat row 6 with last sl st in row 2, turn. *(22 hdc)*

Row 10: Repeat row 6 with last sl st in st at base of row 1, turn. *(24 hdc)*

Row 11: Skip sl st, hdc in each st across, sl st in st at base of row 1. Fasten off.

LEG

Rnd 1: Return dropped fisherman loop to hook; with back of last rnd on Foot facing, ch 1, sc in first 2 sts, sc first worked st of Foot and first st on last row of Heel tog, sc in next 22 sts of Heel, sc last st on Heel and next worked st on Foot tog, sc in last 28 sts of Foot, join with sl st in first sc, **turn.** *(54 sc made)*

Rnd 2: Ch 1, sc in each st around, join, **turn.**

Rnd 3: Ch 1, sc in first 18 sts, hdcfp around sc on rnd before last directly below next st, sc in next 5 sts; with green, skip next 6 sc on row before last, hdcfp around next st, **hdcbp** *(see Notes before rnd 25 of Foot)* around sixth skipped st, hdcfp around each of next 2 sc, skip next st on rnd before last, hdcbp around next st, hdcfp around skipped st; with fisherman, sc in next 5 sts, hdcfp around next sc on rnd before last directly below next st, sc in last 18 sts, join, **turn.**

Rnd 4: Ch 1, sc in each st around, join, **turn.**

Rnd 5: Ch 1, sc in first 18 sts, hdcfp around first fp on rnd before last, sc in next 4 sts; with green, hdcfp around each of next 2 fp or bp *(post sts);* (with fisherman, sc in next st on last rnd; with green, hdcfp around each of next 2 post sts) 2 times; with fisherman, sc in next 4 sts, hdcfp around next fp, sc in last 18 sts, join, **turn.**

Rnd 6: Ch 1, sc in each st around, join, **turn.**

Rnd 7: Ch 1, sc in first 18 sts, hdcfp around first fp on rnd before last, sc in next 3 sts; with green, hdcfp around each of next 2 fp; (with fisherman, sc in next 2 sts; with green, hdcfp around each of next 2 fp) 2 times; with fisherman, sc in next 3 sts, hdcfp around next fp, sc in last 18 sts, join, **turn.**

Rnd 8: Ch 1, sc in first 22 sts; with cranberry, bobble; with fisherman, sc in next 8 sts; with cranberry, bobble; with fisherman, sc in last 22 sts, join, **turn.** *(52 sts, 2 bobbles)*

Rnd 9: Ch 1, sc in first 18 sts, hdcfp around next fp, sc in next 3 sts; skip bobble and next fp, with green, hdcfp around next fp; with fisherman, sc in next 3 sc;

with green, hdcfp around each of next 2 fp; with fisherman, sc in next 3 sts; with green, hdcfp around next fp; with fisherman, sc in next 3 sc, hdcfp around next fp, sc in last 18 sts, join, **turn.**

Rnd 10: Ch 1, sc in first 22 sts; with cranberry, bobble; with fisherman, sc in next 8 sts; with cranberry, bobble; with fisherman, sc in last 22 sts, join, **turn.** *(52 sts, 2 bobbles)*

Rnd 11: Ch 1, sc in first 18 sts, hdcfp around next fp, sc in next 7 sc; with green, hdcfp around each of next 2 fp; with fisherman, sc in next 7 sts, hdcfp around next fp, sc in last 18 sts, join, **turn.**

Rnds 12–21: Repeat rnds 2–11.

Rnds 22–25: Repeat rnds 2–5.

Rnds 26–28: Repeat rnds 8, 9 and 8.

Rnd 29: Repeat rnd 11.

Rnd 30: Ch 1, sc in first 25 sts; with cranberry, bobble; with fisherman, sc in next 2 sts; with cranberry, bobble; with fisherman, sc in last 25 sts, join, **turn.** Fasten off green and cranberry. *(52 sts, 2 bobbles)*

Rnd 31: Ch 1, sc in first 18 sts, hdcfp around next fp, sc in next 16 sts, hdcfp around next fp, sc in last 18 sts, join, **turn.**

Mark end of last row for cuff trim.

Rnds 32–34: For **cuff,** ch 1, sc in each st around, join, **turn.**

Rnd 35: Ch 1, sc in first 15 sts; complete rnd as follows:

A: Counting from st on rnd before last directly below next st, skip next st; with green, hdcfp around next st on rnd before last, with fisherman, sc in next st; with green, hdcfp around same st on rnd before last as last fp;

B: Hdcfp around next st on rnd before last; with fisherman, sc in next st; with green, hdcfp around same st on rnd before last as last fp, with fisherman, sc in next 3 sts;

C : Repeat steps A, B, A and B;

D: Sc in last 12 sts, join, **turn.**

Rnd 36: Ch 1, sc in first 15 sts; with cranberry, (bobble; with fisherman, sc in next 4 sts; with cranberry, bobble; with fisherman, sc in next 3 sts) 3 times, sc in last 12 sts, join, **turn.**

Rnd 37: Ch 1, sc in first 17 sts; (with green, hdcfp around each of next 2 fp; with fisherman, sc in next 7 sts) 3 times, sc in last 10 sts, join, **turn.**

Rnd 38: Ch 1, sc in first 17 sts; with cranberry, (bobble in each of next 2 sts; with fisherman, sc in next 7 sts) 3 times, sc in last 10 sts, join, **turn.** Fasten off green and cranberry.

Rnds 39–40: Ch 1, sc in each st around, join, **turn.** At end of last rnd, fasten off.

Rnd 41: Join cranberry with sc in first st, sc in each st around, join, **do not turn.**

Rnd 42: Ch 1, sc in each st around, join.

Rnd 43: Ch 1, sc in first 14 sts; for **hanger loop,** ch 12, sl st in last sc made, sc in each sc around, join.

Rnd 44: With F hook, sl st in first 14 sts, 24 sc in hanger loop, sl st in each st around, join. Fasten off.

Rnd 45: For **cuff trim,** with G hook, for **topstitch trim,** join green with sl st in first st on marked rnd 31, sl st in each st around, join. Fasten off.

Rnd 46: Working again into rnd 31 just above green sts, with G hook, for **topstitch trim,** join cranberry with sl st in first st, sl st in each st around, join. Fasten off.

Rnd 47: With G hook, join green with sl st in first st on rnd 40 at base of cranberry sts, sl st in each st around, join. Fasten off.

LEAF (make 7)

Row 1: Beginning at stem end, with F hook and green, leaving 5" end for sewing, ch 3, 3 sc in second ch from hook; for **picot, ch 2, sl st in first ch of ch-2;** turn. *(3 sc made)*

Row 2: 2 sc in first st, sc in next st, 2 sc in last st, picot, turn. *(5)*

Row 3: Sc in first 2 sts, hdcfp around center sc on row 1, sc in last 2 sts, picot, turn.

Row 4: Sc in 5 sts, picot, turn.

Row 5: Sc first 2 sts tog, hdcfp around fp on row 3, sc last 2 sts tog, picot, turn. *(3)*

Row 6: Skipping second st, sc first sc and third sc tog, ch 2. Leaving 5" end for sewing, fasten off.

Sew two Leaves to each side of Leg next to bobbles *(see photo)*; sew three Leaves below fp sts on Foot. ●

Wine or Gift Bag

Designed by Darla Sims

A fine wine deserves an equally exquisite wrapping.

FINISHED SIZE: About 5½" wide x 14" high, plus Ties.

MATERIALS: MicroSpun Art. 910 by Lion Brand® Yarn Company or sport yarn: 5 oz. desired color—*Coral #103 shown;* tapestry needle; G crochet hook *(or hook needed to obtain gauge).*

GAUGE: 18 sts = 4"; 18 sc rows = 4".

BAG
Row 1: Loosely ch 51, sc in second ch from hook, sc in each ch across, turn. *(50 sc made)*

Row 2: Ch 1, sc in each st across, turn.

NOTES: *Work each* **hdc front post** *(hdcfp, see Crochet Stitch Guide on page 191) or* **hdc back post** *(hdcbp) around designated st on previous row, pull up to height of row being worked. Always* **skip one st on last row** *for each hdcfp or hdcbp.*

Work all sc sts into sts of last row.

For **bobble variation** *(bobble), 5 dc in same st, remove loop from hook, insert hook from back to front through top loop of first dc of 5-dc group, return loop to hook and pull through st on hook.*

Row 3: Ch 1, sc in first 16 sts, **hdcfp** *(see Notes)* around st on row before last directly below next st, sc in next 5 sts; working on row before last, skip 6 sts past last fp; hdcfp around next st; working behind fp just made, **hdcbp** *(see Notes)* around last skipped st, hdcfp around each of next 2 sts, skip next st on row before last, hdcbp around next st; working in front of bp just made, hdcfp around skipped st, sc in next 5 sts, hdcfp around st on row before last directly below next st, sc in last 16 sts, turn.

Row 4: Ch 1, sc in each st across, turn.

Row 5: Ch 1, sc in first 16 sts, hdcfp around next **post st (ps)** on previous row,

sc in next 4 sts, hdcfp around each of next 2 ps, (sc in next st, hdcfp around each of next 2 ps) 2 times, sc in next 4 sts, hdcfp around next ps, sc in last 16 sts, turn.

Row 6: Ch 1, sc in each st across, turn.

Row 7: Ch 1, sc in first 16 sts, hdcfp around next ps, sc in next 3 sts, hdcfp around each of next 2 ps, (sc in next 2 sts, hdcfp around each of next 2 ps) 2 times, sc in next 3 sts, hdcfp around next ps, sc in last 16 sts, turn.

Row 8: Ch 1, sc in first 20 sts, **bobble** *(see Notes),* sc in same st as bobble, sc in next 8 sts, (sc, bobble) in next st, sc in last 20 sts, turn. *(2 bobbles, 50 sc)*

Row 9: Ch 1, sc in first 16 sts, hdcfp around next ps, sc in next 3 sts, skip bobble, (hdcfp around each of next 2 ps, sc in next 2 sts) 2 times, hdcfp around each of next 2 ps, skip bobble, sc in next 3 sts, hdcfp around next ps, sc in last 16 sts, turn.

Row 10: Ch 1, sc in first 20 sts, (bobble, sc) in next st, sc in next 8 sts, (sc, bobble) in next st, sc in last 20 sts, turn.

Row 11: Ch 1, sc in first 16 sts, hdcfp around next ps; skipping each bobble, sc in next 7 sts, hdcfp around each of next 2 ps, sc in next 7 sts, hdcfp around next ps, sc in last 16 sts, turn.

Row 12: Ch 1, sc in each st across, turn.

Rows 13–62: Repeat rows 3–12 consecutively. At end of last row, fasten off.

Sew ends of rows together to form tube. Flatten tube with seam at center back; sew starting ch together.

Top Trim
Rnd 1: With right side of tube out, join with sc in first st, sc in each st around, join with sl st in first sc. *(50 sts made)*

Rnd 2: (Ch 4, dc) in first st, skip next st, (dc in next st, ch 1, skip next st) around, join with sl st in third ch of ch-4. *(26 ch-1 sps)*

Rnd 3: (Sl st, ch 3, 2 dc, ch 3, sl st in third ch from hook, 3 dc) in first ch sp, sc in next ch sp, *(3 dc, ch 3, sl st in third ch from hook, 3 dc) in next ch sp, sc in next

ch sp; repeat from * around, join with sl st in top of ch-3. Fasten off.

For **Tie** *(make 2),* ch to measure 18", sl st in second ch from hook, sl st in each ch across. Fasten off.

Starting at one side, weave one Tie in and out through ch sps on rnd 2, tie ends together *(see photo);* in same manner, weave other Tie from other side through alternate ch sps, tie ends together. ●

Berry Stitch Pattern

*K*nit berry stitches are formed by working a three-stitch increase in one stitch for the base; then, with or without stitches between, work three stitches together to close the berry and maintain the same stitch count; on the following row, the positions of the increases and decreases are reversed to close the tops of the berries.

To achieve the same effect in crochet, three stitches are worked in the same place, then remove the hook, insert it through the first stitch, replace loop on hook and pull loop through to close the top of the berry.

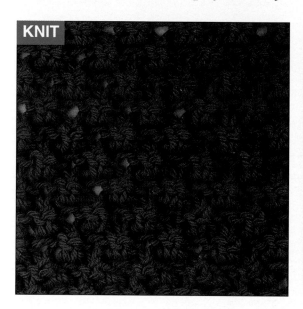
KNIT

CROCHET

Afghan Square: Berry Stitch

READ BEFORE STARTING

Refer to **Chapter 2** for instructions for using Squares to make either Knit or Crochet Version of Large Afghan or Baby Afghan.

For comparison, each Square has instructions for **Knit Version** in blue type, and instructions for **Crochet Version** in black type.

KNIT VERSION

With large needles and color A, cast on 30.

Row 1: *(Right side)* P across.

Row 2: K 1, *(K 1, P 1, K 1) all in next st, P 3 tog; repeat from * across to last

CROCHET VERSION

Row 1: With small hook and color A, ch 31, sc in second ch from hook, sc in each st across, turn. *(30 sc made)*

Row 2: Ch 1, sc in first 2 sts; for **berry variation *(berry)*,** 3 hdc in next st,

st, K 1.

Row 3: P across.

Row 4: K 1, *P 3 tog, (K 1, P 1, K 1) all in next st; repeat from * across to last st, K 1.

Next rows: Repeat rows 1–4 consecutively until piece measures same as gauge, ending with row 2 or row 4.

Bind off.

Work Edging in Basic Finishing on page 28.

remove loop from hook, insert hook from front to back through top of first hdc of 3-hdc group, return dropped loop to hook and pull through all loops on hook, *(berry made)*; (ch 1, skip next st, sc in next st, ch 1, skip next st, berry) 6 times, ch 1, skip next st, sc in last 2 sts, turn. *(30 sts and chs)*

Row 3: Ch 1, sc in first 2 sts, skipping each st unless otherwise stated, (sc in next ch sp, ch 1) across with sc in last 2 sts, turn.

Row 4: Ch 1, sc in first 2 sts, sc in next ch sp, (ch 1, berry in next ch sp, ch 1, sc in next ch sp) 6 times, ch 1, sc in last 2 sts, turn.

Row 5: Ch 1, sc in first 2 sts, skipping each st unless otherwise stated, (sc in next ch sp, ch 1) across with sc in last 2 sts, turn.

Row 6: Ch 1, sc in first 2 sts, berry in next ch sp, (ch 1, sc in next ch sp, ch 1, berry in next ch sp) 6 times, ch 1, sc in last 2 sts, turn.

Next rows: Repeat rows 3–6 consecutively until piece measures same as gauge, ending with row 3 or 5. At end of last row, fasten off.

Work Edging in Basic Finishing on page 28.

Berry Stitch Mittens

Designed by Donna Jones

*Crocheted mittens decorated with the Berry
stitch pattern warm the heart as well as the hands.*

FINISHED SIZES: Fits teen or adult hand
7¼" around palm or **8" around palm.**

MATERIALS: 4 oz. desired color
MicroSpun Art. 910 by Lion Brand® Yarn
Company or sport yarn—*Lime #194 is
shown;* crochet stitch markers; tapestry
needle; small and large crochet hooks in
sizes needed to obtain gauges.

**GAUGES: 7¼" palm: E hook (small-
er),** 22 sc = 4"; 26 sc **back lp** rows = 4".
F hook (larger), 20 sc = 4"; 20 sc rows
= 4".
8" palm: F hook (smaller), 20 sc = 4";
24 sc **back lp** rows = 4". **G hook (larger),** 18 sc = 4"; 16 sc rows = 4".

RIGHT MITTEN
Ribbing

Row 1: With smaller hook, leaving 5" end
for sewing, ch 16, sc in second ch from hook,
sc in each ch across, turn. *(15 sc made)*

Rows 2–38: Working these rows in **back
lps** *(see Crochet Stitch Guide on page 191),*
ch 1, sc in each st across, turn.

At end of last row, pull up long loop and
remove from hook; **do not fasten off.**

Lap edge of last row over starting ch on
first row to form rib; using tapestry needle
with 5" end from row 1, sew together to
form ring.

Hand

Rnd 1: Working in ends of Ribbing rows,
with smaller hook, return loop to hook, ch
1, sc in each row around, join with sl st in
first sc, **turn.** *(38 sc made)*

Rnd 2: With larger hook, ch 1, sc in each
st around, join, **turn.**

NOTES: *For* **berry variation (berry),** *3
hdc in next ch sp (on rnd 3 only, work in sts
instead of ch sps); drop loop from hook,*
*insert hook from front to back through top of
first hdc of 3-hdc group, return dropped loop
to hook and pull through all loops on hook.*

For **Berry Pattern A,** *berry, (ch 1, skip
next st, sc in next ch sp, ch 1, skip next st,
berry) 4 times.*

For **Berry Pattern B,** *sc in next ch sp,
(ch 1, skip next st, berry, ch 1, skip next st,
sc in next ch-sp) 4 times.*

Rnd 3: *(Right side)* Ch 1; working in sts
across **back** of hand, sc in first 2 sts, **berry**
(see Note), (ch 1, skip next st, sc in next st,
ch 1, skip next st, berry) 4 times; working
across **palm,** sc in last 19 sts, join, **turn.**
(38 sts and chs)

Rnd 4: Ch 1, sc in first 19 sts, (ch 1,
skip next st, sc in next ch sp) across to
last 3 sts, ch 1, skip next st, sc in last 2
sts, join, **turn.**

Rnd 5: Ch 1, sc in first 2 sts, work
Berry Pattern B *(see Note),* sc in last 19
sts, join, **turn.**

Rnd 6: Ch 1, sc in first 18 sts; to begin
base of thumb, 3 sc in next st, **mark first
sc** and **last sc** of 3-sc just made; working
across back, ch 1, skip next st, (sc in next
ch sp, ch 1, skip next st) around to last 2
sts, sc in last 2 sts, join, **turn.** *(40)*

NOTE: *When working into marked st,
remove marker, work st, mark st just made.*

Rnd 7: Ch 1, sc in first 2 sts, work Berry
Pattern A *(see Note);* sc in each st around,
join, **turn.**

Rnd 8: Ch 1, sc in each st across palm
and base of thumb to second marker, (ch
1, skip next st, sc in next ch sp) around to
last 3 sts, ch 1, skip next st, sc in last 2 sts,
join, **turn.**

Rnd 9: Ch 1, sc in first 2 sts, work Berry
Pattern B, sc in each st around, join, **turn.**

Rnd 10: Ch 1, sc in each st across to
marker, 2 sc in marked st, move marker to
first sc of 2-sc just made, sc in each st
across to next marker, 2 sc in marked st,
move marker to **last** sc of 2-sc just made;
working across back, (ch 1, skip next st, sc

in next ch sp) around to last 3 sts, ch 1, skip next st, sc in last 2 sts, join, **turn.** *(42)*

Rnds 11–12: Repeat rnds 7 and 8.

Rnd 13: Removing markers as you go, ch 1, sc in first 2 sts, work Berry Pattern B, sc in next 2 sts; for **thumb opening,** ch 3 loosely, skip next 9 sts; sc in last 12 sts, join, **turn.** *(36)*

Rnd 14: Ch 1, sc in first 17 sts and chs, ch 1, skip next st, (sc in next ch sp, ch 1, skip next st) around to last 2 sts, sc in last 2 sts, join, **turn.**

Rnd 15: Ch 1, sc in first 2 sts, work Berry Pattern A, sc in last 17 sts, join, **turn.**

Rnd 16: Ch 1, sc in first 17 sts, ch 1, skip next st, (sc in next ch sp, ch 1, skip next st) around to last 2 sts, sc in last 2 sts, join, **turn.**

Rnd 17: Ch 1, sc in first 2 sts, work Berry Pattern B, sc in last 17 sts, join, **turn.**

Rnd 18: Ch 1, sc in first 17 sts, ch 1, skip next st, (sc in next ch sp, ch 1, skip next st) around to last 2 sts, sc in last 2 sts, join, **turn.**

Rnds 19–27: Repeat rnds 15–18 consecutively, ending with rnd 15.

Rnd 28: Ch 1, sc in first 17 sts, skip next st, (sc in next ch sp, ch 1, skip next st) around to last 2 sts, sc last 2 sts tog, join, **turn.** *(34)*

Rnd 29: Ch 1, sc in first 3 sts and ch sps, berry, (ch 1, skip next st, sc in next ch-sp, ch 1, skip next st, berry) 3 times, sc in last 18 sts, join, **turn.**

Rnd 30: Ch 1, sc first 2 sts tog, sc in next 13 sts, (sc next 2 sts tog) 2 times, sc in next 13 sts and ch sps, sc last 2 sts tog, join, **turn.** *(30)*

Rnd 31: Ch 1, sc first 2 sts tog, sc in next 11 sts, (sc next 2 sts tog) 2 times, sc in next 11 sts, sc last 2 sts tog, join, **turn.** *(26)*

Rnd 32: Ch 1, sc first 2 sts tog, sc in next 9 sts, (sc next 2 sts tog) 2 times, sc in next 9 sts, sc last 2 sts tog, join, **turn.** Fasten off. *(22)*

Flatten rnd 32 at decreases; sew together.

Thumb

Rnd 1: With larger hook and wrong side of sts on thumb opening facing, working on opposite side of ch-3, join with sc in **last** ch of ch-3, sc in last worked st on rnd 12 before skipped sts, sc in next 9 skipped sts, sc in next st beside st already worked, sc in last 2 chs, join, **turn.** *(14 sc made)*

Rnds 2–11: Ch 1, sc in each st around, join, **turn.** At end of last rnd, leaving 6" end, fasten off.

With tapestry needle, weave 6" end through outside loop of each st on rnd 11, pull tight, secure.

LEFT MITTEN
Ribbing

Work same as Right Mitten Ribbing.

Hand

Rnds 1–2: Work same as Right Mitten.

Rnd 3: *(Right side)* Ch 1; working across **palm,** sc in first 19 sts; working across **back** of hand, berry, (ch 1 skip next st, sc in next st, ch 1, skip next st, berry) 4 times, sc in last 2 sts, join, **turn.** *(38 sts and chs)*

Rnd 4: Ch 1, sc in first 2 sts, ch 1, skip next st, (sc in next ch sp, ch 1, skip next st) 8 times, sc in last 19 sts, join, **turn.**

Rnd 5: Ch 1, sc in first 19 sts, work **Berry Pattern B** *(see Note)* across back, sc in last 2 sts, join, **turn.**

Rnd 6: Ch 1, sc in first 2 sts, ch 1, skip next st, (sc in next ch sp, ch 1, skip next st) 8 times; to begin **base of thumb,** 3 sc in next st, mark **first** sc and **last** sc of 3-sc just made, sc in last 18 sts of palm, join, **turn.** *(40)*

Rnd 7: Ch 1, sc in each st across palm and thumb base to second marker, work Berry Pattern A across to last 2 sts, sc in last 2 sts, join, **turn.**

Rnd 8: Ch 1, sc in first 2 sts, (ch 1, skip next st, sc in next ch sp) 8 times, ch 1, skip next st, sc in each st around, join, **turn.**

Rnd 9: Ch 1, sc in first 21 sts, work Berry Pattern B across to last 2 sts, sc in last 2 sts, join, **turn.**

Rnd 10: Ch 1, sc in first 2 sts, (ch 1, skip next st, sc in next ch sp) 8 times, ch 1, skip next st, 2 sc in marked st, move marker to **first** sc of 2-sc just made, sc in next st, 2 sc in next marked st, move marker to **last** sc of 2-sc just made, sc in last 18 sts, join, **turn.** *(42)*

Rnds 11–12: Repeat rnds 7 and 8.

Rnd 13: Removing markers as you go, ch 1, sc in first 12 sts; for **thumb opening,** ch 3 loosely, skip next 9 sts, sc in next 2 sts; work Berry Pattern B, sc in last 2 sts, join, **turn.** *(36)*

Rnd 14: Ch 1, sc in first 2 sts, ch 1, skip next st, (sc in next ch sp, ch 1, skip next st) 8 times, sc in last 17 sts and chs, join, **turn.**

Rnd 15: Ch 1, sc in first 17 sts, work Berry Pattern A, sc in last 2 sts, join, **turn.**

Rnd 16: Ch 1, sc in first 2 sts, ch 1, skip next st, (sc in next ch sp, ch 1, skip next st) 8 times, sc in last 17 sts, join, **turn.**

Rnd 17: Ch 1, sc in first 17 sts, work Berry Pattern B, sc in last 2 sts, join, **turn.**

Rnd 18: Ch 1, sc in first 2 sts, ch 1, skip next st, (sc in next ch sp, ch 1, skip next st) 8 times, sc in last 17 sts, join, **turn.**

Rnds 19–27: Repeat rnds 15–18 consecutively, ending with rnd 15.

Rnd 28: Ch 1, sc first 2 sts tog, (ch 1, skip next st, sc in next ch sp) 8 times, skip next st, sc in last 17 sts, join, **turn.** *(34)*

Rnd 29: Ch 1, sc in first 18 sts, berry, (ch 1, skip next st, sc in next ch-sp, ch 1, skip next st, berry) 3 times, sc in last 3 ch sps and sts, join, **turn.**

Rnds 30–32: Work same as rows 30–32 of Right Mitten.

Flatten rnd 32 at decreases; sew together.

Thumb

Rnd 1: With larger hook, with wrong side of sts on thumb opening facing, working on opposite side of ch-3, join with sc in **first** ch of ch-3, sc in next 2 chs, sc in last worked st on rnd 12 before skipped sts, sc in next 9 sts, sc in next st beside st already worked, join, **turn.** *(14 sc made)*

Rnds 2–11: Ch 1, sc in each st around, join, **turn.** At end of last rnd, leaving 6" end, fasten off.

With tapestry needle, weave 6" end through outside loop of each st on rnd 11, pull tight, secure. ●

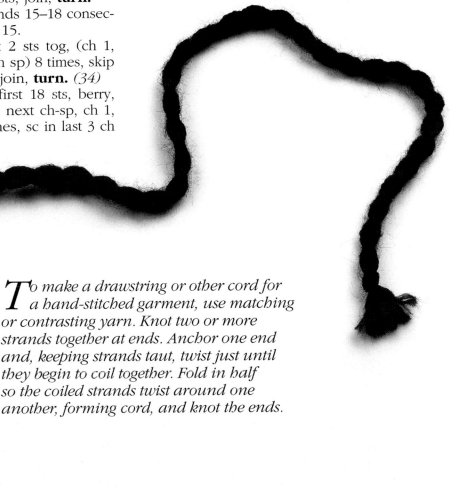

*T*o make a drawstring or other cord for a hand-stitched garment, use matching or contrasting yarn. Knot two or more strands together at ends. Anchor one end and, keeping strands taut, twist just until they begin to coil together. Fold in half so the coiled strands twist around one another, forming cord, and knot the ends.

Beaded Rib Stitch Pattern

*K*nitted bead stitch is a variation of ribbing with bobbles added for texture that resemble beads sewn into the ribs.

To duplicate the look in crochet, we've used half-double crochet stitches worked in front posts to represent the knit stitches and single crochet stitches to represent the purl stitches; the bead stitches are formed over two rows, working five single crochet stitches into the same stitch on the first row, and drawing the tops of the five stitches together on the next row to complete the bead.

KNIT

CROCHET

Afghan Square: Beaded Rib

READ BEFORE STARTING

Refer to **Chapter 2** for instructions for using Squares to make either Knit or Crochet Version of Large Afghan or Baby Afghan.

For comparison, each Square has instructions for **Knit Version** in blue type, and instructions for **Crochet Version** in black type.

KNIT VERSION

With large needles and color B, cast on 28.

Row 1: *(Right side)* P 1, K 1, P 1, (K 2, P 1, K 1, P 1) across.

Row 2: K 1, P 1, K 1, (P 2, K 1, P 1, K 1) across.

CROCHET VERSION

Row 1: With medium hook and color B, ch 29, sc in second ch from hook, sc in each ch across, turn. *(28 sc made)*

Row 2: Ch 1, sc in each st across, turn.

Row 3: *(Right side)* Ch 1, sc in first st; for

Row 3: P 1; for **bead st,** (K 1, P 1, K 1, P 1) all in next st, (counting from tip of right needle, pass second st over first st and off needle) 3 times; push to front of work *(bead st completed),* P 1, (K 2, P 1, bead st, P 1) across.

Row 4: K 1, P 1, K 1, (P 2, K 1, P 1, K 1) across.

Next rows: Repeat rows 1–4 consecutively until piece measures same as gauge, ending last repeat with row 1.

Bind off.

Work Edging in Basic Finishing on page 28.

bead base, 5 sc in next st *(bead base completed);* *(**hdcfp**—*see Special Stitch on page 24*— around st on row before last directly below next st) 3 times, sc in next st, bead base; repeat from * across with sc in last st, turn.

NOTES: *Work **all sc sts** into sts of **last row.***

*To **close bead,** skipping center 3 sc of bead base, sc first sc and last sc of bead base together; push skipped sts to right side of work.*

Row 4: Ch 1, sc in first st, **close bead** *(see Notes),* (sc in next 4 sts, close bead) across with sc in last st, turn.

Row 5: Ch 1, sc in first 2 sc, (hdcfp around each of next 3 fp, sc in next 2 sc) across with sc in last sc, turn.

Rows 6–33: Repeat rows 2–5 consecutively. At end of last row, fasten off.

Piece should measure same as gauge.

Work Edging in Basic Finishing on page 28.

*S*tore each center-pull ball of yarn in its own zip-top bag. Place the ball in, with the strand through the opening, and zip the top shut, leaving a small hole for the working strand. This keeps the ball together as yarn is used.

Santa Hat
Designed by Darla Sims

Spread some holiday cheer with this textured hat.

FINISHED SIZES: Small fits snugly around 18" head; Large fits snugly around 20" head.

MATERIALS: Wool-Ease® Art. 620 by Lion Brand® Yarn Company or worsted yarn: 3 oz. Ranch Red #102, 2 oz. White #100; crochet stitch marker; 3" square of cardboard; tapestry needle; G and H crochet hooks (*or hooks needed to obtain gauges*).

GAUGES: G hook; 12 sts in cuff pattern = 4"; 16 rows in cuff pattern = 4".
H hook; 12 hdc = 4"; 10 hdc rows = 4".

NOTE

Instructions are for small; changes for large are in [ ].

HAT

Rnd 1: With H hook and red, loosely chain 55 [65], join with sl st in first ch to form ring, ch 1, hdc in first ch, mark hdc just made, hdc in each ch around. *(55 [65] sts made)*

*NOTES: Work in continuous rnds, **do not join or turn** unless otherwise stated.*

When working into marked st, remove marker, work st, mark st just made.

Rnd 2: Hdc in each st around.

Next rnds: Repeat rnd 2 until piece measures 3½" from beginning.

Decrease rnd 1: Disregarding ends of rnds, (hdc in next 18 sts, hdc next 2 sts tog) around until piece measures about 6" [6½"] from beginning and 37 [41] sts remain.

Decrease rnd 2: (Hdc in next 15 sts, hdc next 2 sts tog) around until there are 32 [36] sts remaining.

Next rnds: Hdc in each st around until piece measures 16" [17"] from beginning.

Decrease rnd 3: (Hdc in next 4 sts, hdc next 2 sts tog) around until there are 6 sts remaining. At end of last rnd, sc in next st; leave an 8" end, fasten off.

Thread end into tapestry needle, weave through top of each st around, pull tight, secure.

Cuff

Rnd 1: With right side of sts on Hat facing, working on opposite side of starting ch, with G hook, join white with sc in first ch, sc in each ch around, join with sl st in first sc, **turn.** *(55 [65] sc made)*

Rnd 2: Ch 1, sc in each st around, join, **turn.**

*NOTES: Work each **hdc front post** (**hdcfp,** see Crochet Stitch Guide on page 191) around designated st on rnd before last, pull up to height of rnd being worked. Always **skip one st** on last rnd behind each hdcfp.*

*For **bead base,** work 5 sc in next st.*

*To **close bead,** skipping center 3 sc of bead base, sc first sc and last sc of bead base together; push skipped sts to right side of work.*

Rnd 3: *(Right side)* Ch 1; beginning in first st, ***bead base** (see Notes); (**hdcfp**—see Notes—around st on rnd before last directly below next st) 3 times, sc in next st on last rnd; repeat from * around, join, **turn.**

Rnd 4: Ch 1, (sc in next 4 sts, **close bead**—see Notes) around, join, **turn.**

Rnd 5: Ch 1, sc in first st, hdcfp around each of next 3 fp on row before last, (sc in next 2 sts, hdcfp around each of next 3 fp on row before last) around with sc in last st, join, **turn.**

Rnds 6–13: Repeat rnds 2–5 consecutively. At end of last row, fasten off.

Pompom

Wrap white yarn 75 times around 3" cardboard. Run separate 8" strand white through center of loops along one side of cardboard; pull very tight and tie securely. Cut loops along other side and remove cardboard. Trim loops into a round ball.

Using ends of 8" strand, tie Pompom to tip of Hat. ●

Beaded Rib Socks

Designed by Donna Jones

Stitch up a soft pair of socks with the Beaded Rib stitch pattern.

FINISHED SIZES: Make to desired foot length; fits 7¼", 8", or 8¾" around foot at arch.

MATERIALS: 7½ oz. desired color Microspun Art. 910 by Lion Brand® Yarn Company or sport yarn—*Mango #186 is shown;* bobby pins for markers; tapestry needle; F and G crochet hooks *(or hooks needed to obtain gauges).*

GAUGES: F hook, 20 sc = 4"; 24 sc **back lp** rows = 4". **G hook,** 16 sc or Cuff pattern sts = 4"; 16 Cuff pattern rows = 3"; 16 sc rows = 4".

NOTE
Instructions are for 7¼" **arch (small);** changes for **8" arch (medium)** and 8¾" **arch (large)** are in [ ].

SOCK (make 2)
Ribbing
Row 1: With F hook, leaving a 6" end for sewing, ch 8, sc in second ch from hook, sc in each ch across, turn. *(7 sc made)*

Rows 2–36 [2–40, 2–44]: Working these rows in **back lps** *(see Crochet Stitch Guide on page 191),* ch 1, sc in each st across, turn.

At end of last row, ch 1, pull up long loop and remove loop hook; **do not fasten off.**

Lap edge of last row over starting ch on first row; using tapestry needle with 6" end, sew together to form rib.

Cuff
Rnd 1: Place long loop on G hook; working in ends of ribbing rows; for **small size only,** sc first 2 rows tog; for **large size only,** 2 sc in first row; for **all sizes,** sc in each row around, join with sl st in first sc, **turn.** *(35 [40, 45] sts made)*

Rnd 2: Ch 1, sc in each st around, join, **turn.**

NOTES: For **hdcfp** *(see Crochet Stitch Guide);* pull each hdcfp up to height of rnd being worked.

After rnd 3, work all fp sts around fp sts on rnd before last.

For **bead base,** work 5 sc in next st.

To **close bead,** skipping center 3 sc of bead base, sc first sc and last sc of bead base together; push skipped sts to right side of work.

Rnd 3: *(Right side)* Ch 1; beginning in first st, *bead base *(see Notes);* (hdcfp—see Notes—around st on rnd before last directly below next st) 3 times, sc in next st on last rnd; repeat from * around, join, **turn.**

Rnd 4: Ch 1, (sc in next 4 sts, **close bead**—*see Notes)* around, join, **turn.**

Rnd 5: Ch 1, sc in first st, hdcfp around each of next 3 fp on rnd before last, (sc in next 2 sts, hdcfp around each of next 3 fp on rnd before last) around with sc in last st, join, **turn.**

Rnds 6–17: Repeat rnds 2–5 consecutively.

Foot and Heel
Rnd 1: Ch 1; for **small size only,** 2 sc in first st; for **large size only,** sc first 2 sts tog; for **all sizes,** sc in each st around, join with sl st in first sc, **turn.** *(36 [40, 44] sts made)*

Rnds 2–8: Ch 1, sc in each st around, join, **turn.**

Rnd 9: Ch 1, (sc in next 17 [19, 21] sts, 2 sc in next st) 2 times, join, **turn.** *(38 [42, 46] sts)*

Rnd 10: Ch 1, (2 sc in next st, sc in next 18 [20, 22] sts) 2 times, join, **turn.** *(40 [44, 48] sts)*

Row 11: Working short rows to shape **heel,** ch 1, sc in first st, **mark** st just made, sc in next 20 [22, 24] sts leaving last 19 [21, 23] sts unworked, turn. *(21 [23, 25] sts)*

Row 12: Ch 1, skip first st, sc in next st, **mark** sc just made, sc in next 18 [20, 22] sts leaving last sc unworked, turn. *(19 [21, 23] sts)*

Rows 13–20: Ch 1, skip first st, sc in next st, **mark** sc just made *(leave all markers in place until row 21),* sc in each st across to last sc leaving last sc unworked, turn. At end of last row *(3 [5, 7] sc).*

Row 21: Removing marker as each st is worked, sl st in marked st below, 2 sc in first sc, sc in each st across to next marked st, 2 sc in marked st, sl st in next marked st, turn. *(Sl sts are not used or counted as sts—5 [7, 9] sc)*

Rows 22–28: Ch 1, 2 sc in first sc, sc in each st across with 2 sc in last sc, sl st in next marked st, turn. At end of last row *(19 [21, 23] sc).*

Rnd 29: Skipping sl sts, ch 1, sc in each sc across, sc in end of next row; working in unworked sts of rnd 10, sc in each st around, sc first st on row 11 and end of next row tog, join, **turn.** *(40 [44, 48] sc)*

Rnd 30: Ch 1, sc in each st around, join, **turn.**

Next rnds: Repeat rnd 30 until piece measures 6" [7", 8"], or 1½" [1¾", 2"] less than desired foot length from heel to toe. At end of last rnd, **do not fasten off.**

Toe

Rnd 1: Ch 1, sc in same st as sl st; *for **dec, sc next 2 sts tog;** sc in next 15 [17,19] sts, dec*, sc in next st; repeat between **, join, turn. *(36 [40, 44] sc made)*

Rnds 2–6 [2–7, 2–8]: Ch 1, sc in same st as sl st; (dec, sc in each st around to one st before next dec, dec), sc in next st; repeat between ( ), join, **turn.** At end of last rnd *(16).* Fasten off.

Fold Toe flat with decs at sides; matching sts, sew opening closed. ●

History of Socks

*T*he first knit socks were discovered in Egyptian tombs of the 36th century. As early as the 13th century, hand-knitted socks began replacing the woven, cut and sewn stockings throughout the Middle East and Europe. These were a luxury at first, worn only by the aristocracy. By the 16th century hand-knitted socks of wool were being worn by the masses.

European fashion during the 16th and 17th centuries was influenced by Spain. Men's socks were made of knitted silk with emblems of clocks embroidered on them.

As the American colonies were beginning to form, many colonists smuggled hosiery knitting machines out of England to the New World. This created an industry. Often, socks were used as offerings in bartering transactions.

In more modern times, the Red Cross often sent out requests for clothing to send to the armed forces during times of war. Many hand-knitted socks were made for just that purpose.

Socks have always been an important part of an individual's wardrobe. Over the years the knit versions have been converted into crochet versions. Whether choosing needles or a hook, there's no excuse for cold feet.

Chapter Six

Cables, Eyelets, Crossed and Twisted Stitches

*W*hat crocheter doesn't dream of making cables and twisted stitches as soft and lovely as knitted ones? With the tricks and tips in this chapter, you can do just that. Practice your newfound skills with the wonderful designs.

Cables, Eyelets, Crossed and Twisted Stitches

Knitted **cables and cross stitches** can be worked over any number of stitches from two up to six or eight. Any more than eight are not normally used, as larger numbers of stitches become distorted and are difficult to cross on the needles. Cables and cross stitches are knitted by slipping the first half of the stitches onto a cable needle, knitting the second half, then knitting the stitches from the cable needle.

For a crochet counterpart to these stitches, crochet cross stitches worked around the posts of stitches on a previous row are usually chosen. These can be worked with long single crochet post stitches pulled up to the height of the row being worked, as well as half-double, double or treble crochet post stitches, which work equally well, depending on the look desired.

Twisted knit stitches are formed by working the stitch through the back loop rather than the normally used front loop, causing the stitch to twist. Crochet front post stitches have a natural twist which closely resembles a twisted knit stitch.

Simply stated, **eyelets** are merely holes worked into the fabric to produce an open, lacy design.

Knitted **eyelets** are formed by working a yarn-over and a companion decrease to maintain the same stitch count, or omit the decrease if you wish to add a new stitch.

To duplicate this look in crochet, make a chain-1 or chain-2 space and skip a companion stitch on the previous row directly below the chain space.

Cables

KNIT

CROCHET

crossed stitches

Eyelet Cable

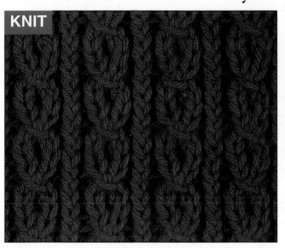

Crossed Stitches

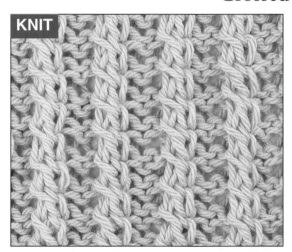

Twisted Stitches

twisted and non-twisted knit stitches

front post stitches

Boxed Cables
Stitch Pattern

*K*nitted four-stitch cables worked over 12 rows on a reverse stockinette stitch background produce a short cable pattern; stagger the design on the next 12 rows to produce a boxed effect.

To achieve the same look in crochet, work a single crochet background and use four-stitch double crochet front post cross stitches for the cable pattern.

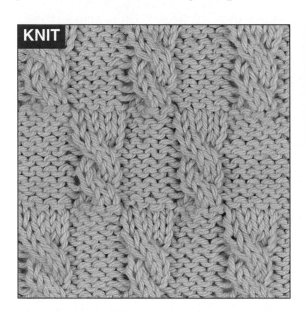

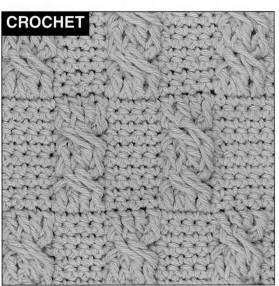

Afghan Square: Boxed Cables

READ BEFORE STARTING

Refer to **Chapter 2** for instructions for using Squares to make either Knit or Crochet Version of Large Afghan or Baby Afghan.

For comparison, each Square has instructions for **Knit Version** in blue type, and instructions for **Crochet Version** in black type.

KNIT VERSION

With large needles and color B, cast on 28.

Row 1: *(Right side)* P 4, (K 4, P 4) 3 times.

Row 2: K each K st and P each P st.

Row 3: *P 4; to **cross cable,** slip next 2 sts onto cable needle and hold at front of

CROCHET VERSION

Row 1: With small hook and color B, ch 29, sc in second ch from hook, sc in each ch across, turn. *(28 sts made)*

Row 2: Ch 1, sc in each st across, turn. ***NOTE:** Work **all sc sts** into sts of **last row.***

Row 3: Ch 1, sc in first 4 sc *(see Note)*, **dcfp** *(see Special Stitch on page 24)* around work, K 2, K 2 from cable needle *(cross cable completed);* (P 4, cross cable) 2 times, P 4.

Rows 4–6: K each K st and P each P st.

Row 7: P 4, (cross cable, P 4) 3 times.

Rows 8–10: K each K st and P each P st.

Row 11: P 8, K 4, P 4, K 4, P 8.

Row 12: K each K st and P each P st.

Row 13: P 8, cross cable, P 4, cross cable, P 8.

Rows 14–16: K each K st and P each P st.

Row 17: P 8, cross cable, P 4, cross cable, P 8.

Rows 18–20: K each K st and P each P st.

Rows 21–30: Repeat rows 1–10.

Bind off.

Piece should measure same as gauge.

Work Edging in Basic Finishing on page 28.

next st on row before last directly below next st, dcfp around each of next 3 sts on row before last, (sc in next 4 sc, dcfp around st on row before last directly below next st, dcfp around each of next 3 sts on row before last) 2 times, sc in last 4 sc, turn.

Row 4: Ch 1, sc in each st across, turn.

Row 5: Ch 1, sc in first 4 sc; to **cross cable,** skip next 2 fp sts on row before last, dcfp around each of next 2 sts; working in front of last 2 fp, dcfp around each of 2 skipped sts *(cross cable completed),* (sc in next 4 sc, cross cable) 2 times, sc in last 4 sc, turn.

Row 6: Ch 1, sc in each st across, turn.

Row 7: Ch 1, sc in first 4 sc, (dcfp around each of next 4 fp, sc in next 4 sc) across, turn.

Row 8: Ch 1, sc in each st across, turn.

Rows 9–12: Repeat rows 5–8.

Row 13: Ch 1, sc in first 8 sc, (dcfp around next st on row before last directly below next st, dcfp around each of next 3 sts, sc in next 4 sc) 2 times, sc in last 4 sc, turn.

Row 14: Ch 1, sc in each st across, turn.

Row 15: Ch 1, sc in first 8 sc, (cross cable, sc in ncxt 4 sc) 2 times, sc in last 4 sc, turn.

Row 16: Ch 1, sc in each st across, turn.

Row 17: Ch 1, sc in first 8 sc, (dcfp around each of next 4 fp, sc in next 4 sc), 2 times, sc in last 4 sc, turn.

Row 18: Ch 1, sc in each st across, turn.

Rows 19–22: Repeat rows 15–18.

Rows 23–31: Repeat rows 3–11. At end of last row, fasten off.

Piece should measure same as gauge.

Work Edging in Basic Finishing on page 28.

Hat and Clutch Purse

Designed by Darla Sims

Create an interesting hat and matching clutch purse with Boxed Cables.

FINISHED SIZES: Clutch Purse is 5½" high x 8½" wide; Hat fits up to 23" head circumference.

MATERIALS: 3 oz. Caramel #124 Wool-Ease® Art. 620 by Lion Brand® Yarn Company or worsted yarn; 1¾" wooden toggle button; cord elastic; tapestry needle; G and H crochet hooks *(or hook needed to obtain H hook gauge).*

GAUGE: H hook, 14 sc = 4"; 14 rows in pattern = 3".

PURSE

Row 1: With H hook, loosely ch 35, sc in second ch from hook, sc in each ch across, turn. *(34 sc made)*

Row 2: Ch 1, sc in each st across, turn.

NOTE: Work all sc sts into sts of last row.

Row 3: *(Right side)* Ch 1, sc in first 3 sc *(see Note),* **(dcfp**—*see Special Stitch on page 24*—around st on row before last directly below next st) 4 times, *sc in next 4 sc, (dcfp around st on row before last directly below next st) 4 times; repeat from * 2 more times, sc in last 3 sc, turn.

Row 4: Ch 1, sc in each st across, turn.

Row 5: Ch 1, sc in first 3 sc, skip next 2 fp sts, dcfp around each of next 2 fp; working in front of last 2 fp made, dcfp around each of 2 skipped fp, (sc in next 4 sc, skip next 2 fp sts, dcfp around each of next 2 fp; working in front of last 2 fp made, dcfp around each of 2 skipped fp) 3 times, sc in last 3 sc, turn.

Row 6: Ch 1, sc in each st across, turn.

Row 7: Ch 1, sc in first 3 sc, dcfp around each of next 4 fp, (sc in next 4 sc, dcfp around each of next 4 fp) 3 times, sc in last 3 sc, turn.

Row 8: Ch 1, sc in each st across, turn.

Row 9: Ch 1, sc in first 7 sc, (dcfp around st on row before last directly below next st) 4 times, *sc in next 4 sc, (dcfp around st on row before last directly below next st) 2 times; repeat from *, sc in last 7 sc, turn.

Row 10: Ch 1, sc in each st across, turn.

Row 11: Ch 1, sc in first 7 sc, skip next 2 fp sts, dcfp around each of next 2 fp, dcfp around each of 2 skipped fp, (sc in next 4 sc, skip next 2 fp sts, dcfp around each of next 2 fp; working in front of last 2 fp made, dcfp around each of 2 skipped fp) 2 times, sc in last 7 sc, turn.

Row 12: Ch 1, sc in each st across, turn.

Row 13: Ch 1, sc in first 7 sc, dcfp around each of next 4 fp, (sc in next 4 sc, dcfp around each of next 4 fp) 2 times, sc in last 7 sc, turn.

Rows 14–61: Repeat rows 2–13 consecutively. At end of last row, **do not turn.**

Rnd 62: With G hook, working around outer edge, ch 1, sc in end of each row across; working on opposite side of ch, 3 sc in first ch, sc in next 16 chs; for **button loop,** ch 6 *(or length needed to fit over toggle button);* sc in next 16 chs, 3 sc in last ch, sc in end of each row across, 3 sc in first st on row 61, sc in each st across with 3 sc in last st, join with sl st in first sc. Fasten off.

Purse Assembly

With right side out, fold Purse on row 41.

On each end, match row 61 to row 21; sew ends of rows together using tapestry needle and yarn. Fold remaining rows over top for flap.

Sew toggle button to center of front to match button loop *(see photo).*

HAT

Rnd 1: Beginning at center, with H hook, ch 4, sl st in first ch to form ring, ch 4, 4 tr in ring, (ch 2, 5 tr in ring) 5 times, ch 2, join with sl st in top of ch-4. *(30 tr, 6 ch-2 sps made)*

Rnd 2: For **petals,** ch 3, tr next 4 tr tog, ch 10, (tr next 5 tr tog, ch 10) 5 times, skip ch-3, join with sl st in first tr-4-tog. *(6 petals, 6 ch-10 sps)*

Rnd 3: (Sl st, ch 3, 9 dc) in first ch-10 sp, 10 dc in each ch-10 sp around, join with sl st in top of ch-3. *(60 dc)*

Rnd 4: Ch 1, sc in first 2 sts, 2 sc in next st, (sc in next 2 sts, 2 sc in next st) around, join with sl st in first sc, **turn.** *(80)*

Rnd 5: Ch 1, sc in each st around, join, **turn.**

Rnd 6: *(Right side)* Ch 1, sc in first 4 sc, (dcfp around sc on row before last directly below next st) 4 times, *sc in next 4 sc, (dcfp around sc on row before last directly below next st) 4 times; repeat from * 8 more times, join, **turn.**

Rnd 7: Ch 1, sc in each st around, join, **turn.**

Rnd 8: Ch 1, sc in first 4 sc, skip next 2 fp sts, dcfp around each of next 2 fp; working in front of last 2 fp, dcfp around each of 2 skipped fp, (sc in next 4 sc, skip next 2 fp sts, dcfp around each of next 2 fp; working in front of last 2 fp, dcfp around each of 2 skipped fp) 9 times, join, **turn.**

*Top of Hat
shown*

Rnd 9: Ch 1, sc in each st around, join, **turn.**

Rnd 10: Ch 1, sc in first 4 sc, dcfp around each of next 4 fp, (sc in next 4 sc, dcfp around each of next 4 fp) 9 times, join, **turn.**

Rnd 11: Ch 1, sc in each st around, join, **turn.**

Rnd 12: Ch 1, dcfp around st on row before last directly below first st, (dcfp around st on row before last directly below next st) 3 times, sc in next 4 sc, *(dcfp around st on row before last directly below next st) 4 times, sc in next 4 sc; repeat from * 8 more times, join, **turn.**

Rnd 13: Ch 1, sc in each st around, join, **turn.**

Rnd 14: Ch 1, skip first 2 fp, dcfp around each of next 2 fp; working in front of last fp, dc fp around each of 2 skipped fp, sc in next 4 sc, (skip next 2 fp sts, dcfp around each of next 2 fp; working in front of last fp, dcfp around each of 2 skipped fp, sc in next 4 sc) 9 times, join with sl st in first fp, **turn.**

Rnd 15: Ch 1, sc in each st around, join, **turn.**

Rnd 16: Ch 1, dcfp around each of first 4 fp, sc in next 4 sc, (dcfp around each of next 4 fp, sc in next 4 sc) 9 times, join, **turn.**

Rnds 17–23: Repeat rnds 5–11. At end of last rnd, **do not turn.**

Rnd 24: Ch 1, **reverse sc** *(see Crochet Stitch Guide on page 191)* in each st around, join with sl st in first st. Fasten off.

Hiding elastic so it does not show on outside, use tapestry needle to weave cord elastic through rnd 24, pull snug as needed to fit around head, secure.

Bow

Row 1: With H hook, ch 40, sc in second ch from hook, sc in each ch across, turn. *(39 made)*

Rows 2–5: Ch 1, sc in each st across, turn. At end of last row, fasten off.

Sew ends of rows together to form ring. Flatten ring with ends of rows at center back.

For **knot,** tightly wrap yarn several times around center of ring; secure.

Sew knot of Bow to lower edge of Hat *(see photo).* ●

Alternating Cables Stitch Pattern

*A*lternating columns of knitted cables on a reversed stockinette stitch background are used for this stitch pattern. The cable columns are comprised of three consecutive crossings followed by six straight rows of raised knit stitches.

To achieve the same look in crochet, work a single crochet background and use half-double crochet front post stitches for the cable columns with cross stitches for each crossing of the cable.

KNIT

CROCHET

Afghan Square: Alternating Cables

READ BEFORE STARTING

Refer to **Chapter 2** for instructions for using Squares to make either Knit or Crochet Version of Large Afghan or Baby Afghan.

For comparison, each Square has instructions for **Knit Version** in blue type, and instructions for **Crochet Version** in black type.

KNIT VERSION

With large needles and white, cast on 28.

Row 1: (Wrong side) K 4, (P 4, K 4) across.

Row 2: P 4; to **cross cable,** slip next 2 sts to cable needle and hold at front of work, K 2, K 2 from cable needle (cross

CROCHET VERSION

Row 1: With small hook and white, ch 29, sc in second ch from hook, sc in each ch across, turn. (28 sts made)

Row 2: Ch 1, sc in each st across, turn.

NOTE: To **cross cable,** skip 2 sts on row before last directly below next 2 sts, **hdcfp** (see cable completed), P 4, K 4, P 4, cross cable, P 4.

Rows 3–6: Repeat rows 1 and 2 alternately.

Row 7: K 4, (P 4, K 4) across.

Row 8: P 4, K 4, P 4, cross cable, P 4, K 4, P 4.

Rows 9–12: Repeat rows 7 and 8 alternately.

Row 13: K 4, (P 4, K 4) across.

Row 14: P 4, cross cable, P 4, K 4, P 4, cross cable, P 4.

Rows 15–18: Repeat rows 13 and 14 alternately.

Rows 19–30: Repeat rows 7–18.
Bind off.
Piece should measure same as gauge.
Work Edging in Basic Finishing on page 28.

Special Stitch on page 24) around each of next 2 sts on row before last; working in front of last fp made, hdcfp around each of 2 skipped sts.

Row 3: Ch 1, sc in first 5 sc, **cross cable** (*see Note*), sc in next 3 sc, hdcfp around next 4 sts on row before last, sc in next 3 sc, cross cable, sc in last 5 sc, turn.

Row 4: Ch 1, sc in each st across, turn.

Row 5: Ch 1, sc in first 5 sc, cross cable, sc in next 3 sc, hdcfp around each of next 4 fp, sc in next 3 sc, cross cable, sc in next 5 sc, turn.

Rows 6–7: Repeat rows 4–5.

Row 8: Ch 1, sc in each st across, turn.

Row 9: Ch 1, sc in first 5 sc, hdcfp around each of next 4 fp, sc in next 3 sc, cross cable, sc in next 3 sc, hdcfp around each of next 4 fp, sc in next 5 sc, turn.

Rows 10–13: Repeat rows 8–9 alternately.

Rows 14–31: Repeat rows 2–13 consecutively, ending with row 7. At end of last row, fasten off.

Piece should measure same as gauge.
Work Edging in Basic Finishing on page 28.

Dog Coat

Designed by Donna Jones

Reward your pampered pooch with a warm and perky coat made with Alternating Cables.

FINISHED SIZES: Small fits dog with up to 14" chest. **Medium** fits 14"–16" chest. **Large** fits 16"–18" chest.

MATERIALS: 6 oz. Butterscotch #189 Wool-Ease® Art. 620 by Lion Brand® Yarn Company or worsted yarn; 6" of ½"-wide Velcro® strip; crochet stitch markers; sewing thread and needle; G crochet hook *(or hook needed to obtain gauge)*.

GAUGE: 4 sc = 1"; 4 rows = 1".

NOTE
Instructions are for **small;** changes for **medium** and **large** are in [ ].

COAT
Row 1: For **body,** beginning at tail, ch 29 [41, 53], 2 sc in second ch from hook, sc in each ch across with 2 sc in last ch, turn. (*30 [42, 54] sts made*)

Row 2: Ch 1, 2 sc in first st, sc in each st across with 2 sc in last st, turn. (*32) [44, 56]*

Row 3: Ch 1, sc in first 2 sts, skip 2 sts on row before last directly below next 2 sts, **hdc front post (hdcfp,** *see Special Stitch on page 24)* around each of next 2 sts; working in front of last 2 fp made, hdcfp around each of 2 skipped sts, (sc in next 2 sts on last row, hdcfp around each of next 4 sts on row before last directly below next 4 sts, sc in next 2 sts on last row, skip 2 sts on row before last directly below next 2 sts, hdcfp around each of next 2 sts; working in front of last 2 fp made, hdcfp around each of 2 skipped sts) 2 [3, 4] times, sc in last 2 sts on last row, turn.

Row 4: Ch 1, sc in each st across, turn.

NOTES: *To* **cross cable,** *skip next 2 fp on row before last, hdcfp around each of next*

2 fp; working in front of last 2 fp made, hdcfp around each of 2 skipped fp.

Work **all sc sts** into sts of **last** row.

Row 5: Ch 1, sc in first 2 sc (see Notes); **cross cable** (see Notes), sc in next 2 sc; (hdcfp around each of next 4 fp, sc in next 2 sc, cross cable, sc in next 2 sc) 2 [3, 4] times, turn.

Rows 6–8: Repeat rows 4, 5, 4.

Row 9: Ch 1, sc in first 2 sc, hdcfp around each of next 4 fp, sc in next 2 sc, (cross cable, sc in next 2 sc, hdcfp around each of next 4 fp, sc in next 2 sc) 2 [3, 4] times, turn.

Row 10: Ch 1, sc in each st across, turn.

Rows 11–14: Repeat rows 9 and 10 alternately.

To **work in pattern,** work rows 3–14 consecutively (see "How to Work in Pattern", Chapter 1, page 16).

Rows [15–18, 15–22]: For **medium and large sizes only,** work in pattern.

NOTE: Mark first st and last st on last row made; when working into marked st on following rows, remove marker, work st, replace marker in st just made.

Row 15 [19, 23]: For **all sizes,** for **chest bands,** ch 3, sc in second ch from hook, sc in next ch, work next row of pattern across with 2 sc in last marked st, move marker to next-to-last st just made, turn. (35) [47, 59]

Rows 16–18 [20–22, 24–26]: Ch 3, sc in second ch from hook, sc in next ch, sc in each st across to marker, work next row of pattern across body to next marker, sc in each st across chest band with 2 sc in last st, turn. At end of last row (44 [56, 68] sts).

Rows 19–20 [23–24, 27–28]: Ch 13, sc in second ch from hook, sc in next 11 chs, sc in each st across to marker, work next row of pattern across body to next marker, sc in each st across chest band, turn. At end of last row (68 [80, 92] sc).

Rows 21–31 [25–39, 29–47]: Ch 1, sc in each st across to marker, work next row of pattern across body to next marker, sc in each st across, turn. At end of last row, fasten off.

Row 32 [40, 48]: Skip first 14 sts, join with sl st in next st, sc in next 3 sts ending at marker, work next row of pattern across

body to next marker, sc in next 2 sts, sc next 2 sts tog leaving last 14 sts unworked, turn. (sl sts are not counted as st—38 [50, 62] sc)

Row 33 [41, 49]: Ch 1, skip first st, sc in next 2 sts, work next row of pattern across body to next marker, sc in next st, sc last 2 sts tog, turn. (36) [48, 60]

Row 34 [42, 50]: Ch 1, skip first st, sc in next st, work next row of pattern across body to next marker, sc last 2 sts tog, turn. Remove markers. (34) [46, 58]

Row 35 [43, 51]: Ch 1, skip first st, work next row of pattern across next 32 [44, 56] sts, sc last 2 sts tog, turn. (32) [44, 56]

Row 36 [44, 52]: Ch 1, work next row of pattern across, turn.

Piece should measure about 9" [11", 13"].

Next rows: If needed, repeat row 36 [44, 52] to desired back length from base of tail to base of neck. At end of last row, **do not fasten off.**

Neck Shaping

Row 1: Ch 1, 2 sc in first st, sc in next 10 [13, 16] sts, (2 sc in next st, sc in next 2 [4, 6] sts) 4 times, sc in next 8 [9, 10] sts, 2 sc in last st, turn. (38 [50, 62] sts made)

Rows 2–4: Ch 1, 2 sc in first st, sc in each st across with 2 sc in last st, turn. At end of last row (42 [54, 66] sc).

Row 5: For **first shoulder band,** ch 1, 2 sc in first st, sc in next 12 [14, 16] sts, sc next 2 sts tog leaving last 27 [37, 47] sts unworked, turn. (15) [17, 19]

Row 6: Ch 1, skip first st, sc in each st across with 2 sc in last st, turn.

Row 7: Ch 1, 2 sc in first st, sc in each st across to last 2 sc, sc last 2 sts tog, turn.

Row 8: Ch 1, skip first st, sc in each st across, turn. (14) [16, 18]

Row 9: Ch 1, sc in each st across to last 2 sts, sc last 2 sts tog, turn. (13) [15, 17]

Rows 10–14: Repeat rows 7 and 8 alternately, ending with row 7. At end of last row (8 [10, 12] sts).

Row 15: Ch 1, sc in each st across, turn.

Rows 16–25 [16–27, 16–29] or to desired length: Repeat row 15 until first shoulder band reaches just to center front at base of neck when Coat is placed on dog.

Last 2 Rows: Ch 1, skip first st, sc in

each st across to last 2 sts, sc last 2 sts tog, turn. At end of last row, fasten off.

Row 5: For **second shoulder band,** skip next 12 [20, 28] sts on row 4, join with sl st in next st, ch 1, sc in next 13 [15, 17] sts, 2 sc in last st, turn. *(15 [17, 19] sc)*

Row 6: Ch 1, 2 sc in first st, sc in each st across to last 2 st, sc last 2 sts tog leaving ch-1 unworked, turn.

Row 7: Ch 1, skip first st, sc in each st across with 2 sc in last st, turn.

Row 8: Ch 1, sc in each st across to last 2 sts, sc last 2 sts tog, turn. *(14) [16, 18]*

Row 9: Ch 1, skip first st, sc in each st across, turn. *(13) [15, 17]*

Rows 10–14: Repeat rows 7 and 8 alternately, ending with row 7. At end of last row *(8 [10, 12] sts).*

Row 15: Ch 1, sc in each st across, turn.

Rows 16–25 [16–27, 16–29] or to desired length: Repeat row 15 until first shoulder band reaches just to center front at base of neck when Coat is placed on dog.

Last 2 Rows: Ch 1, skip first st, sc in each st across to last 2 sts, sc last 2 sts tog, turn. At end of last row, **do not fasten off.**

Edging

With right side of Coat facing, ch 1, sc in each st and in end of each row around with 3 sc in each outer corner and with 2 sc in same place along outer curves or sc 2 sts tog on inner curves as needed for edge to lay flat, join with sl st in first sc. Fasten off.

Collar

Mark center 28 [32, 36] sts across neck edge of Edging.

Row 1: With right side of Coat facing, join with sl st in first marked st, scfp around same st, scfp around each st across ending in last marked st, turn. *(28 [32, 36] scfp made)*

Row 2: Ch 1, 2 sc in first st, sc in next 8 [9, 11] sts, 2 sc in next st, sc in next 8 [10, 10] sts, 2 sc in next st, sc in next 8 [9, 11] sts, 2 sc in last st, turn. *(32) [36, 40]*

Row 3: Ch 1, sc in each st across, turn.

Row 4: Ch 1, 2 sc in first st, sc in next st, (hdcfp around st on row 2 directly below next st, skip one st on last row) 4 times, sc in next 2 [4, 6] sts, 2 sc in next st, (sc in next 4 sts, 2 sc in next st) 3 times, sc in next 2 [4, 6] sts, (hdcfp around st on row 2 directly below next st, skip one st on last row) 4 times, sc in next st, 2 sc in last st, turn. *(38) [42, 46]*

Row 5: Ch 1, 2 sc in first st, sc in next 6 [5, 4] sts, (2 sc in next st, sc in next 5 [6, 7] sts) 5 times, 2 sc in last st, turn. *(45) [49, 53]*

Row 6: Ch 1, sc in first 4 sts; working around previous fp sts, cross cable, sc in each st across to last 8 sts; working around previous fp sts, cross cable, sc in last 4 sts, turn.

Row 7: Ch 1, skip first st, sc in each st across to last 2 sts, sc last 2 sts tog, turn. *(43) [47, 51]*

Row 8: Ch 1, skip first st, sc in next 2 sts, hdcfp around each of next 4 fp sts on previous row, sc in each st across to last 7 sts, hdcfp around each of next 4 fp sts on previous row, sc in next st, sc last 2 sts tog, turn. *(41) [45, 49]*

Row 9: Ch 1, skip first st, sc in each st across to last st, ch 1, sl st in last st. Fasten off.

Row 10: With right side of Collar facing, working in ends of rows and in sts, join with sl st in row 1, sc in rows 2–8 with 2 sc in row 6, 2 sc in first st on row 9, sc in each st across with 2 sc in last st, sc in rows 8–2 with 2 sc in row 6, sl st in row 1. Fasten off.

To counteract the tendency that crocheted corners have to roll, sew ends of rows 2–8 at each end of Collar to shoulder bands.

FINISHING

Cut a piece of velcro strip to fit last row on shoulder bands and separate sides. Using sewing needle and thread, sew fuzzy side of velcro strip to **wrong** side at end of one shoulder band.

Place Coat on dog, overlap shoulder bands to fit and mark position for loopy side of velcro on **right** side at end of other shoulder band to match fuzzy side. Remove Coat from dog and sew loopy side in place.

Cut remaining velcro to fit ends of rows on chest bands and sew in place in same manner as shoulder bands. ●

Entwined Cables Stitch Pattern

Knitted cables combined with diagonal ribs of twisted stitches on a reverse stockinette stitch background form this unique stitch pattern.

To achieve the same look in crochet, work a single crochet background and use half-double crochet front post stitches to create the raised ribs and cables, with half-double crochet cross stitches to cross the cables.

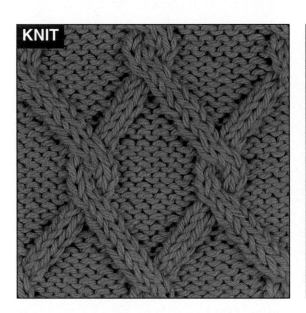

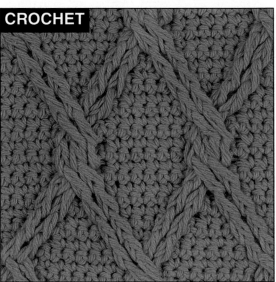

Afghan Square: Entwined Cables

READ BEFORE STARTING

*Refer to **Chapter 2** for instructions for using Squares to make either Knit or Crochet Version of Large Afghan or Baby Afghan.*

*For comparison, each Square has instructions for **Knit Version** in blue type, and instructions for **Crochet Version** in black type.*

KNIT VERSION

With large needles and color A, cast on 26.

Row 1: P 1; to **cross cable,** slip next 2 sts onto cable needle and hold at front of work, K 2, K 2 from cable needle *(cross cable completed),* (P 6, cross cable) 2 times, P 1.

Rows 2–4: K each K st and P each P st.

CROCHET VERSION

Row 1: With small hook and color A, ch 27, sc in second ch from hook, sc in each ch across, turn. *(26 sts made)*

Row 2: Ch 1, sc in each st across, turn. ***NOTE:** Work **all sc sts** into sts of **last row.***

Row 3: Ch 1, sc in first sc—*see Note,* skip first 3 sts on row before last; **hdcfp** *(see*

Row 5: P 1, (cross cable, P 6) 2 times, cross cable, P 1.

Row 6: K each K st and P each P st.

NOTES: *For **Left Twist (LT)**, slip next 2 sts onto cable needle and hold at front of work, P 1, K 2 from cable needle.*

*For **Right Twist (RT)**, slip next st onto cable needle and hold at back of work, K 2, P 1 from cable needle.*

Row 7: P 3, (LT, P 4, RT) 2 times, P 3.

Row 8: K each K st and P each P st.

Row 9: P 4, (LT, P 2, RT, P 2) 2 times, P 2.

Row 10: K each K st and P each P st.

Row 11: P 5, (LT, RT, P 4) 2 times, P 1.

Row 12: K each K st and P each P st.

Row 13: P 6, (cross cable, P 6) 2 times.

Rows 14–16: K each K st and P each P st.

Row 17: P 6, (cross cable, P 6) 2 times.

Row 18: K each K st and P each P st.

Row 19: P 5, (RT, LT, P 4) 2 times, P 1.

Row 20: K each K st and P each P st.

Row 21: P 4, (RT, P 2, LT, P 2) 2 times, P 2.

Row 22: K each K st and P each P st.

Row 23: P 3, (RT, P 4, LT) 2 times, P 3.

Row 24: K each K st and P each P st.

Row 25: P 1, (cross cable, P 6) 2 times, cross cable, P 1.

Rows 26–28: K each K st and P each P st.

Row 29: P 1, (cross cable, P 6) 2 times, cross cable, P 1.

Bind off.

Piece should measure same as gauge.

Work Edging in Basic Finishing on page 28.

Special Stitch on page 24) around each of next 2 sts on row before last; working in front of last 2 fp made, hdcfp around each of last 2 skipped sts, (sc in next 6 sc; counting from last fp, skip next 8 sts on row before last, hdcfp around each of next 2 sts; working in front of last 2 fp made, hdcfp around each of last 2 skipped sts) 2 times, sc in last sc, turn.

Row 4: Ch 1, sc in each st across, turn.

Row 5: Ch 1, sc in first sc, hdcfp around each of next 4 fp, (sc in next 6 sc, hdcfp around each of next 4 fp) 2 times, sc in last sc, turn.

Row 6: Ch 1, sc in each st across, turn.

Row 7: Ch 1, sc in first sc; to **cross cable,** skip next 2 fp, hdcfp around each of next 2 fp; working in front of last 2 fp made, hdcfp around each of 2 skipped fp *(cross cable completed);* (sc in next 6 sc, cross cable) 2 times, sc in last sc, turn.

Row 8: Ch 1, sc in each st across, turn.

Row 9: Ch 1, sc in first 4 sc, skip first 2 fp, (hdcfp around each of next 2 fp, sc in next 4 sc, hdcfp around each of next 2 fp, sc in next 2 sc) 2 times, sc in last 2 sc, turn.

Row 10: Ch 1, sc in each st across, turn.

Row 11: Ch 1, sc in first 5 sc, (hdcfp around each of next 2 fp, sc in next 2 sc, hdcfp around each of next 2 fp, sc in next 4 sc) 2 times, sc in last sc, turn.

Row 12: Ch 1, sc in each st across, turn.

Row 13: Ch 1, sc in first 6 sc, (hdcfp around each of next 4 fp, sc in next 6 sc) 2 times, turn.

Row 14: Ch 1, sc in each st across, turn.

Row 15: Ch 1, sc in first 6 sc, (cross cable, sc in next 6 sc) 2 times, turn.

Rows 16–19: Repeat rows 12–15.

Rows 20–22: Repeat rows 10–12.

Row 23: Ch 1, sc in first 4 sc, (hdcfp around each of next 2 fp, sc in next 4 sc, hdcfp around each of next 2 fp, sc in next 2 sc) 2 times, sc in last 2 sc, turn.

Row 24: Ch 1, sc in each st across, turn.

Row 25: Ch 1, sc in first 3 sc, (hdcfp around each of next 2 fp, sc in next 6 sc, hdcfp around each of next 2 fp) 2 times, sc in last 3 sc, turn.

Row 26: Ch 1, sc in each st across, turn.

Row 27: Ch 1, sc in first sc, skip first 3 sts on row before last, hdcfp around each of next 2 fp; working in front of last 2 fp made, hdcfp around each of last 2 skipped sts, sc in next 6 sc, cross cable, sc in next

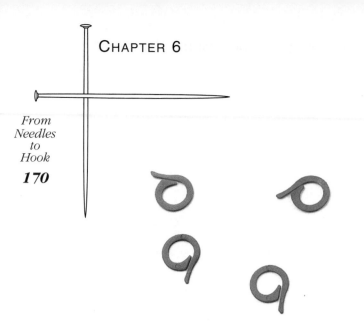

6 sc, skip next 2 fp, hdcfp around each of next 2 sts on row before last; working in front of last 2 fp made, hdcfp around each of 2 skipped fp, sc in last sc, turn.

Row 28: Ch 1, sc in each st across, turn.

Row 29: Ch 1, sc in first sc, hdcfp around each of next 4 fp, (sc in next 6 sc, hdcfp around each of next 4 fp) 2 times, sc in last sc, turn.

Row 30: Ch 1, sc in each st across, turn.

Row 31: Ch 1, sc in first sc, cross cable, (sc in next 6 sc, cross cable) 2 times, sc in last sc. Fasten off.

Piece should measure same as gauge.

Work Edging in Basic Finishing on page 28.

Fringed Pillow

Designed by Darla Sims

Make an accent pillow for your favorite reading nook using Entwined Cables.

FINISHED SIZE: About 14" square, plus Fringe.

MATERIALS: 9 oz. White #100 Imagine Art. 780 by Lion Brand® Yarn Company or fuzzy (mohair) sport yarn; 14" x 14" pillow form; tapestry needle; H and I crochet hooks *(or hook needed to obtain I hook gauge).*

GAUGE: I hook, 14 sts in pattern = 4"; 14 rows in pattern = 4".

SIDE (make 2)

Row 1: With I hook, ch 47, sc in second ch from hook, sc in each ch across, turn. *(46 sc made)*

Row 2: Ch 1, sc in each st across, turn.

NOTES: To **cross cable,** *skip next 2 fp on row before last,* **hdcfp** *around each of next 2 fp; working in front of last 2 fp made, hdcfp around each of 2 skipped fp.*

Work **all sc** *sts into sc of* **last row.**

Row 3: Ch 1, sc in first st, complete row as follows:

A: Skip next 2 sts on last row; working around sts on row before last, **hdcfp** *(see Special Stitch on page 24)* around st directly below third st, hdcfp around

next st; working in front of last 2 fp made, hdcfp around each of 2 sts directly below 2 skipped sts;

B: (Sc in next 6 sts; repeat step A) 4 times, sc in last st, turn.

Row 4: Ch 1, sc in each st across, turn.

Row 5: Ch 1, sc in first sc, hdcfp around each of next 4 fp, (sc in next 6 sc, hdcfp around each of next 4 fp) 4 times, sc in last sc, turn.

Row 6: Ch 1, sc in each st across, turn.

Row 7: Ch 1, sc in first sc, **cross cable** *(see Notes),* (sc in next 6 sc, cross cable) 4 times, sc in last sc, turn.

Row 8: Ch 1, sc in each st across, turn.

Rows 9–20: Repeat rows 5–8 consecutively.

Row 21: Ch 1, sc in first 4 sc, skip first 2 fp on previous row, hdcfp around each of next 2 fp, sc in next 4 sc, (hdcfp around each of next 2 fp, sc in next 2 sc, hdcfp around each of next 2 fp, sc in next 4 sc) 3 times, hdcfp around each of next 2 fp, sc in last 4 sc, turn.

Row 22: Ch 1, sc in each st across, turn.

Row 23: Ch 1, sc in first 5 sc, hdcfp around each of next 2 fp, sc in next 2 sc, (hdcfp around each of next 2 fp, sc in next 4 sc, hdcfp around each of next 2 fp, sc in next 2 sc) 3 times, hdcfp around each of next 2 fp, sc in last 5 sc, turn.

Row 24: Ch 1, sc in each st across, turn.

Row 25: Ch 1, sc in first 6 sc, (hdcfp around each of next 4 fp, sc in next 6 sc)

4 times, turn.

Row 26: Ch 1, sc in each st across, turn.

Row 27: Ch 1, sc in first 6 sc, (cross cable, sc in next 6 sc) 4 times, turn.

Row 28: Ch 1, sc in each st across, turn.

Row 29: Ch 1, sc in first 6 sc, (hdcfp around each of next 4 fp, sc in next 6 sc) 4 times, turn.

Row 30: Ch 1, sc in each st across, turn.

Row 31: Ch 1, sc in first 6 sc, (cross cable, sc in next 6 sc) 4 times, turn.

Row 32: Ch 1, sc in each st across, turn.

Row 33: Ch 1, sc in first 5 sc, (hdcfp around each of next 2 fp, sc in next 2 sc, hdcfp around each of next 2 fp, sc in next 4 sc) 4 times, sc in last sc, turn.

Row 34: Ch 1, sc in each st across, turn.

Row 35: Ch 1, sc in first 4 sc, (hdcfp around each of next 2 fp, sc in next 4 sc, hdcfp around each of next 2 fp, sc in next 2 sc) 4 times, sc in last 2 sc, turn.

Row 36: Ch 1, sc in each st across, turn.

Row 37: Ch 1, sc in first 3 sc, hdcfp around each of next 2 fp, sc in next 6 sc, (hdcfp around each of next 4 fp, sc in next 6 sc) 3 times, hdcfp around each of next 2 fp, sc in last 3 sc, turn.

Row 38: Ch 1, sc in each st across, turn.

Row 39: Ch 1, sc in first sc, hdcfp around each of next 2 fp; working in front of last 2 fp made, hdcfp around second st on row before last, hdcfp around third st, sc in next 6 sc on last row, (cross cable, sc in next 6 sc) 3 times, skip next 2 fp on row before last, hdcfp around each of next 2 sts; working in front of last 2 fp made, hdcfp around each of 2 skipped fp, sc in last sc, turn.

Rows 40–55: Repeat rows 4–7 consecutively. At end of last row, fasten off first Side only; **do not fasten off second Side.**

Rnd 56: Hold pieces with wrong sides together matching sts and ends of rows; working through both layers as one, with H hook, ch 1, 3 sc in first corner, sc in end of each row and in each st around with 3 sc in each corner and inserting pillow form before closing, join with sl st in first sc. Fasten off.

FRINGE

For each **Fringe,** cut a 6" strand of yarn, fold in half; insert crochet hook from front to back through st, pull fold through st, pull ends through fold, pull snug.

Fringe in each st on rnd 56. ●

Baby Cables Stitch Pattern

*C*rossed knit stitches on a reversed stockinette stitch background mimic the look of tiny cable stitches.

To achieve the same look in crochet, use a single crochet background and work long single crochet cross stitches into the row before last for the crossed knit stitches.

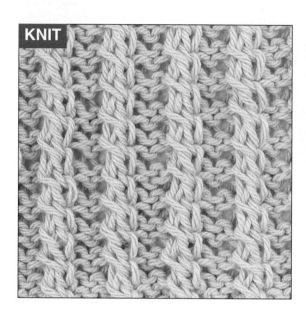

Afghan Square: Baby Cables

READ BEFORE STARTING

Refer to **Chapter 2** for instructions for using Squares to make either Knit or Crochet Version of Large Afghan or Baby Afghan.

For comparison, each Square has instructions for **Knit Version** in blue type, and instructions for **Crochet Version** in black type.

KNIT VERSION

With large needles and color A, cast on 26.

Row 1: *(Wrong side)* K 2, (P 2, K 2) across.

Row 2: P 2, (skip first st on left needle, K in back loop of second st and leave on needle, K in front loop of skipped st and drop both sts from left needle at same time, P 2) across.

CROCHET VERSION

Row 1: With medium hook and color A, ch 27, sc in second ch from hook, sc in each ch across, turn. *(26 sts made)*

Row 2: Ch 1, sc in each st across, turn.

Row 3: Ch 1, sc in first 2 sts, (skip st on row before last directly below next st, **scfp**—*see Special Stitch on page 24*—around next st on row before last; working

Next rows: Repeat rows 1 and 2 alternately until piece measures same as gauge, ending last repeat with row 1.

Bind off.

Work Edging in Basic Finishing on page 28.

in front of last fp made, scfp around skipped st, sc in next 2 sc) across, turn.

NOTE:** Work **all sc sts** into sts of **last row.

Row 4: Ch 1, sc in each st across, turn.

Row 5: Ch 1, sc in first 2 sc, (skip next fp on row before last, scfp around next fp; working in front of last fp made, scfp around skipped fp, sc in next 2 sc) across, turn.

Rows 6–29: Repeat rows 4 and 5 alternately. At end of last row, fasten off.

Piece should measure same as gauge.

Work Edging in Basic Finishing on page 28.

When using a needle to hide yarn ends in a finished crochet or knitted piece, if the back as well as the front will be visible, run the needle through the center of the yarn of several stitches, trying to duplicate the wraps and twists of the stitches as closely as possible; then secure by working in the opposite direction for a couple of stitches and cut the yarn.

If the back of the piece is not visible, simply run the needle under several loops of stitches on the wrong side of the piece, then take a tiny backstitch to secure; run the needle under a couple more loops before cutting the yarn.

Lady's Button-Front Vest

Designed by Darla Sims

Dress up jeans, slacks or skirt with a lovely vest made with Baby Cables.

MATERIALS: Wool-Ease® Art. 620 by Lion Brand® Yarn Company or worsted yarn: amount Caramel #124 needed for size; 5 wooden ⅜" beads or desired buttons; split stitch markers; tapestry needle; F and H crochet hooks *(or hooks needed to obtain gauges).*

GAUGES: F hook; 7 sc = 1½"; 18 sc **back lp** rows = 4". **H hook;** 16 sts in pattern = 4"; 20 rows in pattern = 4".

SIZES

Lady's Small (30"–32" chest):
Yarn: 15½ oz. caramel
Garment chest: 35"
Back length: 21"

Lady's Medium (32"–36" chest):
Yarn: 18 oz. caramel
Garment chest: 39"
Back length: 21½"

Lady's Large (36"–40" chest):
Yarn: 20 oz. caramel
Garment chest: 43"
Back length: 22"

Lady's X-Large (40"–44" chest):
Yarn: 21½ oz. caramel
Garment chest: 47"
Back length: 22½"

NOTE

Instructions are for size **Small;** changes for **Medium, Large** and **X-Large** are in [ ].

BACK

Row 1: With H hook, ch 71 [79, 87, 95], sc in second ch from hook, sc in each ch across, turn. *(70 [78, 86, 94] sts made)*

Row 2: Ch 1, sc in each st across, turn.

*NOTE: Work **all sc sts** into sts of **last row**.*

Row 3: *(Right side)* Ch 1, sc in first sc *(see Note),* skip next st, **long sc front post (lscfp**—*see Special Stitch on page 24)* around st on row 1 directly below next st, working in front of last fp made, lscfp around st on row 1 directly below skipped st, sc in next 2 sc on last row, (skip next sc, lscfp around st on row 1 directly below next st, lscfp around st on row 1 directly below skipped st, sc in next 2 sts) across, turn.

Row 4: Ch 1, sc in each st across, turn.

Row 5: Ch 1, sc in first 2 sc; for **cross st,** skip next fp, lscfp around next fp, working in front of last fp made, lscfp around skipped fp *(cross st made);* sc in next 2 sc, (cross st, sc in next 2 sts) across, turn.

To **work in pattern,** repeat rows 4 and 5 alternately *(see "How to Work in Pattern", Chapter 1, page 16).*

Next rows: Work in pattern until piece measures 10" long, ending with right-side row. At end of last row, fasten off.

Armhole Shaping

Row 1: Skip first 6 [8, 10, 12] sts for underarm; continuing with row 4 of pattern, join with sc in next st, sc in each st across to last 6 [8, 10, 12] sts leaving remaining sts unworked for underarm, turn. *(58 [62, 66, 70] sts)*

Row 2: Ch 1, sc first 2 sts tog, work in pattern across to last 2 sts, sc last 2 sts tog, turn. *(56 [60, 64, 68] sts)*

Row 3: Work in pattern.

Rows 4–9: Repeat rows 2 and 3 alternately. At end of last row *(50 [54, 58, 62] sts).*

Next rows: Work in pattern until piece measures 18½" [19", 19½", 20"] from beginning, ending with right-side row. At end of last row, fasten off.

RIGHT FRONT

Row 1: With H hook, ch 31 [35, 39, 43], sc in second ch from hook, sc in each ch across, turn. *(30 [34, 38, 42] sts made)*

Rows 2–3: Repeat rows 2 and 3 of Back.

Next rows: Work in pattern until piece measures 10" long, ending with right-side row. At end of last row, fasten off.

Armhole and Neck Shaping

Row 1: Skip first 6 [8, 10, 12] sts for **underarm;** continuing with row 4 of pattern, join with sc in next st, sc in each st across, turn. *(24 [26, 28, 30] sts)*

Row 2: Ch 1; for **neck edge** shaping, sc first 2 sts tog, work in pattern across to last 2 sts; for **armhole** shaping, sc last 2 sts tog, turn. *(22 [24, 26, 28] sts)*

Row 3: Work in pattern.

Rows 4–5: Repeat rows 2 and 3. *(20 [22, 24, 26] sts)*

Row 6: Ch 1, sc first 2 sts tog at neck edge, work in pattern across, turn. *(19 [21, 23, 25] sts)*

Row 7: Work in pattern.

Next rows: Repeat rows 6 and 7 alternately until there are 10 [11, 12, 13] sts remaining.

Next rows: Work in pattern until piece measures 18½" [19", 19½", 20"] from beginning, ending with right-side row. At end of last row, fasten off.

LEFT FRONT

Row 1: With H hook, ch 31 [35, 39, 43], sc in second ch from hook, sc in each ch across, turn. *(30 [34, 38, 42] sts made)*

Rows 2–3: Repeat rows 2 and 3 of Back.

Next rows: Work in pattern until piece measures 10" long, ending with right-side row. At end of last row, **do not fasten off.**

Armhole and Neck Shaping

Row 1: Continuing with row 4 of pattern, sc in each st across to last 6 [8, 10, 12] sts leaving remaining sts unworked for **underarm,** turn. *(24 [26, 28, 30] sts)*

Row 2: Ch 1; for **armhole** shaping, sc first 2 sts tog, work in pattern across to last 2 sts; for **neck edge** shaping, sc last 2 sts tog, turn. *(22 [24, 26, 28] sts)*

Row 3: Work in pattern.

Rows 4–5: Repeat rows 2 and 3. *(20 [22, 24, 26] sts)*

Row 6: Ch 1, work in pattern across to last 2 sts at neck edge, sc last 2 sts tog, turn. *(19 [21, 23, 25] sts)*

Row 7: Work in pattern.

Next rows: Repeat rows 6 and 7 alternately until there are 10 [11, 12, 13] sts

remaining.

Next rows: Work in pattern until piece measures 18½" [19", 19½", 20"] from beginning, ending with right-side row. At end of last row, fasten off.

ASSEMBLY

For **shoulder seams,** matching armhole edges, sew last row on Fronts to 10 [11, 12, 13] sts at each end of last row on Back.

For **side seams,** matching ends of rows, sew Fronts to Back from starting chain to underarm.

WAIST RIBBING

Foundation row: Working in starting chs on opposite side of row 1 on assembled piece, with F hook, join with sc in first ch on front, sc in next 4 [5, 6, 7] chs, (sc next 2 chs tog, sc in next 6 [7, 8, 9] chs) across to last 5 chs, sc in last 5 chs, turn. *(115 [131, 147, 163] sts made)*

Row 1: Ch 8, sc in second ch from hook, sc in each ch across, sl st in next 2 sts on foundation row, turn. *(7 sc)*

Row 2: Skip sl sts, sc in **back lp** *(see Crochet Stitch Guide on page 191)* of each st across, turn.

Row 3: Ch 1, sc in **back lps** of next 7 sts, sl st in **both lps** of next 2 sts on foundation row, turn.

Next rows: Repeat rows 2 and 3 alternately across foundation row. At end of last row, fasten off.

ARMHOLE RIBBING (make on each armhole)

Foundation rnd: With F hook, join with sc in side seam; spacing sts so edge lays flat, sc in sts and in ends of rows around armhole, join with sl st in first sc, **turn.**

Row 1: Ch 4, sc in second ch from hook, sc in next 2 chs, sl st in next 2 sts on foundation row, turn. *(3 sc)*

Row 2: Skip sl sts, sc in **back lp** of each sc across, turn.

Row 3: Ch 1, sc in **back lps** of next 3 sc, sl st in **both lps** of next 2 sts on foundation rnd, turn.

Next rows: Repeat rows 2 and 3 alternately around foundation rnd. At end of last row, leaving end for sewing, fasten off. Thread tapestry needle with end.

Lap last row over starting ch to match ribbing; sew together.

FRONT AND NECK RIBBING

Foundation row: Beginning at lower Right Front, with F hook, join with sc in first ch of Bottom Ribbing; spacing sts so edge lays flat *(take extreme care that edge does not flare or pucker)* sc in sts and in ends of rows up Right Front placing 2 sc in same row where neck edge shaping begins on each Front, across Back Neck edge and down Left Front to last st on other end of Bottom Ribbing, turn.

For **buttonholes,** mark sts for placement of five buttonholes on Right Front as follows:

A: Mark **third st** at beginning of foundation row;

B: Mark **first st of 2 sc in same place** at beginning of neck edge shaping;

C: Mark st **half-way between** first two markers;

D: Mark sts **half-way between each of these markers.**

Row 1: Ch 6, sc in second ch from hook, sc in next 4 chs, sl st in next 2 sts on foundation row, turn. *(5 sc)*

Row 2: Skip sl sts, sc in **back lp** of each sc across, turn.

Row 3: Ch 1, sc in **back lps** of next 5 sc, sl st in **both lps** of next 2 sts on foundation row, turn.

Row 4: For **buttonhole row,** skip sl sts; working this row in **back lps,** sc in first sc, ch 2, skip next 2 sc, sc in last 2 sc, turn.

Row 5: Working in **back lps,** ch 1, sc in each st and ch across, sl st in **both lps** of next 2 sts on foundation row, turn.

Next rows: (Repeat rows 2 and 3 alternately across to next marked st; repeat rows 4 and 5) 4 times; repeat rows 2 and 3 alternately across remainder of foundation row. At end of last row, fasten off.

Sew buttons on Left Front Ribbing to match buttonholes. ●

Eyelet Cables
Stitch Pattern

*T*wisted-stitch ribs and passed stitches with an eyelet centered between the ribs form
an intricate cable-look design.
   *To achieve the same look in crochet, post stitches and treble cross stitches mimic the
ribs while chain spaces are used to create the eyelets; chain spaces are worked on
three consecutive rows, then two single crochet stitches are worked around the three
rows of chains, drawing them together to create the eyelet opening.*

KNIT

CROCHET

Afghan Square: Eyelet Cables

READ BEFORE STARTING

   *Refer to **Chapter 2** for instructions for using Squares to make either
Knit or Crochet Version of Large Afghan or Baby Afghan.*
   *For comparison, each Square has instructions for **Knit Version** in blue
type, and instructions for **Crochet Version** in black type.*

KNIT VERSION

With large needles and color A, cast on 28.
   Row 1: *(Right side)* P 1, K 1-**through the
back lp (tbl),** P 1, (K 2, P 1, K 1-tbl, P 1)
across.
   Row 2: K 1, P 1-tbl, K 1, (P 2, K 1, P 1-tbl,
K 1) across.

CROCHET VERSION

   Row 1: With small hook and color A,
ch 29, sc in second ch from hook, (ch 1,
skip next ch, sc in next 4 chs) 5 times,
ch 1, skip next ch, sc in last ch, turn. *(28
sts and chs made)*
   Row 2: Ch 1, sc in each st and in each

Row 3: P 1, K 1-tbl, P 1 (K 1, yo, K 1, P 1, K 1-tbl, P 1) across. *(33 sts on needles)*

Row 4: K 1, P 1-tbl, K 1, (P 3, K 1, P 1-tbl, K 1) across.

Row 5: P 1, K 1-tbl, P 1 (K 3, pass third st on right needle over first 2 sts and off needle, P 1, K 1-tbl, P 1) across. *(28 sts)*

Next rows: Repeat rows 2–5 consecutively until piece measures same as gauge, ending after row 5.

Bind off.

Work Edging in Basic Finishing on page 28.

ch across, turn.

Row 3: Ch 1, sc in first st, dc over last row into ch-sp on row before last; *working in row before last, skip next 3 sts, **trfp** *(see Special Stitch on page 24)* around next st, ch 2, working in front of last trfp, trfp around first skipped st, dc over last row into ch-sp on row before last; repeat from * across with sc in last st on last row, turn.

Row 4: Ch 1, sc in first 3 sts, (ch 2, skip next ch sp, sc in next 3 sts) across, turn.

Row 5: Ch 1, sc in first st; working in row before last, dcfp around next dc, (dcfp around next tr, ch 2, skip ch sp, dcfp around next tr, dcfp around next dc) across with sc in last st on last row, turn.

Row 6: Ch 1, sc in first 3 sts, (ch 2, skip next ch sp, sc in next 3 sts) across, turn.

Row 7: Ch 1, sc in first st; working in row before last, dcfp around next fp, (skip next fp, trfp around next fp, working behind last trfp, 2 sc around all previous loose ch-2 sps at same time; working in front of last tr, trfp around skipped fp, dcfp around next fp) across with sc in last st on last row, turn.

Row 8: Ch 1, sc in first 3 sts, (ch 2, skip next 2 sts, sc in next 3 sts) across, turn.

Row 9: Ch 1, sc in first st; working in row before last, dcfp around next dc, (dcfp around next tr, ch 2, skip ch-2 sp, dcfp around next tr, dcfp around next dc) across with sc in last st on last row, turn.

Next rows: Repeat rows 6–9 consecutively until piece measures same as gauge ending with row 7. At end of last row, fasten off.

Work Edging in Basic Finishing on page 28.

Changing your gauge is as easy as changing your hook size.

Baby Girl or Boy Hat, Mittens, Booties

Designed by Donna Jones

Make a loving baby shower gift with elegant Eyelet Cables.

MATERIALS FOR BOOTIES, MITTENS AND ONE HAT:
4 oz. desired color Babysoft® Art. 920 by Lion Brand® Yarn Company or sport yarn—shown are Pastel Green #156 and Pastel Yellow #157; split stitch markers; small tapestry needle; small and large crochet hooks needed to obtain gauges for size.

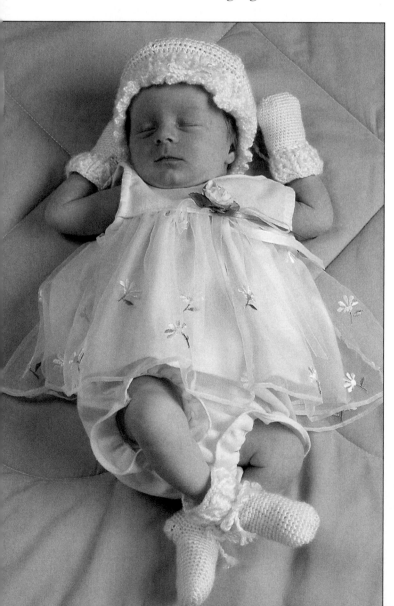

GAUGES: C hook, 28 sc = 4"; 30 sc rows = 4". **D hook,** 24 hdc = 4"; 16 hdc rows = 4". **E hook,** 22 sc = 4"; 24 sc rows = 4". **F hook,** 20 hdc = 4"; 18 hdc rows = 4".

SIZES
Infant newborn:
  Hat fits head up to 15" around;
  Booties are 3" from heel to toe;
  Mittens are 2" wide x 2½" long.
Infant up to 3 months:
  Hat fits head up to 16½" around;
  Booties are 3½" from heel to toe;
  Mittens are 2½" wide x 3" long.

SPECIAL STITCHES
For **treble front post (trfp,** *see Crochet Stitch Guide on page 191)* and **dc front post (dcfp),** work around designated st on row before last; pull up to height of row being worked; skip one st on last row behind fp.

For **treble cross st (trX),** skip next fp, **trfp** *(see above)* around next fp; working behind trfp just made, sc over first ch-1 into opening of ch-3 sp on previous rnd, skip sl sts, sc over last ch-1 into same ch-3 sp; working in front of last trfp made, trfp back around skipped fp.

BASIC CUFF (use with instructions for Booties, Mittens and Hats)
Rnd 1: Ch 1; working in sts *(and in chs if it applies),* sc in each st around, join with sl st in first sc.

Rnd 2: Ch 1, sc in each st around, join.

*NOTES: Work **all sc sts** into sts of **last** rnd. Work **all fp sts** around sts on **rnd before last.***

Rnd 3: Ch 1; working into rnd before last, **dcfp** around first st *(see Note above and Special Stitch on page 24),* skip next st, dcfp around next st, ch 3, dcfp around next st, *(skip next st, dcfp around next st) 2 times, ch

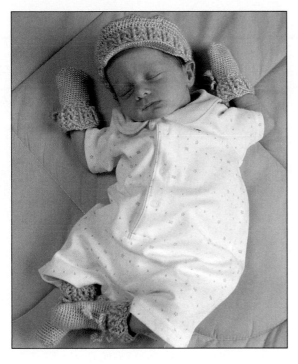

BASIC TWISTED CORD TIE (use with instructions for Booties, Mittens and Girl's Hat)

For each **10" Tie,** cut a 2-yd. long strand of desired color yarn. For **24" Tie,** cut a 5-yd. long strand of desired color yarn.

Fold strand in half; place fold over door knob or hook to hold, or have another person hold it securely.

Holding loose ends together, twist very tightly in one direction; still holding ends, fold in half and let twist naturally from fold. Still holding ends, remove cord from hook or knob; tie loose ends together in a single knot 1" from ends.

For **10" Tie,** tie a second knot 10" from first knot; for **24" Tie,** tie a second knot 24" from first knot.

Trim each end ½" past knot. Separate plys and fray yarn ends to form a tiny tassel.

3, dcfp around next st; repeat from * around to last st, skip last st, join with sl st in first fp.

Rnd 4: Ch 1, sc in first 2 fp, ch 1, sl st in center ch of next ch-3, ch 1, (sc in next 3 fp, ch 1, sl st in center ch of next ch-3, ch 1) around with sc in last st, join with sl st in first sc.

Rnd 5: Ch 1, dcfp around first fp, **trX,** *(see Special Stitches),* (dcfp around next fp, trX) around, join with sl st in first fp.

Rnd 6: Ch 1, sc in first 2 sts, ch 3, skip 2 sc, (sc in next 3 fp, ch 3, skip 2 sc) around with sc in last fp, join with sl st in first sc.

Rnd 7: Ch 1, dcfp around each of first 2 fp, ch 1, sl st in center ch of ch-3, ch 1, (dcfp around each of next 3 fp, ch 1, sl st in center ch of ch-3, ch 1) around to last st, dcfp around last fp, join with sl st in first dc.

Rnd 8: Ch 1, sc in first 2 fp, ch 1, sl st in same ch on previous rnd as next sl st, ch 1, (sc in next 3 fp, ch 1, sl st in same ch on previous rnd as next sl st, ch 1) around with sc in last st, join with sl st in first sc.

Rnd 9: Ch 1, dcfp around first fp, trX, (dcfp around next fp, trX) around, join with sl st in first fp.

Repeat rnds 6–9 as instructed in individual pattern.

Last rnd: Ch 1, sc in each st around, join with sl st in first sc.

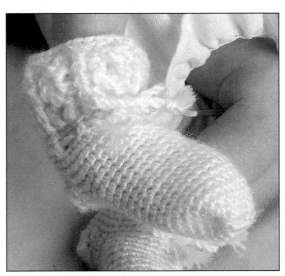

SOCK BOOTIE (make 2)

Rnd 1: With smaller hook and desired color, beginning at toe, ch 8, 2 sc in second ch from hook, sc in next 5 chs, 3 sc in end ch; continuing on opposite side of ch, sc in next 6 chs, **do not join.** *(16 sc made)*

NOTES: *Work in continuous rnds; **do not join or turn** unless otherwise stated.*

Mark first st of each rnd. When working into marked st, remove marker, work st, mark st just made.

Rnd 2: (3 sc in next st, sc in next 7 sts) 2 times. *(20)*

Rnd 3: Sc in next st, 3 sc in next st, sc in next 9 sts, 3 sc in next st, sc in next 8 sts. *(24)*

Rnds 4–17: Sc in each st around.

Rnd 18: For **heel shaping,** sc in next 17 sts leaving remaining sts unworked, **turn;** work heel as follows:

A: Ch 1, skip first st, sc in next 7 sts, **turn; mark ch-1;** *(7 sc)*

B: Ch 1, skip first st, sc in next 5 sts, **turn; mark ch-1;** *(5 sc)*

C: Ch 1, skip first st, sc in next 3 sts, **turn; mark ch-1;** *(3 sc)*

D: Ch 1, sc in first 3 sts, sc in marked ch-1, sc in end of next row, **turn; mark ch-1;** *(5 sc)*

E: Sc in first 5 sts, sc in next marked ch-1, sc in end of next row, **turn;** *(7 sc)*

F: Sc in first 7 sts, sc in next marked ch-1, **turn;** *(8 sc)*

G: Sc in first 8 sts, sc in next marked ch-1, **turn;** *(9 sc)*

H: Sc in first 9 sts, sc in end of step G, sc again into last worked st on rnd 17, sc in last 7 sts on rnd 17, **do not turn;** *(18 sc)* **Remove all ch-1 markers.**

Rnd 19: Sc in first 9 sts, sc again into next worked st, sc in end of step A, sc in last 18 sts of step H. *(29 sc)*

Rnd 20: Sc in each st around.

Rnd 21: Sc in first 16 sts, sl st in next st. Rnds now begin here.

Rnd 22: For **beading rnd,** ch 3, (hdc in next st, ch 1, skip next st) around, join with sl st in second ch of ch-3. *(30 sts and ch sps)*

Rnds 23–31: For **cuff,** work rnds 1–9 of Basic Cuff.

Rnd 32: Work last rnd of Basic Cuff.
Make Basic Twisted Cord 10" Tie.
Weave Tie in and out through beading rnd, tie in bow at front.

MITTEN (make 2)

Rnd 1: With smaller hook and desired color, beginning at fingertips, ch 8, 2 sc in second ch from hook, sc in next 5 chs, 3 sc in end ch; continuing on opposite side of ch, sc in next 6 chs, **do not join.** *(16 sc made)*

NOTES: *Work in continuous rnds;* **do**

not join or turn unless otherwise stated.

Mark first st of each rnd. When working into marked st, remove marker, work st, mark st just made.

Rnd 2: (3 sc in next st, sc in next 7 sts) 2 times. *(20)*

Rnd 3: Sc in next st, 3 sc in next st, sc in next 9 sts, 3 sc in next st, sc in next 8 sts. *(24)*

Rnd 4: Sc in next 2 sts, 3 sc in next st, sc in next 11 sts, 3 sc in next st, sc in next 9 sts. *(28)*

Rnds 5–18: Sc in each st around. At end of last rnd, sl st in next st.

Rnd 19: For **beading rnd,** ch 3, (hdc in next st, ch 1, skip next st) 6 times, hdc in next st, ch 1, (hdc in next st, ch 1, skip next st) around, join with sl st in second ch of ch-3. *(30 sts and chs)*

Rnds 20–28: For **Cuff,** work rnds 1–9 of Basic Cuff.

Rnd 29: Work last rnd of Basic Cuff.
Make Basic Twisted Cord 10" Tie.
Weave Tie in and out through beading rnd, tie in bow at center.

HAT (for Boy or Girl)

Rnd 1: Beginning at center top of crown, with larger hook and desired color yarn, ch 3, sl st in first ch to form ring, ch 1, 10 hdc in ring, join with sl st in first hdc. *(10 hdc made)*

Rnd 2: Ch 1, (hdc, ch 1, hdc) in first st, hdc in next st, *(hdc, ch 1, hdc) in next st, hdc in next st; repeat from * around, join with sl st in first hdc. *(15 hdc, 5 ch sps)*

Rnds 3–7: (Sl st, ch 1, hdc) in first ch sp, hdc in each st around with (hdc, ch 1, hdc) in each ch sp, hdc over sl st into first ch sp, ch 2, join with sl st in first hdc. At end of last rnd *(65 hdc, 5 ch sps)*.

Rnds 8–12: Sl st in first ch sp, ch 1, hdc in each st across to next ch sp, (hdc in ch sp, ch 1, hdc in each st across to next ch sp) around, hdc over sl st into first ch sp, ch 2, join with sl st in first hdc. At end of last rnd *(90 hdc, 5 ch sps)*.

Rnds 13–14: Ch 2, (hdc in each st across to next ch sp, ch 1, skip ch sp) 5 times, join with sl st in second ch of ch-2.

Rnd 15: Ch 1; skipping each ch sp, hdc in each st around, join with sl st in first hdc. *(90 hdc)*

Rnds 16–24: For **cuff,** with smaller hook, work rnds 1–9 of Basic Cuff.

Rnd 25: Work last rnd of Basic Cuff. Fasten off for Boy; **do not fasten off for Girl.**

Girl's Hat Ruffle

Rnd 1: With smaller hook and right side of sts facing, for **beading rnd,** ch 3, hdc in next st, (ch 1, skip next st, hdc in next st) around, ch 1, join with sl st in second ch of ch-3. *(46 ch sps, 46 hdc)*

Rnd 2: Ch 3; skipping each ch sp, (dc, ch 2) 3 times in next hdc, *sc in next hdc, ch 2, (dc, ch 2) 3 times in next hdc; repeat from * around, sc in same ch as first ch-3, join with sl st in first ch of ch-3. Fasten off.

Make Basic Twisted Cord 24" Tie.

Weave Tie in and out through beading rnd, tie in bow at front.

Boy's Hat Brim

Row 1: With smaller hook and right side of sts facing, skip first 30 sts on last rnd of Cuff, join with scfp around next st, scfp around each of next 29 sts leaving last 30 sts on Cuff unworked, turn. *(30 scfp)*

Row 2: Ch 1, skip first st, (sc in next 6 sts, 2 sc in next st) 3 times, sc in next 6 sts, skip next st, sc in last st, turn. *(31)*

Row 3: Ch 1, skip first st, sl st in next st, sc in next 7 sts, (2 sc in next st, sc in next 5 sts) 3 times, sc in next 2 sts, sl st in next st leaving last st unworked, turn. *(30 sc, 2 sl sts)*

Row 4: Ch 1, skip first sl st, sl st in next sc, sc in next 9 sts, 2 sc in next st, sc in next 8 sts, 2 sc in next st, sc in next 9 sts, sl st in next sc leaving last sl st unworked, turn. Fasten off.

Row 5: Join with sl st around post of last unworked sc before Brim on last rnd of Hat, sc in end of each row on Brim to row 4, 2 sc in row 4, sc in each st across row 4, 2 sc in end of row 4, sc in each row across, sl st in next unworked st on last rnd of Hat. Fasten off. ●

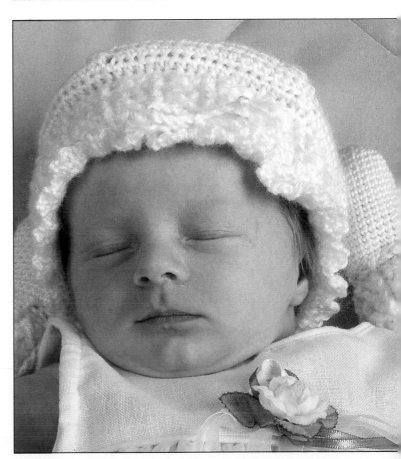

Diamond Columns Stitch Pattern

Twisted knit stitches help to raise the geometric diamond design above the reverse stockinette background. To achieve a similar effect in crochet, long half-double crochet post stitches are worked into previous rows to raise the diamond design above the single crochet stitches of the background.

KNIT

CROCHET

Afghan Square: Diamond Columns

READ BEFORE STARTING

Refer to **Chapter 2** for instructions for using Squares to make either Knit or Crochet Version of Large Afghan or Baby Afghan.

For comparison, each Square has instructions for **Knit Version** in blue type, and instructions for **Crochet Version** in black type.

KNIT VERSION

With large needles and white, cast on 25.

Row 1: *(Right side)* P 2, K 7-**through the back loops (-tbl),** P 3, K 1-tbl, P 3, K 7-tbl, P 2.

Row 2: K each K st and P each P st *(as they appear on the needle).*

Row 3: P 2, K 7-tbl, P 3, K 1-tbl, P 3, K 7-tbl, P 2.

CROCHET VERSION

Row 1: With medium hook and white, ch 26, sc in second ch from hook, sc in each ch across, turn. *(25 sts made)*

Row 2: Ch 1, sc in each st across, turn.

*NOTE: Work **all sc sts** into sts of **last row.***

Row 3: Ch 1, sc in first 2 sc, *beginning in st directly below next st, **hdcfp** (see Special Stitch on page 24) around each of next 7 sts

Row 4: K each K st and P each P st.

Row 5: P 3, K 5-tbl, P 4, K 1-tbl, P 4, K 5-tbl, P 3.

Row 6: K each K st and P each P st.

Row 7: P 4, K 3-tbl, P 5, K 1-tbl, P 5, K 3-tbl, P 4.

Row 8: K each K st and P each P st.

Row 9: P 5, K 1-tbl, P 5, K 3-tbl, P 5, K 1-tbl, P 5.

Row 10: K each K st and P each P st.

Row 11: P 5, K 1-tbl, P 4, K 5-tbl, P 4, K 1-tbl, P 5.

Row 12: K each K st and P each P st.

Row 13: P 5, K 1-tbl, P 3, K 7-tbl, P 3, K 1-tbl, P 5.

Row 14: K each K st and P each P st.

Row 15: P 5, K 1-tbl, P 3, K 7-tbl, P 3, K 1-tbl, P 5.

Row 16: K each K st and P each P st.

Row 17: P 5, K 1-tbl, P 3, K 7-tbl, P 3, K 1-tbl, P 5.

Row 18: K each K st and P each P st.

Row 19: P 5, K 1-tbl, P 4, K 5-tbl, P 4, K 1-tbl, P 5.

Row 20: K each K st and P each P st.

Row 21: P 5, K 1-tbl, P 5, K 3-tbl, P 5, K 1-tbl, P 5.

Row 22: K each K st and P each P st.

Row 23: P 4, K 3-tbl, P 5, K 1-tbl, P 5, K 3-tbl, P 4.

Row 24: K each K st and P each P st.

Row 25: P 3, K 5-tbl, P 4, K 1-tbl, P 4, K 5-tbl, P 3.

Row 26: K each K st and P each P st.

Row 27: P 2, K 7-tbl, P 3, K 1-tbl, P 3, K 7-tbl, P 2.

Row 28: K each K st and P each P st.

Row 29: P 2, K 7-tbl, P 3, K 1-tbl, P 3, K 7-tbl, P 2.

Row 30: K each K st and P each P st.
Piece should measure same as gauge.
Bind off.
Work Edging in Basic Finishing on page 28.

on row before last*, sc in next 3 sc *(see Note)*, hdcfp around st on row before last directly below next st, sc in next 3 sc; repeat between * *, sc in last 2 sc, turn.

Row 4: Ch 1, sc in each st across, turn.

Row 5: Ch 1, sc in first 2 sc, hdcfp around each of next 7 fp, sc in next 3 sc, hdcfp around next fp, sc in next 3 sc; hdcfp around each of next 7 fp, sc in last 2 sc, turn.

Row 6: Ch 1, sc in each st across, turn.

Row 7: Ch 1, sc in first 3 sc, (skip next fp, hdcfp around each of next 5 fp), sc in next 4 sc, hdcfp around next fp, sc in next 4 sc; repeat between ( ), sc in last 3 sc, turn.

Row 8: Ch 1, sc in each st across, turn.

Row 9: Ch 1, sc in first 4 sc, (skip next fp, hdcfp around each of next 3 fp), sc in next 5 sc, hdcfp around next fp, sc in next 5 sc; repeat between ( ), sc in last 4 sc, turn.

Row 10: Ch 1, sc in each st across, turn.

Row 11: Ch 1, sc in first 5 sc, (skip next fp, hdcfp around next fp), sc in next 5 sc, hdcfp around st on row before last directly below next st, hdcfp around next fp, hdcfp around next st on row before last, sc in next 5 sc; repeat between ( ), sc in last 5 sc, turn.

Row 12: Ch 1, sc in each st across, turn.

Row 13: Ch 1, sc in first 5 sc, hdcfp around next fp, sc in next 4 sc, hdcfp around st on row before last directly below next st, hdcfp around each of next 3 fp, hdcfp around next st on row before last, sc in next 4 sc, hdcfp around next fp, sc in last 5 sc, turn.

Row 14: Ch 1, sc in each st across, turn.

Row 15: Ch 1, sc in first 5 sc, hdcfp around next fp, sc in next 3 sc, hdcfp around st on row before last directly below next st, hdcfp around each of next 5 fp, hdcfp around next st on row before last, sc in next 3 sc, hdcfp around next fp, sc in last 5 sc, turn.

Row 16: Ch 1, sc in each st across, turn.

Row 17: Ch 1, sc in first 5 sc, hdcfp around next fp, sc in next 3 sc, hdcfp around each of next 7 fp, sc in next 3 sc, hdcfp around next fp, sc in last 5 sc, turn.

Rows 18–19: Repeat rows 16 and 17.

Row 20: Ch 1, sc in each st across, turn.

Row 21: Ch 1, sc in first 5 sc, hdcfp around next fp, sc in next 4 sc, skip next fp, hdcfp around each of next 5 fp, sc in next 4

sc, hdcfp around next fp, sc in last 5 sc, turn.

Row 22: Ch 1, sc in each st across, turn.

Row 23: Ch 1, sc in first 5 sc, hdcfp around next fp, sc in next 5 sc, skip next fp, hdcfp around each of next 3 fp, sc in next 5 sc, hdcfp around next fp, sc in last 5 sc, turn.

Row 24: Ch 1, sc in each st across, turn.

Row 25: Ch 1, sc in first 4 sc, (hdcfp around st on row before last directly below next st, hdcfp around next fp, hdcfp around next st on row before last), sc in next 5 sc, skip next fp, hdcfp around next fp, sc in next 5 sc; repeat between ( ), sc in last 4 sc, turn.

Row 26: Ch 1, sc in each st across, turn.

Row 27: Ch 1, sc in first 3 sc, (hdcfp around st on row before last directly below next st, hdcfp around each of next 3 sts, hdcfp around next st on row before last), sc in next 4 sc, hdcfp around next fp, sc in next 4 sc; repeat between ( ), sc in last 3 sc, turn.

Row 28: Ch 1, sc in each st across, turn.

Row 29: Ch 1, sc in first 2 sc, (hdcfp around st on row before last directly below next st, hdcfp around each of next 5 fp, hdcfp around next st on row before last), sc in next 3 sc, hdcfp around next fp, sc in next 3 sc; repeat between ( ), sc in last 2 sc. Fasten off.

Rows 30–31: Repeat rows 4 and 5. Piece should measure same as gauge. Work Edging in Basic Finishing on page 28.

Cuddle Kitty Pet Bed
Designed by Donna Jones

Pamper your beloved kitty with his or her very own crocheted bed using the Diamond Columns stitch pattern.

FINISHED SIZE: About 10" wide x 14½" long x 4" deep.

MATERIALS: Wool-Ease® Chunky Art. 630 by Lion Brand® Yarn Company or bulky yarn: 16 oz. Nantucket #178, 1 oz. Fisherman #099; bobby pins for markers; 2 pieces each 10" x 14" of thick quilt batting; polyester fiberfill; sewing needle and thread; tapestry needle; I crochet hook *(or hook needed to obtain gauge).*

GAUGE: 9 sc = 3"; 10 rows = 3".

BED TOP

Row 1: *(Right side)* Beginning at front edge, with nantucket, ch 44, sc in second ch from hook, sc in each ch across, turn. *(43 sts made)*

Row 2: Ch 1, sc in each st across, turn.

NOTE: *Work each* **hdc front post (hdcfp,** *see Crochet Stitch Guide on page 191) around designated st on row before last, pull up to height of row being worked. Always* **skip one st** *on last row behind each hdcfp.*

Row 3: Ch 1, sc in first 4 sts, skip first 4 sts on row before last, **hdcfp** *(see Note)*

around each of next 7 sts on row before last, (sc in next 3 sts on last row, hdcfp around next st on row before last directly below next st, sc in next 3 sts on last row, skip next 3 sts on row before last, hdcfp around each of next 7 sts on row before last) across to last 4 sts, sc in last 4 sts, turn.

Row 4: Ch 1, sc in each st across, turn.

Row 5: Ch 1, sc in first 4 sts, hdcfp around each of next 7 fp on row before last, (sc in next 3 sts on last row, hdcfp around next fp on row before last, sc in next 3 sts on last row, hdcfp around next 7 fp on row before last) across to last 4 sts, sc in last 4 sts, turn.

Row 6: Ch 1, sc in each st across, turn.

Row 7: Ch 1, sc in first 5 sts, skip first fp on row before last, hdcfp around each of next 5 fp, (sc in next 4 sts on last row, hdcfp around next fp on row before last, sc in next 4 sts on last row, skip next fp on row before last, hdcfp around each of next 5 fp) across to last 5 sts, sc in last 5 sts on last row, turn.

Row 8: Ch 1, sc in each st across, turn.

Row 9: Ch 1, sc in first 6 sts, skip first fp on row before last, hdcfp around each of next 3 fp, (sc in next 5 sts on last row, hdcfp around next fp on row before last, sc in next 5 sts on last row, skip next fp on row before last, hdcfp around each of next 3 fp) across to last 6 sts, sc in last 6 sts on last row, turn.

Row 10: Ch 1, sc in each st across, turn.

Row 11: Ch 1, sc in first 7 sts, skip first fp on row before last, hdcfp around next fp, (sc in next 5 sts on last row, skip next 5 sts on row before last, hdcfp around each of next 3 sts on row before last—*sc and fp and sc count as 3 sts,* sc in next 5 sts on last row, skip next fp on row before last, hdcfp around next fp) across to last 7 sts, sc in last 7 sts on last row, turn.

Row 12: Ch 1, sc in each st across, turn.

Row 13: Ch 1, sc in first 7 sts, hdcfp around next fp on row before last, (sc in next 4 sts on last row, skip next 4 sts on row before last, hdcfp around each of next 5 sts on rnd before last—*sc and 3 fp and sc count as 5 sts,* sc in next 4 sts on last row, hdcfp around next fp on row before last) across to last 7 sts, sc in last 7 sts on last row, turn.

Row 14: Ch 1, sc in each st across, turn.

Row 15: Ch 1, sc in first 7 sts, hdcfp around next fp on row before last, (sc in next 3 sts on last row, skip next 3 sts on row before last, hdcfp around each of next 7 sc or fp on row before last, sc in next 3 sts on last row, hdcfp around next fp on row before last) across to last 7 sts, sc in last 7 sts on last row, turn.

Rows 16-20: Repeat rows 14 and 15 alternately; ending with row 14.

Row 21: Ch 1, sc in first 7 sts, hdcfp around next fp on row before last, (sc in next 4 sts on last row, skip next fp on row before last, hdcfp around each of next 5 fp, sc in next 4 sts on last row, hdcfp around next fp on row before last) across to last 7 sts, sc in last 7 sts on last row, turn.

Row 22: Ch 1, sc in each st across, turn.

Row 23: Ch 1, sc in first 7 sts, hdcfp around next fp on row before last, (sc in next 5 sts on last row, skip next fp on row before last, hdcfp around each of next 3 fp, sc in next 5 sts on last row, hdcfp around next fp on row before last) across to last 7 sts, sc in last 7 sts, turn.

Row 24: Ch 1, sc in each st across, turn.

Row 25: Ch 1, skip first st, sc next 2 sts tog, sc in next 3 sts, skip first 6 sts on row before last, hdcfp around each of next 3 sts and fp, (sc in next 5 sts on last row, skip next fp on row before last, hdcfp around next fp, sc in next 5 sts on last row, skip next 5 sts on row before last, hdcfp around each of next 3 sts and fp) across to last 6 sts, sc in next 3 sts, sc next 2 sts tog leaving last st unworked, turn. *(39 sts)*

Row 26: Ch 1, sc in each st across, turn.

Row 27: Ch 1, skip first st, sc next 2 sts tog, skip first 3 sts on row before last, hdcfp around each of next 5 sts, (sc in next 4 sts on last row, hdcfp around next fp on row before last, sc in next 4 sts on last row, skip next 4 sts on row before last, hdcfp around each of next 5 sts) across to last 3 sts, sc next 2 sts tog leaving last st unworked, turn. *(35)*

Row 28: Ch 1, sc in each st across, turn.

Row 29: Ch 1, skip first st, sc next 2 sts tog, skip first 2 fp on row before last, hdcfp around each of next 4 sts, (sc in next 3 sts on last row, hdcfp around next fp on row before last, sc in next 3 sts on last row, skip next 3 sts on row before last), hdcfp around each of next 7 sts; repeat between ( ), hdcfp around each of next 4 sts, sc next 2 sts tog leaving last st unworked, turn. *(31)*

Row 30: Ch 1, sc in each st across, turn.

Row 31: Ch 1, skip first st, sc next 2 sts tog, skip first 2 fp on row before last, hdcfp around each of next 2 fp, (sc in next 3 sts on last row, hdcfp around next fp on row before last, sc in next 3 sts on last row, skip next 3 sts on row before last), hdcfp around each of next 7 fp on row before last; repeat between ( ), hdcfp around each of next 2 fp, sc next 2 sts tog leaving last st unworked, **do not turn.** *(27)*

Rnd 32: Working around outer edge, ch 1, sc in each st around with 2 sc at each corner and 36 sc evenly spaced in ends of rows across each side, join with sl st in first sc. Fasten off. *(150)*

With sewing needle and thread, taking care that stitches are not visible on right side, baste two layers of quilt batting to wrong side of Bed Top; trim batting edges ½" smaller than Top all around.

BED BOTTOM

Row 1: With nantucket, beginning at **front,** ch 44, sc in second ch from hook, sc in each ch across, turn. *(43 sts made)*

Rows 2–24: Ch 1, sc in each st across, turn.

Row 25: Sl st in first st, ch 1, sc next 2 sts tog,

sc in each st across to last 3 sts, sc next 2 sts tog leaving last st unworked, turn. *(39 sc, 1 sl st)*

Row 26: Ch 1, sc in each sc across leaving sl st unworked, turn.

Rows 27–31: Repeat rows 25 and 26 alternately, ending with row 25. At end of last row *(27 sts)*.

Rnd 32: Working around outer edge, ch 1, sc in each st around with 2 sc at each corner and 36 sc evenly spaced in ends of rows across each side, join with sl st in first sc. Fasten off. *(150)*

Joining rnd 1: Hold Bed Bottom on wrong side of Bed Top with edges matching and batting between; with right side of Top facing, holding yarn behind work and working through Top and Bottom as one, join white with sl st in first st on rnd 32 of Top, sl st in each st around, join with sl st in first sl st. Fasten off. *(150 sts)*

Mark first and last sl sts of the center 43 sl sts worked across straight front edge.

Joining rnd 2: With front edge toward you and Top facing up, working **this rnd** in **back lps** *(see Crochet Stitch Guide)* of sl sts, join nantucket with sc in 10th st from marked st at right end of front edge, sc in each st around remainder of front, sides and back, join with sl st in first sc, **turn; do not fasten off.**

OUTER SIDES

Row 1: Working **this row** in **back lps** of joining rnd 2, ch 1, sc in first 127 sc leaving last 23 sts unworked, turn. *(127 sc)*

NOTE: When working fp sts, take care to leave remaining lps of joining row 2 exposed.

Row 2: *(Right side)* Ch 1, sc in first 7 sts, hdcfp around sc on joining row 2 directly below next st, (sc in next 3 sts on last row, skip next 3 sts on joining row 2, hdcfp around each of next 7 sc on joining row 2, sc in next 3 sts on last row, hdcfp around next sc on joining row 2 directly below next st) across to last 7 sts, sc in last 7 sts on last row, turn.

Row 3: Ch 1, sc in each st across, turn.

Row 4: Ch 1, sc in first 7 sts, hdcfp around next fp on row before last, (sc in next 4 sts on last row, skip next fp on row before last, hdcfp around next 5 fp, sc in next 4 sts on last row, hdcfp around next

fp on row before last) across to last 7 sts, sc in last 7 sts on last row, turn.

Row 5: Ch 1, sc in each st across, turn.

Row 6: Ch 1, sc first 2 sts tog, sc in next 5 sts, hdcfp around next fp on row before last, (sc in next 5 sts on last row, skip next fp on row before last, hdcfp around each of next 3 fp, sc in next 5 sts on last row, hdcfp around next fp on row before last) across to last 7 sts, sc in next 5 sts, sc last 2 sts tog, turn. *(125)*

Row 7: Ch 1, sc first 2 sts tog, sc in each st across to last 2 sts, sc last 2 sts tog, turn. *(123)*

Row 8: Ch 1, sc first 2 sts tog, sc in next 3 sts, hdcfp around next fp on row before last, (sc in next 6 sts on last row, skip next fp on row before last, hdcfp around next fp, sc next 2 sts tog, sc in next 4 sts on last row, hdcfp around next fp on row before last) across to last 5 sts, sc in next 3 sts, sc last 2 sts tog, **do not turn.** Fasten off. *(113)*

Row 9: With right side of row 8 facing, join nantucket with sl st in next unworked st on joining rnd 2, sc in end of each row and in each st across to other end of Outer Side, sl st in next unworked st on joining rnd 2. Fasten off. *(129 sc)*

Trim row: With right side of row 8 facing, join fisherman with sl st in first sc of row 8, sc in each sc across. Fasten off.

INNER SIDES

Row 1: Fold Outer Sides out over edge of Bed so wrong side is showing; with front edge of Bed Top toward you, working this row in **remaining lps** of worked sts on joining rnd 2, skip sl st of Outer Sides row 8, join nantucket with sc in first remaining lp, sc in each lp across to next sl st, turn. *(127 sc)*

Rows 2–8: Repeat rows 2–8 of Outer Sides.

Row 9: With right side of row 8 facing, join nantucket with sc in end of row 1, sc in end of each row and in each st across to other end of row 1, turn. *(129 sc)*

Fold Outer Sides up.

Row 10: To join Inner and Outer Sides, with Outer Sides facing, matching stitches of last rows and stuffing lightly with fiberfill as you go, working through all layers as one and through **back lps** of Trim row and through **both lps** of Outer Sides and Inner Sides ch 1, sc in each st across. Fasten off. ●

Knit Stitch Guide

CAST ON

1.

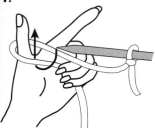

2.

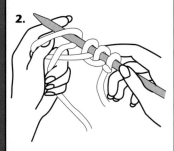

KNIT—K

PURL—P

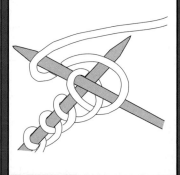

KNIT DECREASE—Dec or K 2 tog: Insert needle from front to back through 2 sts at one time, complete as knit st.

PURL DECREASE—Dec or P 2 tog: Insert needle through 2 sts at one time, complete as purl st.

KNIT INCREASE—K inc: Knit in front and back of lps of next st.

BIND OFF: K or P 2 sts; *insert left needle in first st on right needle (Step 1), slip first st over second st and drop off needle (Step 2), knit or purl next st; repeat from * until desired sts have been bound off.

1.

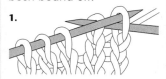

2.

MAKE 1 INVISIBLE INCREASE—M1: With left needle, pick up lp between sts on last row, twisting the lp; knit or purl in back bar of picked-up lp.

STANDARD ABBREVIATIONS

beg	beginning
ch, chs	chain, chains
dec	decrease
inc	increase
K	knit
lp, lps	loop, loops
P	purl
psso	pass slipped st over
rnd, rnds	round, rounds
skp	slip 1 knitwise, knit 1, pass slipped st over knit st and off needle
sp, sps	space, spaces
st st	stockinette stitch
st, sts	stitch, stitches
tog	together
yo	yarn over

KNITTING NEEDLES

Metric Sizes	US Sizes
1.75 mm	0
2.00 mm	1
2.50 mm	2
3.00 mm	3
3.50 mm	4
4.00 mm	5
4.50 mm	6
5.00 mm	8
5.50 mm	9
6.00 mm	10
7.00 mm	10½
8.00 mm	11
9.00 mm	13
10.00 mm	15

Crochet Stitch Guide

STANDARD ABBREVIATIONS

beg . . . . beginning
ch, chs . . . . . chain, chains
dc . . . . double crochet
dec . . . . decrease
hdc . . . . half double crochet
inc . . . . increase
lp, lps . . . . loop, loops
rnd, rnds . . . round, rounds
sc . . . . single crochet
sl st . . . . slip stitch
sp, sps . . . . . . space, spaces
st, sts . . . . . . stitch, stitches
tog . . . . together
tr . . . . treble crochet
yo . . . . yarn over

sc next 2 sts tog......(insert hook in next st, yo, pull through st) 2 times, yo, pull through all 3 lps on hook.

hdc next 2 sts tog.....(yo, insert hook in next st, yo, pull through st) 2 times, yo, pull through all 5 lps on hook.

dc next 2 sts tog......(yo, insert hook in next st, yo, pull through st, yo, pull through 2 lps on hook) 2 times, yo, pull through all 3 lps on hook.

Front post stitch—fp: Back post stitch—bp:
When working post st, insert hook from right to left around post of st on previous row.

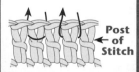

Back   **Front**

Post of Stitch

Chain—ch: Yo, pull through lp on hook.

Slip stitch—sl st:
Insert hook in st, yo, pull through both lps on hook.

Single crochet—sc:
Insert hook in st, yo, pull through st, yo, pull through both lps on hook.

Reverse single crochet—reverse sc:
Working from left to right, insert hook in next st, complete as sc.

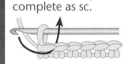

Front loop—front lp: Back loop—back lp:

Front Loop   **Back Loop**

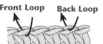

Half double crochet—hdc:
Yo, insert hook in st, yo, pull through st, yo, pull through all 3 lps on hook.

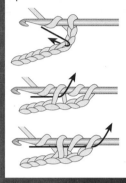

Double crochet—dc:
Yo, insert hook in st, yo, pull through st, (yo, pull through 2 lps) 2 times.

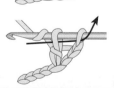

Treble crochet—tr:
Yo 2 times, insert hook in st, yo, pull through st, (yo, pull through 2 lps) 3 times.

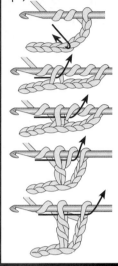

Double treble crochet—dtr:
Yo 3 times, insert hook in st, yo, pull through st, (yo, pull through 2 lps) 4 times.

Change colors:
Drop first color; with second color, pull through last 2 lps of st.

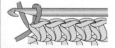

The patterns in this book are written using American crochet stitch terminology.
For our international customers, hook sizes, stitches and yarn definitions should be converted as follows:

But, as with all patterns,
test your gauge (tension) to be sure.

US	= INTERNATIONAL
sl st (slip stitch)	= sc (single crochet)
sc (single crochet)	= dc (double crochet)
hdc (half double crochet)	= htr (half treble crochet)
dc (double crochet)	= tr (treble crochet)
tr (treble crochet)	= dtr (double treble crochet)
dtr (double treble crochet)	= ttr (triple treble crochet)
skip	= miss

THREAD/YARNS

Bedspread Weight	= No. 10 Cotton or Virtuoso
Sport Weight	= 4 Ply or thin DK
Worsted Weight	= Thick DK or Aran

MEASUREMENTS

1" = 2.54 cm
1 yd. = .9144 m
1 oz. = 28.35 g

CROCHET HOOKS

Metric	US	Metric	US
.60mm	14	3.00mm	D/3
.75mm	12	3.50mm	E/4
1.00mm	10	4.00mm	F/5
1.50mm	6	4.50mm	G/6
1.75mm	5	5.00mm	H/8
2.00mm	B/1	5.50mm	I/9
2.50mm	C/2	6.00mm	J/10

Instructional Index

*This listing refers you
to additional tips and
technique instructions.*

Sampler Afghan Squares Index

*A quick reference to locate
your favorite individual square.*

Crochet Projects Index

*Quickly find the page
for your next project.*